The Giver

LOIS LOWRY

WORKBOOK

Contents

뉴베리 상이란? · 4

이 책의 구성 · 6

이 책의 활용법 · 8

chapter one
• Quiz & Words List · 10

chapter two
• Quiz & Words List · 22

chapter three
• Quiz & Words List · 30

chapter four
• Quiz & Words List · 38

chapter five
• Quiz & Words List · 48

chapter six
• Quiz & Words List · 56

chapter seven
• Quiz & Words List · 68

chapter eight
• Quiz & Words List · 78

chapter nine
• Quiz & Words List · 88

chapter ten
- Quiz & Words List · **96**

chapter eleven
- Quiz & Words List · **104**

chapter twelve
- Quiz & Words List · **112**

chapter thirteen
- Quiz & Words List · **120**

chapter fourteen
- Quiz & Words List · **132**

chapter fifteen
- Quiz & Words List · **144**

chapter sixteen
- Quiz & Words List · **150**

chapter seventeen
- Quiz & Words List · **158**

chapter eighteen
- Quiz & Words List · **168**

chapter nineteen
- Quiz & Words List · **174**

chapter twenty
- Quiz & Words List · **182**

chapter twenty one
- Quiz & Words List · **192**

chapter twenty two
- Quiz & Words List · **202**

chapter twenty three
- Quiz & Words List · **210**

영어원서 읽기 TIPS · **218**
Answer Key · **224**

뉴베리 상이란?

'아동 도서계의 노벨상!' 미국 최고 권위의 아동 문학상

뉴베리 상(Newbery Award)은 미국 도서관 협회에서 해마다 미국 아동 문학 발전에 가장 크게 이바지한 작가에게 수여하는 아동 문학상입니다. 1922년에 시작된 이 상은 미국에서 가장 오랜 역사를 지닌 아동 문학상이자, '아동 도서계의 노벨상'이라 불릴 만큼 높은 권위를 자랑하는 상입니다.

뉴베리 상은 그 역사와 권위만큼이나 심사 기준이 까다롭기로 유명한데, 심사단은 책의 주제 의식은 물론 정보의 깊이와 스토리의 정교함, 캐릭터와 문체의 적정성 등을 꼼꼼히 평가하여 수상작을 결정합니다.

그해 최고의 작품으로 선정된 도서에게는 '뉴베리 메달(Newbery Medal)'이라고 부르는 금색 메달을 수여하며, 최종 후보에 올랐던 주목할 만한 작품들에게는 '뉴베리 아너(Newbery Honor)'라는 이름의 은색 마크를 수여합니다.

뉴베리 상을 받은 도서는 미국의 모든 도서관에 비치되어 더 많은 독자들을 만나게 되며, 대부분 수십에서 수백만 부가 판매되는 베스트셀러가 됩니다. 뉴베리 상을 수상한 작가는 그만큼 필력과 작품성을 인정받게 되어, 수상 작가의 다른 작품들 또한 수상작 못지않게 커다란 주목과 사랑을 받습니다.

왜 뉴베리 수상작인가?
쉬운 어휘로 쓰인 '검증된' 영어원서!

뉴베리 수상작들은 '검증된 원서'로 국내 영어 학습자들에게 큰 사랑을 받고 있습니다. 뉴베리 수상작이 원서 읽기에 좋은 교재인 이유는 무엇일까요?

1. 아동 문학인 만큼 어휘가 어렵지 않습니다.
2. 어렵지 않은 어휘를 사용하면서도 '문학상'을 수상한 만큼 문장의 깊이가 상당합니다.
3. 적당한 난이도의 어휘와 깊이 있는 문장으로 구성되어 있기 때문에 초등 고학년부터 성인까지, 영어 초보자부터 실력자까지 모든 영어 학습자들이 읽기에 좋습니다.

실제로 뉴베리 수상작은 국제중·특목고에서는 입시 필독서로, 대학교에서는 영어 강독 교재로 다양하고 폭넓게 활용되고 있습니다. 이런 이유로 뉴베리 수상작은 한국어 번역서보다 오히려 원서가 훨씬 많이 판매되는 기현상을 보이고 있습니다.

'베스트 오브 베스트'만을 엄선한 「뉴베리 컬렉션」

「뉴베리 컬렉션」은 뉴베리 메달 및 아너 수상작, 그리고 뉴베리 수상 작가의 유명 작품들을 엄선하여 한국 영어 학습자들을 위한 최적의 교재로 재탄생시킨 영어 원서 시리즈입니다.

1. 어휘 수준과 문장의 난이도, 분량 등 국내 영어 학습자들에게 적합한 정도를 종합적으로 검토하여 선정하였습니다.
2. 기존 원서 독자층 사이의 인기도까지 감안하여 최적의 작품들을 선별하였습니다.
3. 판형이 좁고 글씨가 작아 읽기 힘들었던 원서 디자인을 대폭 수정하여, 판형을 시원하게 키우고 읽기에 최적화된 영문 서체를 사용하여 가독성을 극대화하였습니다.
4. 함께 제공되는 워크북은 어려운 어휘를 완벽하게 정리하고 이해력을 점검하는 퀴즈를 덧붙여 독자들이 원서를 보다 쉽고 재미있게 읽을 수 있도록 구성하였습니다.
5. 기존에 높은 가격에 판매되어 구입이 부담스러웠던 오디오북을 부록으로 제공하여 리스닝과 소리 내어 읽기에까지 원서를 두루 활용할 수 있도록 했습니다.

로이스 로리(Lois Lowry)는 1937년 하와이 호놀룰루에서 태어난 미국의 청소년 문학 작가입니다. 언니의 죽음을 자전적으로 다룬 첫 소설 「그 여름의 끝(A Summer to Die)」으로 단숨에 독자들을 사로잡은 그녀는, 2차 세계대전을 배경으로 인간의 존엄성과 가치를 되새기게 하는 문제작 「별을 헤아리며(Number the Stars)」로 1990년 첫 번째 뉴베리 메달을 수상했습니다. 이어 1994년에는 인간의 어두운 면을 파헤치며 미래 사회에 대한 질문을 던진 수작 「기억 전달자(The Giver)」로 다시 뉴베리 메달을 수상했는데, 한 작가가 뉴베리 아너도 아닌 메달을 두 번이나 수상한 것은 극히 이례적인 일로 그녀의 뛰어난 작품성을 확인할 수 있는 단적인 예라고 할 수 있습니다.

「The Giver」는 로이스 로리에게 두 번째 뉴베리 메달을 안겨준 작품이자 가장 성공한 작품으로, 전 세계적으로 530만부 이상 판매되었습니다.

모두 똑같이 행복한 삶을 살기 위해 감정과 기억이 철저히 통제된 유토피아 사회에서 유일하게 감정을 느끼게 되는 소년의 이야기를 다룬 이 소설은, 청소년 소설로는 극히 드문 공상 과학적인 독특한 소재를 담고 있으며 한 번 들면 마지막까지 책을 놓지 못하게 만드는 흡인력과 탄탄한 구성력이 돋보이는 소설입니다.

특히 이 책은 국내 원서 독자가 극히 드물던 10년 전부터 이미 입소문을 타기 시작해 지금은 원서 읽기를 시작하면 한번쯤은 반드시 거치는 필독서로 자리 잡았으며, 국제중·특목고 등에서 추천 도서에 가장 많이 오르는 책이기도 합니다.

이 책의 구성

원서 본문

내용이 담긴 원서 본문입니다.

원어민이 읽는 일반 원서와 같은 텍스트지만, 암기해야 할 중요 어휘들은 볼드체로 표시되어 있습니다. 이 어휘들은 지금 들고 계신 워크북에 챕터별로 정리되어 있습니다.

학습 심리학 연구 결과에 따르면, 한 단어씩 따로 외우는 단어 암기는 거의 효과가 없다고 합니다. 단어를 제대로 외우기 위해서는 문맥(Context) 속에서 단어를 암기해야 하며, 한 단어당 문맥 속에서 15번 이상 마주칠 때 완벽하게 암기할 수 있다고 합니다.

이 책의 본문에서는 중요 어휘를 볼드체로 강조하여, 문맥 속의 단어들을 더 확실히 인지(Word Cognition in Context)하도록 돕고 있습니다. 또한 대부분의 중요 단어들은 다른 챕터에서도 반복해서 등장하기 때문에 이 책을 읽는 것만으로도 자연스럽게 어휘력을 향상시킬 수 있습니다.

또한 본문 하단에는 내용 이해를 돕기 위한 '각주'가 첨가되어 있습니다. 각주는 굳이 암기할 필요는 없지만, 알아 두면 도움이 될 만한 정보를 설명하고 있습니다. 각주를 참고하면 스토리를 더 깊이 있게 이해할 수 있어 원서를 읽는 재미가 배가됩니다.

워크북(Workbook)

Check Your Reading Speed

해당 챕터의 단어 수가 기록되어 있어, 리딩 속도를 측정할 수 있습니다. 특히 리딩 속도를 중시하는 독자들이 유용하게 사용할 수 있습니다.

Build Your Vocabulary

본문에 볼드 표시되어 있던 단어들이 정리되어 있습니다. 리딩 전·후에 반복해서 보면 원서를 더욱 쉽게 읽을 수 있고, 어휘력도 빠르게 향상될 것입니다.

단어는 〈스펠링 – 빈도 – 발음기호 – 품사 – 한글 뜻 – 영문 뜻〉 순서로 표기되어 있으며 빈도 표시(★)가 많을수록 필수 어휘입니다. 반복해서 등장하는 단어는 빈도 대신 '복습'으로 표기되어 있습니다. 품사는 아래와 같이 표기했습니다.

n. 명사 | a. 형용사 | ad. 부사 | vi. 자동사 | vt. 타동사 | v. 자·타동사 모두 쓰이는 동사
conj. 접속사 | prep. 전치사 | int. 감탄사 | phrasal v. 구동사 | idiom 숙어 및 관용구

Comprehension Quiz

간단한 퀴즈를 통해 읽은 내용에 대한 이해력을 점검해 볼 수 있습니다.

이 책의 활용법

「뉴베리 컬렉션」 이렇게 읽어 보세요!

아래와 같이 프리뷰(Preview) → 리딩(Reading) → 리뷰(Review) 세 단계를 거치면서 읽으면, 더욱 효과적으로 영어 실력을 향상할 수 있습니다.

1. 프리뷰(Preview) : 오늘 읽을 내용을 먼저 점검하자!

- 워크북을 통해 오늘 읽을 챕터에 나와 있는 단어들을 쭉 훑어봅니다. 어떤 단어들이 나오는지, 내가 아는 단어와 모르는 단어는 어떤 것들이 있는지 가벼운 마음으로 살펴봅니다.
- 평소처럼 하나하나 쓰면서 암기하려고 하지는 마세요! 익숙하지 않은 단어들을 주의 깊게 보되, 어차피 리딩을 하면서 점차 익숙해질 단어라는 것을 기억하며 빠르게 훑어봅니다.
- 뒤 챕터로 갈수록 '복습'이라고 표시된 단어들이 늘어나는 것을 알 수 있습니다. '복습' 단어인데도 여전히 익숙하지 않다면 더욱 신경을 써서 봐야겠죠? 매일매일 꾸준히 읽는다면, 익숙한 단어들이 점점 많아진다는 것을 몸으로 느낄 수 있습니다.

2. 리딩(Reading) : 내용에 집중하며 빠르게 읽어 나가자!

- 프리뷰를 마친 후 바로 리딩을 시작합니다. 방금 살펴봤던 어휘들을 문장 속에서 다시 만나게 되는데, 이 과정에서 단어의 쓰임새와 어감을 자연스럽게 익히게 됩니다.
- 모르는 단어나 이해되지 않는 문장이 나오더라도 멈추지 말고 전체적인 맥락을 파악하면서 속도감 있게 읽어 나가세요. 이해되지 않는 문장들은 따로 표시를 하되, 일단 넘어가고 계속 읽는 것이 좋습니다. 뒷부분을 읽다 보면 자연히 이해가 되는 경우도 있고, 정 이해가 되지 않는 부분은 리딩을 마친 이후에 따로 리뷰하는 시간을 가지면 됩니다. 문제집을 풀듯이 모든 문장을 분석하면서 원서를 읽는 것이 아니라, 리딩을 할 때는 리딩에만, 리뷰를 할 때는 리뷰에만 집중하는 것이 필요합니다.
- 볼드 처리된 단어의 의미가 궁금하더라도 워크북을 바로 펼치지 마세요. 정 궁금하다면 한 번씩 참고하는 것도 나쁘진 않지만, 워크북과 원서를 번갈아 보면서 읽는 것은 리딩의 흐름을 끊고 단어 하나하나에 집착하는 좋지 않은 리딩 습관을 심어 줄 수 있습니다.
- 같은 맥락에서 번역서를 구해 원서와 동시에 번갈아 보는 것도 좋은 방법이 아닙니다. 한글 번역을 가지고 있다고 해도 일단 영어로 읽을 때는 영어에만 집중하고 어느 정도 분량을 읽은 후에 번역서와 비교하도록 하세요. 모든 문장을

일일이 번역해서 완벽하게 이해하려는 것은 오히려 좋지 않은 리딩 습관을 심어 주어 장기적으로는 바람직하지 않은 결과를 얻을 수 있습니다. 처음부터 완벽하게 이해하려고 하는 것보다는 빠른 속도로 2~3회 반복해서 읽는 방식이 실력 향상에 더 도움이 됩니다. 만일 반복해서 읽어도 내용이 전혀 이해되지 않아 곤란하다면 책 선정에 문제가 있다고 할 수 있습니다. 그럴 때는 좀 더 쉬운 책을 골라 실력을 다진 뒤 다시 도전하는 것이 좋습니다.

• 초보자라면 분당 150단어의 리딩 속도를 목표로 잡고 리딩을 합니다. 분당 150단어는 원어민이 말하는 속도로, 영어 학습자들이 리스닝과 스피킹으로 넘어가기 위해 가장 기초적으로 달성해야 하는 단계입니다. 분당 50~80단어 정도의 낮은 리딩 속도를 가지고 있는 경우는 대부분 영어 실력이 부족해서라기보다 '잘못된 리딩 습관'을 가지고 있어서 그렇습니다. 이해력이 조금 떨어진다고 하더라도 분당 150단어까지는 속도에 대한 긴장감을 놓치지 말고 속도감 있게 읽어 나가도록 하세요.

3. 리뷰(Review) : 이해력을 점검하고 꼼꼼하게 다시 살펴보자!

• 해당 챕터의 Comprehension Quiz를 통해 이해력을 점검해 봅니다.
• 오늘 만난 어휘들을 다시 한번 복습합니다. 이때는 읽으면서 중요하다고 생각했던 단어를 연습장에 써 보면서 꼼꼼하게 외우는 것도 좋습니다.
• 이해가 되지 않는다고 표시해 두었던 부분도 주의 깊게 분석해 봅니다. 다시 한번 문장을 꼼꼼히 읽고, 어떤 이유에서 이해가 되지 않았는지 생각해 봅니다. 따로 메모를 남기거나 노트를 작성하는 것도 좋은 방법입니다.
• 사실 꼼꼼히 리뷰하는 것은 매우 고된 과정입니다. 원서를 읽고 리뷰하는 시간을 가지는 것이 영어 실력 향상에 많은 도움이 되기는 하지만, 이 과정을 철저히 지키려다가 원서 읽기의 재미를 반감시키는 것은 바람직하지 않습니다. 그럴 때는 차라리 리뷰를 가볍게 하는 것이 좋을 수 있습니다. '내용에 빠져서 재미있게', 문제집에서는 상상도 못할 '많은 양'을 읽으면서, 매일매일 조금씩 꾸준히 실력을 키워 가는 것이 원서를 활용하는 기본적인 방법이며, 영어 공부의 왕도입니다. 문제집 풀듯이 원서 읽기를 시도하고 접근해서는 실패할 수밖에 없습니다.
• 이런 방식으로 원서를 끝까지 다 읽었다면, 다시 반복해서 읽거나 오디오북을 활용하는 등 다양한 방식으로 원서 읽기를 확장해 나갈 수 있습니다. 이에 대한 자세한 안내가 워크북 말미에 실려 있습니다.

chapter one

1. Why was Jonas frightened of the plane he saw a year ago?
   - (A) The people of the community had never seen a plane before.
   - (B) The pilot had flown too close to the ground.
   - (C) The plane he saw was a single pilot jet whereas the people of the community had only seen cargo planes.
   - (D) The plane had almost crashed in the community and the people were in grave danger.

2. How did the citizens know what to do after they saw the plane?
   - (A) A community leader took them to a nearby building.
   - (B) The citizens knew to go indoors during an emergency
   - (C) The afternoon community workers told the citizens to go indoors.
   - (D) The citizens followed the instructions they heard over a loud speaker.

3. What was required of Asher when he was late to class?
   - (A) He had to sing the morning anthem alone.
   - (B) He had to make a public apology to his teacher and classmates.
   - (C) He was forced to write a letter of apology to the teacher.
   - (D) He had to report to the leader of the school before entering his classroom.

4. Jonas first thought he was _____ about the Ceremony of Twelve, but then decided he was _____.

(A) distraught; frightened

(B) frightened; apprehensive

(C) apprehensive; nervous

(D) distraught; apprehensive

5. After every meal, the family members must _____.

(A) discuss the feelings they had experienced that day

(B) talk about what they had done at work or at school that day

(C) talk about the events that made them angry that day

(D) share their daydreams with each other

6. Why might Jonas's father need to release the new born child?

(A) The child was not healthy when he was born.

(B) The child wasn't growing as fast as he should, and he was not sleeping soundly.

(C) The child wasn't growing as fast as he should, and was not eating or drinking properly.

(D) The child was too large for his age and was not sleeping soundly.

7. Which of the following is NOT a reason why a person would be released?

(A) A citizen is released when they commit a third transgression.

(B) The elderly are released nearing the end of their life. It is a time for people to celebrate their life.

(C) A new born child is released when he or she is not growing quickly enough.

(D) A citizen is released when they do not have the capacity to connect with others.

1분에 몇 단어를 읽는지 리딩 속도를 측정해보세요.

$$\frac{2,396 \text{ words}}{\text{reading time (} \quad \text{) sec}} \times 60 = (\quad) \text{ WPM}$$

• *Build Your Vocabulary*

frighten**
[fráitn]

v. 놀라게 하다, 섬뜩하게 하다; 기겁하다 (frightened a. 깜짝 놀란, 겁이 난)
If something or someone frightens you, they cause you to suddenly feel afraid, anxious, or nervous.

sicken*
[síkən]

v. 메스꺼워지다, 병나다 (sickening a. 병나게 하는, 메스꺼운)
If something sickens you, it makes you feel disgusted.

unidentified
[ʌ̀naidéntəfàid]

a. (국적 · 소유 · 신원이) 불확실한, 미확인의
If you describe someone or something as unidentified, you mean that nobody knows who or what they are.

aircraft*
[έərkræft]

n. 항공기 (비행기 · 비행선 · 기구 · 헬리콥터 등의 총칭)
An aircraft is a vehicle which can fly, for example an airplane or a helicopter.

overfly
[òuvərflái]

vt. (overflew–overflown) (비행기가) …의 상공을 날아가다; 영공을 침해하다
When an aircraft overflies an area, it flies over it.

squint*
[skwint]

v. 곁눈질하다, 실눈으로 보다; a. 사시의; 곁눈질하는
If you squint at something, you look at it with your eyes partly closed.

sleek*
[sli:k]

a. 매끄러운; 날씬한, 유선형의
Sleek vehicles, furniture, or other objects look smooth, shiny, and expensive.

blur*
[blə:r]

n. 흐림, 침침함; 더러움, 얼룩; v. 흐릿해지다
A blur is a shape or area which you cannot see clearly because it has no distinct outline or because it is moving very fast.

blast**
[blæst]

n. 폭발, 폭파; 폭풍, 돌풍; v. 폭파하다
A blast is a big explosion, especially one caused by a bomb.

fascinate*
[fǽsənèit]

v. 매혹하다, 반하게 하다 (fascinated a. 매혹된, 마음을 빼앗긴)
If something fascinates you, it interests and delights you so much that your thoughts tend to concentrate on it.

occasional**
[əkéiʒənəl]

a. 가끔의, 때때로의 (occasionally ad. 때때로, 가끔)
Occasional means happening sometimes, but not regularly or often.

cargo**
[ká:rgou]

n. (선박 · 항공기의) 짐, 화물
The cargo of a ship or plane is the goods that it is carrying.

riverbank
[rívərbæ̀ŋk]

n. 강둑, 강기슭
A riverbank is the land along the edge of a river.

intrigue*
[intríːg]

v. 호기심을[흥미를] 돋우다; 음모를 꾸미다; n. 음모
If something intrigues you, it interests you and you want to know more about it.

unload*
[ʌnlóud]

v. (차·배 등의) 짐을 내리다; (총에서) 탄알을 빼내다
If you unload goods from a vehicle, or you unload a vehicle, you remove the goods from the vehicle, usually after they have been transported from one place to another.

squat*
[skwɑt]

a. 땅딸막한; 쪼그리고 앉은; v. 웅크리다, 쪼그리고 앉다
If you describe someone or something as squat, you mean they are short and thick, usually in an unattractive way.

fat-bellied
[fætbélid]

a. 배 부분이 팽창된, 뚱뚱한
fat (a. 살찐, 뚱뚱한) + bellied (a. 배가 …한)

needle-nosed
[níːdlnouzd]

a. 코가 뾰족한
needle (n. 바늘) + nosed (a. …같은 코의)

anxious**
[ǽŋkʃəs]

a. 걱정하는, 염려하는; 열망하는, 간절히 바라는
(anxiously ad. 걱정스럽게, 불안해하며)
If you are anxious, you are nervous or worried about something.

rasp
[ræsp]

v. 귀에 거슬리는 소리로 말하다; 삐걱거리다; n. 강판; 끽끽 줄질하는 소리
(rasping a. 귀에 거슬리는)
If someone rasps, their voice or breathing is harsh and unpleasant to listen to.

obedient**
[oubíːdiənt]

a. 순종하는, 고분고분한 (obediently ad. 고분고분하게)
A person or animal who is obedient does what they are told to do.

dwelling**
[dwéliŋ]

n. 거처, 주소, 사는 집
A dwelling is a place where someone lives.

populate*
[pápjəlèit]

v. …에 거주하다, 살다, 장소를 차지하다
If an area is populated by certain people or animals, those people or animals live there, often in large numbers.

abandon**
[əbǽndən]

vt. 버리다; 단념하다, 그만두다 (abandoned a. 버려진)
If you abandon a place, thing, or person, you leave the place, thing, or person permanently or for a long time.

upturned
[ʌptə́ːrnd]

a. 뒤집힌; 파헤쳐진
Something that is upturned is upside down.

revolve*
[riválv]

v. 회전하다; 공전(公轉)하다
When something revolves or when you revolve it, it moves or turns in a circle around a central point or line.

churn
[tʃəːrn]

v. (속이) 뒤틀리다; (물·파도 등이) 마구 휘돌다, 휘젓다; 거품이 나게 하다
If you say that your stomach is churning, you mean that you feel sick.

tremble*
[trémbəl]
v. 떨다, 떨리다; n. 떨림
If you tremble, you shake slightly because you are frightened or cold.

crackle*
[krǽkəl]
v. 딱딱 소리를 내다; n. 딱딱[우지직]하는 소리
If something crackles, it makes a rapid series of short, harsh noises.

reassure*
[rìːəʃúər]
vt. 안심시키다
If you reassure someone, you say or do things to make them stop worrying about something.

urgent**
[ə́ːrdʒənt]
a. 긴급한, 절박한
If something is urgent, it needs to be dealt with as soon as possible.

misread
[misríːd]
vt. 잘못 읽다; 잘못 해석하다, 오해하다
If you misread something that has been written or printed, you look at it and think that it says something that it does not say.

navigational
[næ̀vəgéiʃənl]
a. 항공[항해]의, 운항의
Navigational means relating to the act of navigating a ship or an aircraft.

desperate**
[déspərit]
a. 필사적인; 자포자기의, 절망적인 (desperately ad. 필사적으로)
If you are desperate for something or desperate to do something, you want or need it very much indeed.

needless to say
idiom 말할 필요도 없이, 물론
You use needless to say when you want to emphasize that what you are about to say is obvious and to be expected in the circumstances.

release**
[rilíːs]
vt. 놓아주다, 해방시키다, 풀어놓다; n. 석방
If a person or animal is released from somewhere where they have been looked after, they are set free or allowed to go.

amuse**
[əmjúːz]
vt. 즐겁게 하다, 재미나게 하다 (amusing a. 재미있는, 즐거운)
If something amuses you, it makes you want to laugh or smile.

grim**
[grim]
a. 암울한, 음산한; 엄한, 엄격한
If you say that something is grim, you think that it is very bad, ugly, or depressing.

contribute**
[kəntríbjut]
v. 기여[공헌]하다; 기부[기증]하다
If you contribute to something, you say or do things to help to make it successful.

punish**
[pʌ́niʃ]
v. 벌하다, 응징하다, 처벌하다 (punishment n. 처벌, 징계)
To punish someone means to make them suffer in some way because they have done something wrong.

overwhelm**
[òuvərhwélm]
vt. 압도하다, 제압하다; 질리게 하다 (overwhelming a. 압도적인, 저항할 수 없는)
If something is overwhelming, it affects you very strongly, and you do not know how to deal with it.

scold**
[skould]
v. 꾸짖다, 잔소리하다
If you scold someone, you speak angrily to them because they have done something wrong.

jeer*
[dʒiər]

v. 조롱하다, 조소하다, 놀리다; n. 조롱, 빈정거리는 말
To jeer at someone means to say or shout rude and insulting things to them to show that you do not like or respect them.

stumble**
[stʌmbəl]

v. 발부리가 걸리다, 비틀거리며 걷다; n. 비틀거림
If you stumble, you put your foot down awkwardly while you are walking or running and nearly fall over.

clumsy*
[klʌmzi]

a. 꼴사나운, 어색한, 서투른
A clumsy person moves or handles things in a careless, awkward way, often so that things are knocked over or broken.

hang one's head

idiom 부끄러워 고개를 숙이다
When you feel embarrassed or ashamed, you hang your head.

guilt**
[gilt]

n. 죄책감, 유죄
Guilt is an unhappy feeling that you have because you have done something wrong or think that you have done something wrong.

embarrass**
[imbǽrəs]

v. 당황스럽게[쑥스럽게] 만들다, 곤란하게 하다 (embarrassment n. 난처함, 당황)
If something or someone embarrasses you, they make you feel shy or ashamed.

apologize**
[əpálədʒàiz]

v. 사과하다, 사죄하다
When you apologize to someone, you say that you are sorry that you have hurt them or caused trouble for them.

pedal*
[pédl]

v. 페달을 밟다; n. 페달, 발판
When you pedal a bicycle, you push the pedals around with your feet to make it move.

palpable
[pǽlpəbəl]

a. 명백한, 곧 알 수 있는; 손으로 만질 수 있는
You describe something as palpable when it is obvious or intense and easily noticed.

sink***
[siŋk]

v. 가라앉다, 침몰하다 (sinking a. 가라앉는)
If something sinks, it disappears below the surface of a mass of water.

streak**
[stri:k]

v. 질주하다; 줄을 긋다; n. 경향, 기미; 줄
If something or someone streaks somewhere, they move there very quickly.

scramble**
[skrǽmbəl]

v. 뒤섞다, 뒤죽박죽으로 만들다; 기어오르다; (경쟁하듯) 서로 밀치다
If you scramble, you gather something together in a hurried or disorderly fashion.

phrase**
[freiz]

n. 구절, 관용구
A phrase is a short group of words that people often use as a way of saying something.

barely**
[béərli]

ad. 간신히, 가까스로; 거의 …않다
You use barely to say that something is only just true or only just the case.

recognizable*
[rékəgnàizəbəl]

a. 인식할 수 있는, 알아볼 수 있는
If something can be easily recognized or identified, you can say that it is easily recognizable.

grin**
[grin]

v. (이를 드러내고) 싱긋 웃다, 활짝 웃다; n. 싱긋 웃음
When you grin, you smile broadly.

dash***
[dæʃ]

v. 돌진하다, 서둘러 가다; 내던지다; n. 돌진, 질주
If you dash somewhere, you run or go there quickly and suddenly.

breathless*
[bréθlis]

a. 숨도 못 쉴 정도의, 숨 가쁜 (breathlessly ad. 숨 가쁘게)
If you are breathless, you have difficulty in breathing properly, for example because you have been running or because you are afraid or excited.

chant*
[tʃænt]

v. 노래를 부르다; 일제히 외치다; n. (규칙적으로 반복되는) 구호, 문구; 노래
If you chant or if you chant something, you sing a religious song or prayer.

anthem**
[ǽnθəm]

n. 성가, 찬송가
An anthem is a song which is used to represent a particular nation, society, or group and which is sung on special occasions.

patriotic*
[pèitriátik]

a. 애국적인, 애국심이 강한
Someone who is patriotic loves their country and feels very loyal towards it.

hymn**
[him]

n. (교회의) 찬송가, 찬미가
A hymn is a religious song that Christians sing in church.

apology**
[əpálədʒi]

n. 사죄, 사과
An apology is something that you say or write in order to tell someone that you are sorry that you have hurt them or caused trouble for them.

inconvenience*
[ìnkənví:njəns]

vt. …에게 불편을 느끼게 하다, 폐를 끼치다; n. 불편, 불편한 것
If someone inconveniences you, they cause problems or difficulties for you.

patient***
[péiʃənt]

a. 인내심[참을성] 있는; n. 환자 (patiently ad. 참을성 있게, 끈기 있게)
If you are patient, you stay calm and do not get annoyed, for example when something takes a long time, or when someone is not doing what you want them to do.

hatchery
[hǽtʃəri]

n. (물고기 · 닭의) 부화장
A hatchery is a place where people control the hatching of eggs, especially fish eggs.

salmon**
[sǽmən]

n. 연어
A salmon is a large silver-colored fish.

distraught
[distrɔ́:t]

a. 정신이 혼란한, 제정신이 아닌
If someone is distraught, they are so upset and worried that they cannot think clearly.

smooth*
[smu:ð]

v. 매끄럽게 하다[되다]; a. 매끄러운; 유창한
You use smooth to describe something that is going well and is free of problems or trouble.

rumple
[rʌ́mpəl]

vt. (옷·종이 등을) 구기다, (머리털 등을) 헝클어 놓다; n. 구김살, 주름
If you rumple someone's hair, you move your hand backwards and forwards through it as your way of showing affection to them.

tunic
[tjú:nik]

n. 튜닉 (고대 그리스나 로마인들이 입던, 무릎까지 내려오는 헐렁한 가운 같은 웃옷)
A tunic is a loose piece of clothing covering the body down to the knees, usually without sleeves.

recite* *
[risáit]

vt. 읊다, 낭독(낭송, 암송)하다
When someone recites a poem or other piece of writing, they say it aloud after they have learned it.

in unison

idiom 일제히, 한목소리로
If two or more people do something in unison, they do it together at the same time.

distract*
[distrǽkt]

vt. (마음·주의를) 흐트러뜨리다, 딴 데로 돌리다
(distracted a. 주의가 빗나간, 마음이 산란한)
If something distracts you or your attention from something, it takes your attention away from it.

recollection* *
[rèkəlékʃən]

n. 회상, 회고
If you have a recollection of something, you remember it.

port* *
[pɔ:rt]

n. 항구 (여기서는 '자전거를 세우는 곳' 이라는 의미로 사용)
A port is a harbor area where ships load and unload goods or passengers.

eager* *
[í:gər]

a. 열망하는, 간절히 하고 싶어 하는
If you are eager to do or have something, you want to do or have it very much.

shudder* *
[ʃʌ́dər]

n. 떨림, 전율; vi. 떨다, 몸서리치다
A shudder is a shaking movement you make because you are cold, frightened or disgusted.

apprehensive*
[æprihénsiv]

a. 우려하는, 염려하는
Someone who is apprehensive is afraid that something bad may happen.

ritual*
[rítʃuəl]

n. (종교적인) 의식, 행사
A ritual is a religious service or other ceremony which involves a series of actions performed in a fixed order.

wheedle
[hwí:dl]

vt. 구슬리다, 꾀다, 솔깃한 말로 속이다
If you say that someone wheedles, you mean that they try to persuade someone to do or give them what they want.

complicated* *
[kámpləkèitid]

a. 복잡한, 이해하기 어려운
If you say that something is complicated, you mean it has so many parts or aspects that it is difficult to understand or deal with.

sift^{**}
[sift]

v. 체로 치다, 거르다, 선별하다 (sift through phrasal v. …을 엄밀히 조사하다)
If you sift through something such as evidence, you examine it thoroughly.

wiggle
[wígəl]

v. 꿈틀꿈틀 움직이다, (좌우·상하로) 조금씩 움직이다
If you wiggle something or if it wiggles, it moves up and down or from side to side in small quick movements.

impatient^{**}
[impéiʃənt]

a. 성급한, 조급한, 참을성 없는 (impatience n. 성급함, 조바심)
If you are impatient, you are annoyed because you have to wait too long for something.

obey^{***}
[oubéi]

v. 복종하다, 따르다
If you obey a person, a command, or an instruction, you do what you are told to do.

fist^{**}
[fist]

n. (쥔) 주먹
Your hand is referred to as your fist when you have bent your fingers in towards the palm in order to hit someone, to make an angry gesture, or to hold something.

clench[*]
[klentʃ]

v. (손을) 꽉 쥐다; (이를) 악물다; n. 단단히 쥐기; 이를 악물기
When you clench your fist or your fist clenches, you curl your fingers up tightly, usually because you are very angry.

defiant[*]
[difáiənt]

a. 도전적인, 반항적인, 시비조의
If you say that someone is defiant, you mean they show aggression or independence by refusing to obey someone.

frown^{**}
[fraun]

vi. 눈살을 찌푸리다, 얼굴을 찡그리다; n. 찌푸린 얼굴
When someone frowns, their eyebrows become drawn together, because they are annoyed or puzzled.

shrug[*]
[ʃrʌg]

v. (양 손바닥을 내보이면서 어깨를) 으쓱하다; n. 으쓱하기
If you shrug, you raise your shoulders to show that you are not interested in something or that you do not know or care about something.

usage^{**}
[júːsidʒ]

n. 사용(법), 쓰임새, 용법
Usage is the degree to which something is used or the way in which it is used.

ponder[*]
[pándər]

v. 숙고하다, 곰곰이[깊이] 생각하다
If you ponder something, you think about it carefully.

straightfor-ward[*]
[stréitfɔ́ːrwərd]

a. 똑바른; 정직한, 솔직한; 직접의
If you describe something as straightforward, you approve of it because it is easy to do or understand.

resolve^{**}
[rizálv]

v. (문제 등을) 풀다, 해결하다; 결심하다, 결의하다
To resolve a problem, argument, or difficulty means to find a solution to it.

attentive^{**}
[əténtiv]

a. 주의를 기울이는, 경청하는; 배려하는, 친절한 (attentively ad. 주의 깊게)
If you are attentive, you are paying close attention to what is being said or done.

nurture*
[nə́:rtʃər]
vt. 양육하다, 기르다; n. 양육, 양성 (nurturer n. 양육자)
If you nurture something such as a young child or a young plant, you care for it while it is growing and developing.

gender*
[dʒéndər]
n. 성(性), 성별
A person's gender is the fact that they are male or female.

disposition**
[dìspəzíʃən]
n. 성질, 기질, 경향; 배열, 배치
Someone disposition is the way that they tend to behave or feel.

sleep soundly
idiom 깊이 잠들다
If someone's sleep soundly, they are sleeping very deeply.

supplementary*
[sʌ̀pləméntəri]
a. 보충하는, 추가의 n. 보충되는 사람[것]
Supplementary things are added to something in order to improve it.

committee***
[kəmíti]
n. 위원회
A committee is a group of people who meet to make decisions or plans for a larger group or organization that they represent.

murmur*
[mə́:rmər]
v. 중얼거리다; 투덜거리다; n. 중얼거림
If you murmur something, you say it very quietly, so that not many people can hear what you are saying.

sympathetic**
[sìmpəθétik]
a. 공감하는, 동조하는; 동정적인, 동정어린
(sympathetically ad. 동정하여, 교감하여)
If you are sympathetic to someone who is in a bad situation, you are kind to them and show that you understand their feelings.

occasion***
[əkéiʒən]
n. 특수한 경우, 때; 행사, 의식
An occasion is a time when something happens, or a case of it happening.

elder**
[éldər]
n. 연장자, 웃어른; a. 나이가 더 많은 (elderly a. 나이가 지긋한)
A person's elder is someone who is older than them, especially someone quite a lot older.

celebration**
[sèləbréiʃən]
n. 축하, 축전, 기념행사
The celebration of something is praise and appreciation which is given to it.

rare**
[rɛər]
a. 드문, 진귀한 (rarely ad. 드물게, 좀처럼 …하지 않는)
Something that is rare is not common and is therefore interesting or valuable.

permission**
[pə:rmíʃən]
n. 허가, 허락, 승인
If someone is given permission to do something, they are allowed to do it.

assign**
[əsáin]
v. 맡기다, 배정하다, 임명하다, 지정하다
If you assign a piece of work to someone, you give them the work to do.

insight*
[ínsàit]
n. 통찰력; 이해, 간파
If someone has insight, they are able to understand complex situations.

vital**
[váitl]

a. 극히 중대한, 필수적인; 생명 유지와 연관된
If you say that something is vital, you mean that it is necessary or very important.

spouse*
[spaus]

n. 배우자, 남편, 아내
Someone's spouse is the person they are married to.

capacity**
[kəpǽsəti]

n. 능력, 역량; 수용력, 용량
Your capacity for something is your ability to do it, or the amount of it that you are able to do.

innocent**
[ínəsnt]

a. 순진한, 천진난만한; 결백한
If someone is innocent, they have no experience or knowledge of the more complex or unpleasant aspects of life.

giggle*
[gígəl]

v. 낄낄 웃다; n. 낄낄 웃음
If someone giggles, they laugh in a childlike way, because they are amused, nervous, or embarrassed.

prominent**
[prámənənt]

a. 현저한, 두드러진
Something that is prominent is very noticeable or is an important part of something else.

justice***
[dʒʌ́stis]

n. 사법, 재판; 정의, 공정
Justice is the legal system that a country uses in order to deal with people who break the law.

offender*
[əféndər]

n. 범죄자, 위반자
An offender is a person who has committed a crime.

adequate**
[ǽdikwit]

a. 적당한, 충분한; 어울리는 (adequately ad. 적당히, 충분히)
If something is adequate, there is enough of it or it is good enough to be used or accepted.

restore**
[ristɔ́:r]

vt. 되돌리다, 복구하다, 회복시키다
To restore someone or something to a previous condition means to cause them to be in that condition once again.

frustration*
[frʌstréiʃən]

n. 좌절, 실패; 낙담, 좌절감
Frustration is the feeling of being annoyed or angry because you cannot do or achieve what you want.

confess**
[kənfés]

v. 자백하다, 고백하다, 인정하다
If someone confesses to doing something wrong, they admit that they did it.

transgression
[trænsgréʃən]

n. 위반, 범죄
Transgression is the action of going beyond or overstepping some boundary or limit.

shiver**
[ʃívər]

v. (추위 · 공포로) 후들후들 떨다; 전율하다; n. 떨림, 전율
When you shiver, your body shakes slightly because you are cold or frightened.

disgrace[**]
[disgréis]

n. 불명예, 치욕, 창피; vt. 수치가 되다; 욕보이다
You say that someone is a disgrace to someone else when you want to emphasize that their behavior causes the other person to feel ashamed.

unspeakable[*]
[ʌnspíːkəbəl]

a. 형언하기 어려운, 이루 말할 수 없는
If you describe something as unspeakable, you are emphasizing that it is extremely unpleasant.

stroke[**]
[strouk]

① vt. 쓰다듬다, 어루만지다; n. 쓰다듬기, 달램 ② n. 타격, 일격, 치기
If you stroke someone or something, you move your hand slowly and gently over them.

soothe[**]
[suːð]

v. 달래다, 어르다
If you soothe someone who is angry or upset, you make them feel calmer.

appropriate[**]
[əpróuprièit]

a. 적당한, 적절한, 알맞은; vt. 사용하다, 충당하다
Something that is appropriate is suitable or acceptable for a particular situation.

descriptive[*]
[diskríptiv]

a. 서술[묘사]하는, 설명적인
Descriptive language or writing indicates what someone or something is like.

ceremony[**]
[sérəmòuni]

n. 의식, 의례
A ceremony is a formal event such as a wedding.

awe
[ɔː]

vt. 경외심을 갖게 하다; n. 경외, 외경심 (awed a. 외경심에 휩싸인)
If you are awed by someone or something, they make you feel respectful and amazed, though often rather frightened.

lie[***]
[lai]

vi. (lay-lain) 놓여 있다, 위치하다; 눕다, 누워 있다
LAY(v. 놓다, 눕히다)와 헷갈리기 쉬우므로 유의하자.

beckon[*]
[békən]

v. 손짓[고갯짓, 몸짓]으로 부르다, 신호하다
If you beckon to someone, you signal to them to come to you.

chapter two

1. What happens at the Ceremony of One?

   (A) All newchildren who were born in the previous year are given names and assigned to nurturer.
   (B) The community celebrates the release of the newchildren who are not fully grown.
   (C) All newchildren who were born in the previous year are given names and assigned to a family unit.
   (D) All newchildren who were born in the previous year are assigned to a family unit and are given names by the new parents.

2. How did Jonas's father break a rule?

   (A) He found out Lily's name before receiving her at the Ceremony of One.
   (B) He found out which newchild he would receive during the Ceremony of One.
   (C) He tried to find out if Gabe would be released before the Ceremony of One.
   (D) He found out Gabe's name before the Ceremony of One.

3. Which rule is not taken very seriously?

   (A) Family members must share their feelings after their evening meal.
   (B) Citizens must be precise with their use of vocabulary.
   (C) A newchild's name must not be used before the Ceremony of One.
   (D) Children are not allowed to use bicycles before the age of nine.

4. How could an important rule change?

(A) A committee studies the rule and seeks advice from The Receiver of Memory.

(B) A committee studies the rule and makes changes to it if necessary.

(C) A committee changes the rule with guidance from Elders.

(D) The elders vote on changing the rule.

5. Which of the following was NOT true about Jonas's father when he was young?

(A) He spent most of his volunteer hours at the Nurturing Center.

(B) He knew his aptitude in nurturing before the Ceremony of Eleven.

(C) He expected the assignment of Nurturer and was pleased with the decision.

(D) Before the Ceremony of Eleven, his parents told him it was obvious what his assignment would be.

6. Which of the following is NOT true about how the Elders decide a citizen's assignment?

(A) They interview the children about their aspirations.

(B) They took notes while watching the children.

(C) They hold meetings with school instructors.

(D) They watch the children during recreation time and volunteer hours.

7. What did Jonas's parents warn him about?

(A) He might not like his assignment.

(B) His group of friends might change after his assignment.

(C) He was not able to appeal his assignment if he did not enjoy it.

(D) His assignment would be easy work and might be boring for him.

1분에 몇 단어를 읽는지 리딩 속도를 측정해보세요.

$$\frac{2{,}293 \text{ words}}{\text{reading time (\quad) sec}} \times 60 = (\qquad) \text{ WPM}$$

• *Build Your Vocabulary*

pour***
[pɔːr]

v. 따르다, 붓다, 쏟다
If you pour a liquid or other substance, you make it flow steadily out of a container by holding the container at an angle.

observe***
[əbzə́ːrv]

vt. 관찰하다, 목격하다
If you observe a person or thing, you watch them carefully, especially in order to learn something about them.

ceremony**
[sérəmòuni]

n. 의식, 의례
A ceremony is a formal event such as a wedding.

release**
[rilíːs]

vt. 놓아주다, 해방시키다, 풀어놓다; n. 석방
If a person or animal is released from somewhere where they have been looked after, they are set free or allowed to go.

nurture**
[nə́ːrtʃər]

vt. 양육하다, 기르다; n. 양육, 양성, 교육 (nurturer n. 양육자)
If you nurture something such as a young child or a young plant, you care for it while it is growing and developing.

wobbly
[wábəli]

a. 흔들거리는, 동요하는, 불안정한
Something that is wobbly moves unsteadily from side to side.

unsteady*
[ʌnstédi]

a. 불안정한, 비틀비틀하는
If you are unsteady, you have difficulty doing something, for example walking, because you cannot completely control your legs or your body.

blanket**
[blǽŋkit]

n. 담요, 모포
A blanket is a large square or rectangular piece of thick cloth, especially one which you put on a bed to keep you warm.

application**
[æplikéiʃən]

n. 지원(서), 신청(서); 적용, 응용
An application for something such as a job or membership of an organization is a formal written request for it.

approve**
[əprúːv]

v. 찬성하다, 승인하다
If someone in a position of authority approves a plan or idea, they formally agree to it and say that it can happen.

sneak*
[sniːk]

v. 몰래 움직이다, 몰래하다; 고자질하다; n. 밀고자
If you sneak somewhere, you go there very quietly on foot, trying to avoid being seen or heard.

confide**
[kənfáid]

v. (비밀을) 털어놓다; 신임하다, 신뢰하다
If you confide in someone, you tell them a secret.

committee**
[kəmíti]

n. 위원회
A committee is a group of people who meet to make decisions or plans for a larger group or organization that they represent.

as a matter of fact

idiom 사실은, 실제로
As a matter of fact is used when you are telling somebody something interesting, new or important.

guilty**
[gílti]

a. 죄진 듯한, 가책을 느끼는; 유죄의
If you feel guilty, you feel unhappy because you think that you have done something wrong or have failed to do something which you should have done.

enhance*
[enhǽns]

vt. 높이다, 강화하다, 향상하다
To enhance something means to improve its value, quality, or attractiveness.

fascinate**
[fǽsənèit]

v. 매혹하다, 반하게 하다 (fascinated a. 매혹된, 마음을 빼앗긴)
If something fascinates you, it interests and delights you so much that your thoughts tend to concentrate on it.

awe**
[ɔː]

vt. 경외심을 갖게 하다; n. 경외, 외경심
If you are awed by someone or something, they make you feel respectful and amazed, though often rather frightened.

glance***
[glæns]

v. 흘긋 보다, 잠깐 보다; n. 흘긋 봄
If you glance at something or someone, you look at them very quickly and then look away again immediately.

adherence
[ædhíərəns]

n. 고수, 집착; 충성, 지지
Adherence is the fact of behaving according to a particular rule, agreement, or belief.

relieve**
[rilíːv]

vt. (걱정 · 고통 등을) 덜다, 완화하다
If something relieves an unpleasant feeling or situation, it makes it less unpleasant or causes it to disappear completely.

grin**
[grin]

v. (이를 드러내고) 싱긋 웃다, 활짝 웃다; n. 싱긋 웃음
When you grin, you smile broadly.

acquire**
[əkwáiər]

vt. 얻다, 획득하다; 습득하다, 배우다
If you acquire something, you buy or obtain it for yourself, or someone gives it to you.

establish***
[istǽbliʃ]

vt. 수립하다; 설립하다; 제정하다
If someone establishes something such as an organization, a type of activity, or a set of rules, they create it or introduce it in such a way that it is likely to last for a long time.

assemble**
[əsémbəl]

v. 모이다, 집합하다; 모으다, 조립하다
When people assemble or when someone assembles them, they come together in a group, usually for a particular purpose such as a meeting.

clap**
[klæp]

v. 박수를 치다; 가볍게 치다[두드리다]
When you clap, you hit your hands together to show appreciation or attract attention.

barely복습
[béərli]

ad. 간신히, 가까스로; 거의 ···않다
You use barely to say that something is only just true or only just the case.

fist복습
[fist]

n. (쥔) 주먹
Your hand is referred to as your fist when you have bent your fingers in towards the palm in order to hit someone, to make an angry gesture, or to hold something.

impatient복습
[impéiʃənt]

a. 성급한, 조급한, 참을성 없는
If you are impatient, you are annoyed because you have to wait too long for something.

technically*
[téknikəli]

ad. 엄밀히 말해서; 전문적으로, 기술적으로
Technically means according to an exact understanding of rules or facts.

elder복습
[éldər]

n. 연장자, 웃어른; a. 나이가 더 많은
A person's elder is someone who is older than them, especially someone quite a lot older.

govern**
[gʌ́vərn]

v. 다스리다, 통치하다 (governing a. 통치하는, 관리하는)
To govern a place such as a country, or its people, means to be officially in charge of the place, and to have responsibility for making laws, managing the economy, and controlling public services.

eventually**
[ivéntʃuəli]

ad. 결국, 마침내
Eventually means at the end of a situation or process or as the final result of it.

fret**
[fret]

v. 애타다, 안달하다; 속 타게 하다, 초조하게 하다; n. 애달음, 초조
If you fret about something, you worry about it.

shiver복습
[ʃívər]

v. 전율하다; (추위·공포로) 후들후들 떨다; n. 떨림, 전율
When you shiver, your body shakes slightly because you are cold or frightened.

fidget
[fídʒit]

v. 꼼지락거리다, 만지작거리다, 안절부절 못하다
If you fidget, you keep moving your hands or feet slightly or changing your position slightly, for example because you are nervous, bored, or excited.

attentive복습
[əténtiv]

a. 주의를 기울이는, 경청하는; 배려하는, 친절한
If you are attentive, you are paying close attention to what is being said or done.

element***
[éləmənt]

n. 요소, 성분; 원소
If something has an element of a particular quality or emotion, it has a certain amount of this quality or emotion.

suspense *
[səspéns]

n. 긴장감, 조마조마한 상태; 미결, 미정
Suspense is a state of excitement or anxiety about something that is going to happen very soon, for example about some news that you are waiting to hear.

assign 복습
[əsáin]

v. 맡기다, 배정하다, 임명하다, 지정하다 (assignment n. 임무, 과제, 할당된 일)
If you assign a piece of work to someone, you give them the work to do.

confess 복습
[kənfés]

v. 자백하다, 고백하다, 인정하다
If someone confesses to doing something wrong, they admit that they did it.

aptitude *
[ǽptitùːd]

n. 소질, 적성
Someone's aptitude for a particular kind of work or activity is their ability to learn it quickly and to do it well.

vehicle **
[víːikəl]

n. 탈것, 차량
A vehicle is a machine such as a car, bus, or truck which has an engine and is used to carry people from place to place.

construction **
[kənstrʌ́kʃən]

n. 건설, 건축; 건축물
Construction is the building of things such as houses, factories, roads, and bridges.

volunteer **
[vὰləntíər]

n. 지원자, 자원 봉사자; v. 자발적으로 나서다; a. 자발적인
A volunteer is someone who offers to do a particular task or job without being forced to do it.

observation **
[ὰbzərvéiʃən]

n. 관찰, 감시
Observation is the action or process of carefully watching some-one or something.

applaud **
[əplɔ́ːd]

v. 박수를 보내다, 성원하다
When a group of people applaud, they clap their hands in order to show approval, for example when they have enjoyed a play or concert.

envy **
[énvi]

vt. 부러워하다, 선망하다; 질투하다; n. 부러움, 선망; 질투
If you envy someone, you wish that you had the same things or qualities that they have.

thrill **
[θril]

v. 감동[감격, 흥분]시키다; 오싹하다; n. 전율 (thrilled a. 흥분한, 감격한)
If something thrills you, it gives you a feeling of great pleasure and excitement.

rare 복습
[rɛər]

a. 드문, 진귀한 (rarely ad. 드물게, 좀처럼 …하지 않는)
Something that is rare is not common and is therefore interesting or valuable.

reassure 복습
[rìːəʃúər]

vt. 안심시키다
If you reassure someone, you say or do things to make them stop worrying about something.

appeal ***
[əpíːl]

n. 항소, 상소; 애원, 간청; vi. 애원하다, 호소하다
An appeal is a formal request for a decision to be changed.

chuckle**
[tʃʌkl]

vi. 낄낄 웃다; n. 낄낄 웃음
When you chuckle, you laugh quietly.

giggle^{복습}
[gígəl]

v. 낄낄 웃다; n. 낄낄 웃음
If someone giggles, they laugh in a childlike way, because they are amused, nervous, or embarrassed.

lose track of

idiom ···을 놓치다, 잊다
If you lose track of someone or something, you no longer know where they are or what is happening.

justice^{복습}
[dʒʌ́stis]

n. 사법, 재판; 정의, 공정
Justice is the legal system that a country uses in order to deal with people who break the law.

occasional^{복습}
[əkéiʒənəl]

a. 가끔의, 때때로의 (occasionally ad. 때때로, 가끔)
Occasional means happening sometimes, but not regularly or often.

stroke^{복습}
[strouk]

① vt. 쓰다듬다, 어루만지다; n. 쓰다듬기, 달램 ② n. 타격, 일격, 치기
If you stroke someone or something, you move your hand slowly and gently over them.

neat**
[ni:t]

a. 산뜻한, 깔끔한 (neatly ad. 깔끔하게)
A neat place, thing, or person is tidy and smart, and has everything in the correct place.

trim**
[trim]

v. 다듬다, 정돈하다, 손질하다
If you trim something you cut off small amounts of it in order to make it look neater and tidier.

fond***
[fɑnd]

a. 정다운, 다정한; 좋아하는 (fondly ad. 다정하게)
If you are fond of someone, you feel affection for them.

shelf**
[ʃelf]

n. 선반
A shelf is a flat piece which is attached to a wall or to the sides of a cupboard for keeping things on.

stuff***
[stʌf]

vt. 채워 넣다, 속을 채우다; n. 물건, 물질 (stuffed a. 속을 채운)
If you stuff a container or space with something, you fill it with something or with a quantity of things until it is full.

imaginary**
[imǽdʒənèri]

a. 상상의, 가공의
An imaginary person, place, or thing exists only in your mind or in a story, and not in real life.

affectionate**
[əfékʃənit]

a. 다정한, 애정 어린 (affectionately ad. 애정을 담아서)
If you are affectionate, you show your love or fondness for another person in the way that you behave towards them.

briefcase*
[brí:fkèis]

n. 서류 가방
A briefcase is a case used for carrying documents in.

chapter three

1. Why would Lily get chastised for mentioning the appearance of Jonas's eyes?

   (A) There is a rule against mentioning differences between individuals.
   (B) Citizens are forbidden to speak about the appearance of others.
   (C) Lily often makes fun of Jonas.
   (D) It is considered rude to mention differences between individuals.

2. Why did Lily's mother respond sharply when Lily said she hoped to be a Birthmother?

   (A) There was little honor in becoming a Birthmother and the women were very lazy until they entered the House of the Old.
   (B) There was little honor in becoming a Birthmother and the women would become laborers after their third birth.
   (C) Lily was told she would be assigned Nurturer instead of Birthmother.
   (D) There was great honor in becoming a Birthmother and Lily insulted their importance in the community.

3. Lily's mother suggested Lily could start volunteer hours to better understand the assignment of _____, but Jonas thought she would be better suited for the assignment of _____.

   (A) Birthmother; Nurturer
   (B) Speaker; Nurturer
   (C) Nurturer; Speaker
   (D) Speaker; Birthmother

4. Which of the following did NOT happen after Jonas took the apple from the Recreation Area?

   (A) An announcement was made to remind male elevens they were not to take snacks from the Recreation Area.
   (B) Jonas's parents chastised Jonas for breaking the rules.
   (C) Jonas apologized to the Recreation Director.
   (D) Jonas felt humiliated and disposed of the apple.

5. Why was Jonas bewildered when he played with Asher?

   (A) He felt when he heard the announcement on the loudspeaker.
   (B) He was not scolded by his parents after the announcement.
   (C) The apple had somehow changed when it was in the air, but Asher did not notice the change.
   (D) The apple had slightly changed size and shape, but Asher did not notice the change.

1분에 몇 단어를 읽는지 리딩 속도를 측정해보세요.

$$\frac{1,621 \text{ words}}{\text{reading time (\quad) sec}} \times 60 = (\qquad) \text{ WPM}$$

• *Build Your Vocabulary*

squeal* \
[skwi:l]

v. 깩깩거리다, 끼익하는 소리를 내다; 비명을 지르다 \
If someone or something squeals, they make a long, high-pitched sound.

glare** \
[glɛər]

v. 노려보다; 번쩍번쩍 빛나다; n. 섬광; 노려봄 \
If you glare at someone, you look at them with an angry expression on your face.

chastise* \
[tʃæstáiz]

vt. 벌하다, 꾸짖다, 혼내주다 \
If you chastise someone, you speak to them angrily or punish them for something wrong that they have done.

strap** \
[stræp]

vt. 끈으로 묶다, 잡아매다; n. 가죽 끈, 혁대 (unstrap vt. 끈을 벗기다, 풀다) \
If you strap something somewhere, you fasten it there with a narrow piece of leather or cloth.

peer* \
[piər]

vi. 응시하다, 자세히 보다 \
If you peer at something, you look at it very hard.

exception** \
[iksépʃən]

n. 예외, 이례, 특례; 제외 \
An exception is a particular thing, person, or situation that is not included in a general statement, judgment, or rule.

unsettling \
[ʌnsétliŋ]

a. 동요시키는, 심란하게 하는 \
If you describe something as unsettling, you mean that it makes you feel rather worried or uncertain.

individual** \
[ìndəvídʒuəl]

n. 개인; a. 개개의; 개인의 \
An individual is a person.

insensitive \
[insénsətiv]

a. 무감각한, 둔감한 \
If you describe someone as insensitive, you are criticizing them for being unaware of or unsympathetic to other people's feelings.

chatter** \
[tʃætər]

n. 재잘거림, 수다; v. 수다를 떨다, 재잘거리다; 지저귀다 \
A chatter is a quick and continuous talk, usually about things which are not important.

port복습 \
[pɔ:rt]

n. 항구 (여기서는 '자전거를 세우는 곳' 이라는 의미로 사용) \
A port is a harbor area where ships load and unload goods or passengers.

glance^{복습}
[glæns]

v. 흘긋 보다, 잠깐 보다; n. 흘긋 봄
If you glance at something or someone, you look at them very quickly and then look away again immediately.

tease**
[tiːz]

v. 놀리다, 골리다, 괴롭히다; n. 골리기, 놀림
To tease someone means to laugh at them or make jokes about them in order to embarrass, annoy, or upset them.

shrug^{복습}
[ʃrʌg]

v. (양 손바닥을 내보이면서 어깨를) 으쓱하다; n. 으쓱하기
If you shrug, you raise your shoulders to show that you are not interested in something or that you do not know or care about something.

startle**
[stáːrtl]

v. 깜짝 놀라게 하다; 움찔하다; n. 깜짝 놀람 (startled a. 놀란)
If something sudden and unexpected startles you, it surprises and frightens you slightly.

forbidden**
[fərbídn]

a. 금지된
If something is forbidden, you are not allowed to do it or have it.

rarity
[rɛ́ərəti]

n. 아주 드묾, 진귀한 것
If someone or something is a rarity, they are interesting or valuable because they are so unusual.

depth**
[depθ]

n. 깊이; 깊은 곳, 깊음
The depth of something such as a river or hole is the distance downwards from its top surface, or between its upper and lower surfaces.

lurk**
[ləːrk]

vi. 숨다, 잠복하다; n. 잠복, 밀행
If someone lurks somewhere, they wait there secretly so that they cannot be seen, usually because they intend to do something bad.

self-conscious*
[sélfkánʃəs]

a. 남의 시선을 의식하는, 자의식이 강한
Someone who is self-conscious is easily embarrassed and nervous because they feel that everyone is looking at them and judging them.

blanket^{복습}
[blǽŋkit]

n. 담요, 모포
A blanket is a large square or rectangular piece of thick cloth, especially one which you put on a bed to keep you warm.

stuff^{복습}
[stʌf]

vt. 채워 넣다, 속을 채우다; n. 물건, 물질 (stuffed a. 속을 채운)
If you stuff a container or space with something, you fill it with something or with a quantity of things until it is full.

hippo
[hípou]

n. (= hippopotamus) [동물] 하마
A hippo is a very large African animal with short legs and thick, hairless skin.

assign^{복습}
[əsáin]

v. 맡기다, 배정하다, 임명하다, 지정하다
If you assign a piece of work to someone, you give them the work to do.

volunteer^{복습}
[váləntíər]

n. 지원자, 자원 봉사자; v. 자발적으로 나서다; a. 자발적인
A volunteer is someone who offers to do a particular task or job without being forced to do it.

amuse^{수능}
[əmjúːz]

vt. 즐겁게 하다, 재미나게 하다
If something amuses you, it makes you want to laugh or smile.

petulant
[pétʃələnt]

a. 심통을 내는, 심술을 부리는, 잘 토라지는 (petulantly ad. 토라지며)
Someone who is petulant is unreasonably angry and upset in a childish way.

acknowledge**
[əknálidʒ]

vt. 인정하다, 알리다; 감사하다
If you acknowledge a fact or a situation, you accept or admit that it is true or that it exists.

reluctant*
[rilʌ́ktənt]

a. 마음이 내키지 않는, 마지못해 하는 (reluctantly ad. 마지못해서)
If you are reluctant to do something, you are unwilling to do it and hesitate before doing it, or do it slowly and without enthusiasm.

tummy
[tʌ́mi]

n. 배, 복부
Your tummy is the part of the front of your body below your waist.

affectionate^{수능}
[əfékʃənit]

a. 다정한, 애정 어린 (affectionately ad. 애정을 담아서)
If you are affectionate, you show your love or fondness for another person in the way that you behave towards them.

kneel**
[niːl]

vi. (knelt-knelt) 무릎 꿇다
When you kneel, you bend your legs so that your knees are touching the ground.

drone*
[droun]

v. 윙윙거리다, 낮은 소리로 단조롭게 말하다
If something drones, it makes a low, continuous, dull noise.

self-important
[sélfimpɔ́ːrtənt]

a. 거드름 피우는, 자만심이 강한
If you say that someone is self-important, you disapprove of them because they behave as if they are more important than they really are.

reminder*
[rimáindər]

n. 상기시키는 조언; 생각나게 하는 것
Something that serves as a reminder of another thing makes you think about the other thing.

neat^{수능}
[niːt]

a. 산뜻한, 깔끔한 (neatly ad. 깔끔하게)
A neat place, thing, or person is tidy and smart, and has everything in the correct place.

satisfaction**
[sæ̀tisfǽkʃən]

n. 만족, 만족을 주는 것
Satisfaction is the pleasure that you feel when you do something or get something that you wanted or needed to do or get.

dangle*
[dǽŋgəl]

v. (달랑달랑) 매달(리)다; n. 매달린 것
If something dangles from somewhere or if you dangle it somewhere, it hangs or swings loosely.

humiliation*
[hjuːmìliéiʃən]

n. 창피, 굴욕
Humiliation is the embarrassment and shame you feel when someone makes you appear stupid, or when you make a mistake in public.

hoard[*]
[hɔːrd]

v. 저장하다, 축적하다; n. 저장, 축적
If you hoard things such as food or money, you save or store them, often in secret, because they are valuable or important to you.

sufficient[***]
[səfíʃənt]

a. 충분한, 흡족한
If something is sufficient for a particular purpose, there is enough of it for the purpose.

appropriate[복습]
[əpróuprièit]

a. 적당한, 적절한, 알맞은; vt. 사용하다, 충당하다
Something that is appropriate is suitable or acceptable for a particular situation.

remorse[*]
[rimɔ́ːrs]

n. 후회, 양심의 가책
Remorse is a strong feeling of sadness and regret about something wrong that you have done.

dispose[**]
[dispóuz]

v. 처리하다; 배치하다
If you dispose of something, you get rid of something that you do not want.

apology[복습]
[əpάlədʒi]

n. 사죄, 사과
An apology is something that you say or write in order to tell someone that you are sorry that you have hurt them or caused trouble for them.

incident[**]
[ínsədənt]

n. 일어난 일, 작은 사건
An incident is something that happens, often something that is unpleasant.

bewilder[**]
[biwíldər]

vt. 당황하게 하다, 어리둥절하게 하다
If something bewilders you, it is so confusing or difficult that you cannot understand it.

procedure[**]
[prəsíːdʒər]

n. 순서, 차례; 절차
A procedure is a way of doing something, especially the usual or correct way.

deserve[**]
[dizə́ːrv]

vt. …을 할[받을] 만하다, …할 가치가 있다
If you say that a person or thing deserves something, you mean that they should have it or receive it because of their actions or qualities.

countless[**]
[káuntlis]

a. 셀 수 없는, 무수한
Countless means very many.

effortless
[éfərtlis]

a. 노력하지 않는, 힘들이지 않는, 쉬운
Something that is effortless is done easily and well.

coordination[*]
[kouɔ̀ːrdənéiʃən]

n. 조직화, 합동, 조화
Coordination is the ability to use the different parts of your body together efficiently.

adequate[복습]
[ǽdikwit]

a. 적당한, 충분한; 어울리는 (adequately ad. 적당히, 충분히)
If something is adequate, there is enough of it or it is good enough to be used or accepted.

sphere**
[sfiər]

n. 구, 구체; 영역
A sphere is an object that is completely round in shape like a ball.

nondescript
[nàndiskrípt]

a. 별 특징 없는
If you describe something or someone as nondescript, you mean that their appearance is rather dull, and not at all interesting or attractive.

tunic艸
[tjúːnik]

n. 튜닉 (고대 그리스나 로마인들이 입던, 무릎까지 내려오는 헐렁한 가운 같은 웃옷)
A tunic is a loose piece of clothing covering the body down to the knees, usually without sleeves.

remarkable**
[rimáːrkəbəl]

a. 비범한, 뛰어난; 주목할 만한
Someone or something that is remarkable is unusual or special in a way that makes people notice them and be surprised or impressed.

toss**
[tɔːss]

v. 던지다, 내던지다; (머리 등을) 갑자기 쳐들다
If you toss something somewhere, you throw it there lightly, often in a rather careless way.

blink*
[bliŋk]

v. 눈을 깜박거리다; (등불 · 별 등이) 깜박이다; n. 깜박거림
When you blink or when you blink your eyes, you shut your eyes and very quickly open them again.

eyesight*
[áisàit]

n. 시력, 시야
Your eyesight is your ability to see.

squint艸
[skwint]

v. 곁눈질을 하다, 실눈으로 보다; a. 사시의; 곁눈질하는
If you squint at something, you look at it with your eyes partly closed.

identification*
[aidèntəfikéiʃən]

n. 신분 증명, 신원 확인; 동일함
The identification of something is the recognition that it exists, is important, or is true.

attach**
[ətǽtʃ]

vt. 붙이다, 달다; 소속시키다
If you attach something to an object, you join it or fasten it to the object.

mystify
[místəfài]

vt. 혼란스럽게 만들다, 어리둥절하게 하다
If you are mystified by something, you find it impossible to explain or understand.

ignore**
[ignɔ́ːr]

vt. 무시하다, 모르는 체하다
If you ignore someone or something, you pay no attention to them.

conviction**
[kənvíkʃən]

n. 신념, 확신; [법] 유죄 판결
A conviction is a strong belief or opinion.

dwelling艸
[dwéliŋ]

n. 거처, 주소, 사는 집
A dwelling is a place where someone lives.

bruise**
[bruːz]

v. 멍들게 하다, 타박상을 입히다; n. 타박상, 멍 (bruised a. 멍든)
If a fruit, vegetable, or plant bruises or is bruised, it is damaged by being handled roughly, making a mark on the skin.

magnifying glass
[mǽgnəfàiiŋglæs]

n. 확대경, 돋보기
magnifying (a. 확대하는) + glass (n. 유리)

meaningful *
[míːniŋfəl]

a. 의미심장한; 의미 있는, 중요한 (meaningfully ad. 의미심장하게)
A meaningful look or gesture is one that is intended to express something, usually to a particular person, without anything being said.

hover **
[hʌ́vər]

v. 맴돌다, 서성이다, 배회하다
If you hover, you stay in one place and move slightly in a nervous way.

stir ***
[stəːr]

v. 휘젓다, 움직이다; n. 움직임; 휘젓기
If you stir, you move slightly, for example because you are uncomfortable or beginning to wake up.

whimper *
[hwímpər]

v. 훌쩍이다, 울먹이다; 낑낑거리다
If someone whimpers, they make quiet unhappy or frightened sounds, as if they are about to start crying.

formula **
[fɔ́ːrmjələ]

n. 유아용 유동식; 공식, 방식
Formula is a powder which you mix with water to make artificial milk for babies.

equipment **
[ikwípmənt]

n. 장비, 설비
Equipment consists of the things which are used for a particular purpose, for example a hobby or job.

proceed ***
[prousíːd]

vi. 진행되다, 계속하다, 나아가다
If an activity, process, or event proceeds, it goes on and does not stop.

reflective *
[riflktiv]

a. 사색적인, 돌아보는, 반성하는; 반사하는
If you are reflective, you are thinking deeply about something.

renewal *
[rinjúːəl]

n. 새롭게 하기, 재개, 부활, 갱신
If there is a renewal of an activity or a situation, it starts again.

solemn **
[sɑ́ləm]

a. 엄숙한, 근엄한
Someone or something that is solemn is very serious rather than cheerful or humorous.

chapter four

1. Why did Jonas not speak with Benjamin about working at the Rehabilitation Center?

    (A) It was against the rules to talk about the details of people's jobs.

    (B) Jonas wasn't interested in the work done at the rehabilitation center.

    (C) Jonas would be harshly chastised for breaking the rule against rudeness.

    (D) Jonas didn't want to be in a situation where Benjamin could break the rule against bragging.

2. How could someone know Jonas volunteered at the House of the Old?

    (A) The attendant at the front desk takes record of the volunteers and posts the records at the Hall of Open Records.

    (B) Jonas must sign in on a sign-in sheet and his hours are calculated at the Hall of Open Records.

    (C) Jonas must record his volunteer hours at the Hall of Open Records after they are complete each day.

    (D) The Elders are responsible to give the Elevens volunteer assignments and secretly calculate the Elevens' volunteer hours.

3. How do people in the community get their food?

    (A) The dwellings in the community must grow their own food in public gardens.

    (B) The dwellings in the community have their food delivered by the Food Distribution Center.

    (C) Each family unit must buy and cook food from the Food Distribution Center.

    (D) The people of the community eat their meals at the Food Distribution Center.

4. What did Jonas like about the experience of bathing the Old?

    (A) He liked to speak plainly with the elderly at the House of the Old.

    (B) He only liked doing volunteer hours with Fiona.

    (C) He liked the safety and trust he felt while bathing the people at the House of the Old.

    (D) He liked the relaxation he felt in the bathing room at the House of the Old.

5. Which of the following is true about a release at the House of the Old?

    (A) The life story of the Old being released is told.

    (B) The Old are usually depressed when one of their friends is released.

    (C) The stories about the person being released are always interesting and exciting.

    (D) The celebration is generally boring and the Old never enjoy taking part in the celebration.

6. Put the following events of a release at the House of the Old in order:

    (A) ___ Some of the Old make short speeches.

    (B) ___ The life story of the Old being released is told.

    (C) ___ The Old being released makes a good-bye speech.

    (D) ___ A toast is made.

    (E) ___ The Old who is being released is taken away to the Releasing Room.

    (F) ___ The Old raise their glasses and cheer.

    (G) ___ The Old chant an anthem.

1분에 몇 단어를 읽는지 리딩 속도를 측정해보세요.

$$\frac{1{,}953 \text{ words}}{\text{reading time (} \qquad \text{) sec}} \times 60 = (\qquad) \text{ WPM}$$

• *Build Your Vocabulary*

leisurely*
[líːʒərli]
a. 느긋한, 유유한, 여유 있는; ad. 천천히, 유유히
A leisurely action is done in a relaxed and unhurried way.

spot***
[spɑt]
vt. 발견하다, 분별하다; n. 반점, 얼룩; 장소, 지점
If you spot something or someone, you notice them.

fool around
idiom (하찮은 일로) 시간을 낭비하다, 빈둥거리며 세월을 보내다
If you fool around, you waste time or behave in a silly way.

luxury**
[lʌ́kʃəri]
n. 사치, 호사; 사치품
A luxury is a pleasure which you do not often have the opportunity to enjoy.

regulate*
[régjəlèit]
vt. 규제하다, 단속하다; 조절하다
To regulate an activity or process means to control it, especially by means of rules.

invariably**
[invɛ́əriəbli]
ad. 변함없이; 늘, 반드시
If something invariably happens or is invariably true, it always happens or is always true.

guidance**
[gáidns]
n. 안내, 지도, 길잡이
Guidance is help and advice.

self-confidence
[sélfkánfədəns]
n. 자신(감)
If you have self-confidence, you behave confidently because you feel sure of your abilities or value.

maturity*
[mətʃúərəti]
n. 성숙(함), 다 자란 상태
Someone's maturity is their quality of being fully developed in their personality and emotional behavior.

gravitate
[grǽvətèit]
v. 인력에 끌리다, (사람 등이) …에 자연히 끌리다
If you gravitate towards a particular place, thing, or activity, you are attracted by it and go to it or get involved in it.

rehabilitation*
[rìːhəbílətèiʃən]
n. 사회 복귀, 갱생; 복직, 복위
Rehabilitation is the process of assisting someone to improve and recover lost function after an event, illness or injury that has caused functional limitations.

injure*
[índʒər]
vt. 상처를 입히다, 해치다
If you injure a person or animal, you damage some part of their body.

rumor**
[rʌ́mər]

vt. 소문을 내다; n. 소문, 루머
If a fact is rumoured, people are talking about it although they do not know if it is true.

hasten**
[héisn]

v. 재촉하다, 독촉하다; 서두르다
If you hasten to do something, you are quick to do it.

permit**
[pə:rmít]

v. 허가하다, 허락하다; n. 허가(증)
If someone permits something, they allow it to happen.

bypass*
[báipæs]

vt. 우회하다, (단계를) 건너뛰다; n. 우회 도로
If you bypass someone or something that you would normally have to get involved with, you ignore them, often because you want to achieve something more quickly.

impress**
[imprés]

v. 깊은 인상을 주다, 감명을 주다 (impressed a. 감명[감동]을 받은)
If something impresses you, you feel great admiration for it.

accomplish***
[əkámpliʃ]

vt. 이루다, 성취하다, 완수하다 (accomplishment n. 성취, 업적)
If you accomplish something, you succeed in doing it.

awkward**
[ɔ́:kwərd]

a. 어색한, 불편한, 곤란한
Someone who feels awkward behaves in a shy or embarrassed way.

brag*
[bræg]

v. 자랑하다, 자만하다, 허풍떨다
If you brag, you say in a very proud way that you have something or have done something.

punishable
[pʌ́niʃəbəl]

a. 벌 줄 수 있는, 처벌할 만한, 처벌해야 할
If a crime is punishable in a particular way, anyone who commits it is punished in that way.

chastise^{복습}
[tʃæstáiz]

vt. 벌하다, 꾸짖다, 혼내주다 (chastisement n. 혼내 줌, 체벌)
If you chastise someone, you speak to them angrily or punish them for something wrong that they have done.

steer**
[stiər]

v. 조종하다, 이끌다, 나아가다
When you steer a car, boat, or plane, you control it so that it goes in the direction that you want.

occasion^{복습}
[əkéiʒən]

n. 특수한 경우, 때; 행사, 의식
An occasion is a time when something happens, or a case of it happening.

govern^{복습}
[gʌ́vərn]

v. 다스리다, 통치하다
To govern a place such as a country, or its people, means to be officially in charge of the place, and to have responsibility for making laws, managing the economy, and controlling public services.

structure**
[strʌ́ktʃər]

n. 건물; 구조, 체계; vt. 구성하다
A structure is something that has been built.

auditorium**
[ɔ̀:ditɔ́:riəm]

n. 강당, 회관; 청중석, 관객석
An auditorium is a large room, hall, or building which is used for events such as meetings and concerts.

nametag
[neimtæg]

n. 이름표
name (n. 이름) + tag (n. 꼬리표, 번호표)

distribution**
[dìstrəbjú:ʃən]

n. 분배, 배급; 분포
The distribution of things involves giving or delivering them to a number of people or places.

carton
[ká:rtən]

n. 큰 상자; 한 통
A carton is a large, strong cardboard box in which goods are stored and transported.

upright**
[ʌ́pràit]

a. 똑바른, 꼿꼿한, 수직으로 선
If you are sitting or standing upright, you are sitting or standing with your back straight, rather than bending or lying down.

attendant**
[əténdənt]

n. 안내원, 수행원; 참석자
An attendant is someone whose job is to serve or help people in a place such as a petrol station, a car park, or a cloakroom.

seal**
[si:l]

n. 도장, 직인; 봉인; v. 봉하다, 도장을 찍다
When you seal an envelope, you close it by folding part of it over and sticking it down, so that it cannot be opened without being torn.

signature**
[sígnətʃər]

n. 서명, 사인
Your signature is your name, written in your own characteristic way, often at the end of a document to indicate that you wrote the document.

tabulate
[tǽbjəlèit]

vt. 표로 만들다, 일람표로 만들다
To tabulate information means to arrange it in columns on a page so that it can be analyzed.

applause**
[əplɔ́:z]

n. 박수(갈채); 칭찬
Applause is the noise made by a group of people clapping their hands to show approval.

celebration^{수능}
[sèləbréiʃən]

n. 축하, 축전, 기념행사
The celebration of something is praise and appreciation which is given to it.

disgrace^{수능}
[disgréis]

n. 불명예, 치욕, 창피; vt. 수치가 되다; 욕보이다
You say that someone is a disgrace to someone else when you want to emphasize that their behavior causes the other person to feel ashamed.

cloud***
[klaud]

v. 흐리다, 흐려지다, 어둡게 하다; n. 구름
If you say that something clouds a situation, you mean that it makes it unpleasant.

celebrate**
[séləbrèit]

v. 기념하다, 축하하다
If you celebrate, you do something enjoyable because of a special occasion.

craft**
[kræft]

n. 공예; 기능, 기교
A craft is an activity such as weaving, carving, or pottery that involves making things skilfully with your hands.

furnish**
[fə́:rniʃ]

v. 갖추다, 비치하다; 공급하다, 제공하다
If you furnish a room or building, you put furniture and furnishings into it.

carpeting
[káːrpitiŋ]

n. 카펫류, 양탄자 재료
You use carpeting to refer to a carpet, or to the type of material that is used to make carpets.

serene**
[siríːn]

a. 고요한, 잔잔한; 조용한, 평온한
Someone or something that is serene is calm and quiet.

tease
[tiːz]

v. 놀리다, 골리다, 괴롭히다; n. 골리기, 놀림
To tease someone means to laugh at them or make jokes about them in order to embarrass, annoy, or upset them.

suspect**
[səspékt]

v. 짐작하다; 의심하다 혐의를 두다; n. 용의자
You use suspect when you are stating something that you believe is probably true, in order to make it sound less strong or direct.

caretaker
[kɛ́ərtèikər]

n. 돌보는 사람, 간호인; 관리인
A caretaker is someone who is responsible for looking after another person, for example, a person who is disabled, ill, or very young.

hunch*
[hʌntʃ]

v. 둥글게 구부리다; n. 예감, 직감
If you hunch forward, you raise your shoulders, put your head down, and lean forwards, often because you are cold, ill, or unhappy.

shuffle*
[ʃʌ́fl]

v. 질질 끌다, 발을 끌며 걷다; (카드를) 뒤섞다
If you shuffle somewhere, you walk there without lifting your feet properly off the ground.

blank**
[blæŋk]

a. 멍한, 얼빠진; 공허한, 공백의; n. 공백
If you look blank, your face shows no feeling, understanding, or interest.

blind***
[blaind]

a. 눈먼, 장님인; vt. 눈멀게 하다
Someone who is blind is unable to see because their eyes are damaged.

moist**
[mɔist]

a. 축축한, 습한, 습기 있는
Something that is moist is slightly wet.

scent**
[sent]

n. 냄새, 향기; v. 냄새 맡다; 냄새를 풍기다
The scent of a person or animal is the smell that they leave and that other people sometimes follow when looking for them.

smock*
[smɑk]

n. 겉옷, 작업복
A smock is a loose garment worn by people such as artists to protect their clothing.

shelf
[ʃelf]

n. 선반
A shelf is a flat piece which is attached to a wall or to the sides of a cupboard for keeping things on.

kneel
[niːl]

vi. 무릎 꿇다
When you kneel, you bend your legs so that your knees are touching the ground.

tub[*]
[tʌb]

n. 목욕통, 욕조; 통
A tub is a long, usually rectangular container which you fill with water and sit in to wash your body.

pad[*]
[pæd]

vt. 패드를 대다, 완충제를 넣다; n. 덧대는 것, 패드
If you pad something, you put something soft in it or over it in order to make it less hard, to protect it, or to give it a different shape.

lounging chair
[laundʒiŋtʃɛər]

n. 안락의자
lounging (a. 편하게 하는) + chair (n. 의자)

robe^{**}
[roub]

n. 예복, 관복; 길고 헐거운 겉옷
A robe is a loose piece of clothing which covers all of your body and reaches the ground.

steady^{***}
[stédi]

vt. 흔들리지 않게 하다, 안정시키다; a. 한결같은, 고른; 확고한
If you steady something or if it steadies, it stops shaking or moving about.

cushion^{**}
[kúʃən]

vt. 쿠션으로 받치다, 충격을 완화하다; n. 쿠션; 완충물
If you cushion something, you cover or hide it with or like a cushion.

headrest
[hédrèst]

n. 머리 받침
A headrest is the part of the back of a seat on which you can lean your head, especially one on the front seat of a car.

squeeze^{**}
[skwi:z]

vt. 꽉 쥐다, 짜다, 압착하다; 쑤셔 넣다; n. 압착, 짜냄
If you squeeze something, you press it firmly, usually with your hands.

frail^{**}
[freil]

a. 노쇠한; 약한, 부서지기 쉬운
Someone who is frail is not very strong or healthy.

bathe^{**}
[beið]

v. 목욕시키다, 씻다; (열·빛 등이) 뒤덮다, 감싸다
If you bathe someone, especially a child, you wash them in a bath.

fragile[*]
[frǽdʒəl]

a. 부서지기[깨지기] 쉬운
Something that is fragile is easily broken or damaged.

soothing
[súːðiŋ]

a. 달래는, 위로하는, 진정시키는
Something that is soothing has a calming, assuaging, or relieving effect.

slippery[*]
[slípəri]

a. 미끄러운, 미끈거리는
Something that is slippery is smooth, wet, or oily and is therefore difficult to walk on or to hold.

naked^{**}
[néikid]

a. 나체의, 벌거벗은; 적나라한 (nakedness n. 벌거숭이; 있는 그대로임)
Someone who is naked is not wearing any clothes.

nuisance^{**}
[njúːsəns]

n. 폐, 성가심
If you say that someone or something is a nuisance, you mean that they annoy you or cause you a lot of problems.

glimpse***
[glimps]

v. 흘끗 보다, 잠깐보다; n. 흘끗 봄, 잠깐 봄
If you glimpse someone or something, you see them very briefly and not very well.

tender***
[téndər]

a. 부드러운, 상냥한, 다정한 (tenderly ad. 상냥하게)
Someone or something that is tender expresses gentle and caring feelings.

absorbent
[əbsɔ́ːrbənt]

a. 잘 빨아들이는, 흡수력 있는
Absorbent material soaks up liquid easily.

drift**
[drift]

v. 모르는 사이에 빠져들다; 표류하다, 떠돌다; n. 표류; 흐름
If someone or something drifts into a situation, they get into that situation in a way that is not planned or controlled.

mischievous*
[místʃivəs]

a. 짓궂은, 장난이 심한,; 유해한
A mischievous person likes to have fun by playing harmless tricks on people or doing things they are not supposed to do.

recall***
[rikɔ́ːl]

vt. 생각해내다, 상기하다, 소환하다; n. 회상, 상기
When you recall something, you remember it and tell others about it.

meaningful*
[míːniŋfəl]

a. 의미 있는, 중요한; 의미심장한
If you describe something as meaningful, you mean that it is serious, important, or useful in some way.

prim
[prim]

a. (특히 여자가) 새침 떠는, 점잔빼는 (primly ad. 새침데기처럼)
If you describe someone as prim, you disapprove of them because they behave too correctly and are too easily shocked by anything rude.

confide*
[kənfáid]

v. (비밀을) 털어놓다; 신임하다, 신뢰하다
If you confide in someone, you tell them a secret.

rinse*
[rins]

vt. 헹구어 내다, 씻어내다; n. 헹굼
When you rinse something, you wash it in clean water in order to remove dirt or soap from it.

lay***
[lei]

v. (laid-laid) 놓다, 눕히다; 알을 낳다
If you lay something somewhere, you put it there in a careful, gentle, or neat way.

murmur*
[mə́ːrmər]

v. 중얼거리다; 투덜거리다; n. 중얼거림
If you murmur something, you say it very quietly, so that not many people can hear what you are saying.

toast*
[toust]

n. 건배, 축배; v. 건배하다
When you drink a toast to someone or something, you drink some wine or another alcoholic drink as a symbolic gesture, in order to show your appreciation of them or to wish them success.

chant*
[tʃænt]

v. 노래를 부르다; 일제히 외치다; n. (규칙적으로 반복되는) 구호, 문구; 노래
If you chant or if you chant something, you sing a religious song or prayer.

anthem^{복습}
[ǽnθəm]

n. 성가, 찬송가
An anthem is a song which is used to represent a particular nation, society, or group and which is sung on special occasions.

fond^{복습}
[fɑnd]

a. 좋아하는; 정다운, 다정한
If you are fond of something, you like it or you like doing it very much.

thrill^{복습}
[θril]

v. 감동[감격, 흥분]시키다; 오싹하다; n. 전율 (thrilled a. 흥분한, 감격한)
If something thrills you, it gives you a feeling of great pleasure and excitement.

bare***
[bɛər]

a. 발가벗은; 있는 그대로의
If a part of your body is bare, it is not covered by any clothing.

bow***
[bou]

v. (인사로 혹은 좌절·수치심에) 머리를 숙이다, 굽히다; n. 절, 경례; 몸을 굽힘
When you bow, you move your head or the top half of your body forwards and downwards.

frown^{복습}
[fraun]

vi. 얼굴을 찡그리다, 눈살을 찌푸리다; n. 찌푸린 얼굴
When someone frowns, their eyebrows become drawn together, because they are annoyed or puzzled.

enlarge**
[enlá:rdʒ]

v. 크게 하다, 확대하다
When you enlarge something or when it enlarges, it becomes bigger.

sly**
[slai]

a. 익살맞은; 음흉한, 다 알고 있다는 듯이 (slyly ad. 장난스럽게; 음흉한)
A sly look or expression shows that you know something that other people do not know.

chortle
[tʃɔ́:rtl]

v. 깔깔 웃다; 아주 좋아하다
To chortle means to laugh in a way that shows you are very pleased.

hoot*
[hu:t]

v. (폭소 혹은 비웃음의 표시로) 올빼미 같은 소리를 내다, (우우하고) 야유하다
If you hoot, you make a loud high-pitched noise when you are laughing or showing disapproval.

chapter five

1. Why didn't Jonas participate in the ritual of sharing dreams often?

   (A) He was always embarrassed about his dreams and did not want to share them with his parents.
   (B) He did not dream often.
   (C) He never understood his dreams and he didn't want to be chastised for being inarticulate.
   (D) He did not have to share his dreams if he didn't want to.

2. Which of the following was NOT true about Jonas's dream?

   (A) There were rows and rows of tubs.
   (B) The room was warm and damp.
   (C) Jonas had a bare chest.
   (D) Jonas was sweating.

3. Why was Jonas almost angry in his dream?

   (A) Fiona was laughing at Jonas's bare chest.
   (B) Fiona splashed water at Jonas.
   (C) Jonas and Fiona were fighting in his dream.
   (D) Fiona would not allow Jonas to bathe her and she laughed at him.

4. What feeling was new to Jonas about his dream?

    (A) Anger.

    (B) Wanting.

    (C) Humiliation.

    (D) Being frightened.

5. What are Stirrings?

    (A) Feeling strong hatred towards a person.

    (B) Desire for another person.

    (C) Frustration when interacting with people.

    (D) Feeling guilty about a problem.

6. The treatment for Stirrings is a daily_____. A person in the community stops treatment when they_____.

    (A) Injection; stop experiencing Stirrings

    (B) Injection; enter the House of the Old

    (C) Pill; enter the House of the Old

    (D) Pill; stop experiencing Stirrings

7. Why were Jonas's feelings about Stirrings confused?

    (A) He was proud to experience Stirrings and to start taking pills but wished he never experienced it.

    (B) He was scared to feel Stirrings but didn't want to take the pills for it.

    (C) He enjoyed the feeling of Stirrings and wanted to lie to his parents about it.

    (D) He was proud to experience Stirrings and to start taking pills but he also liked the feelings.

1분에 몇 단어를 읽는지 리딩 속도를 측정해보세요.

$$\frac{1,407 \text{ words}}{\text{reading time ( ) sec}} \times 60 = (\qquad) \text{ WPM}$$

• *Build Your Vocabulary*

ritual^{빈출}
[rítʃuəl]

n. (종교적인) 의식, 행사
A ritual is a religious service or other ceremony which involves a series of actions performed in a fixed order.

contribute^{빈출}
[kəntríbjut]

v. 기여[공헌]하다; 기부[기증]하다
If you contribute to something, you say or do things to help to make it successful.

rare^{빈출}
[rɛər]

a. 드문, 진귀한 (rarely ad. 드물게, 좀처럼 …하지 않는)
Something that is rare is not common and is therefore interesting or valuable.

fragment**
[frǽgmənt]

n. 부서진 조각, 파편, 단편
A fragment of something is a small piece or part of it.

afloat*
[əflóut]

a. (물위·공중에) 뜬, 떠있는
If someone or something is afloat, they remain partly above the surface of water and do not sink.

grasp**
[græsp]

v. 붙잡다, 움켜쥐다; n. 움켜잡기
If you grasp something, you take it in your hand and hold it very firmly.

vivid**
[vívid]

a. 생생한, 선명한 (vividly ad. 생생하게, 선명하게)
If you describe memories and descriptions as vivid, you mean that they are very clear and detailed.

wander***
[wάndər]

v. 돌아다니다, 방황하다; n. 유랑, 방랑
If you wander in a place, you walk around there in a casual way, often without intending to go in any particular direction.

recount*
[rikáunt]

v. 자세히 말하다, 이야기하다; 다시 세다
If you recount a story or event, you tell or describe it to people.

lengthy*
[léŋkθi]

a. 긴, 오랜; 장황한, 지루한
You use lengthy to describe an event or process which lasts for a long time.

frighten^{빈출}
[fráitn]

v. 놀라게 하다, 섬뜩하게 하다; 기겁하다 (frightening a. 깜짝 놀라게 하는)
If something or someone frightens you, they cause you to suddenly feel afraid, anxious, or nervous.

phrase^{복습}
[freiz]

n. 구절, 관용구
A phrase is a short group of words that people often use as a way of saying something.

disquiet
[diskwáiət]

vt. 평온을 잃게 하다; n. 동요, 불안 (disquieting a. 불안하게 하는, 걱정하게 하는)
If something disquiets you, it makes you feel anxious.

infraction
[infrǽkʃən]

n. 위반, 침해
An infraction is a violation or infringement of a law, agreement, or set of rules.

reluctant^{복습}
[rilʌ́ktənt]

a. 마음이 내키지 않는, 마지못해 하는 (reluctantly ad. 마지못해서)
If you are reluctant to do something, you are unwilling to do it and hesitate before doing it, or do it slowly and without enthusiasm.

punish^{복습}
[pʌ́niʃ]

v. 벌하다, 응징하다, 처벌하다 (punishment n. 처벌, 징계)
To punish someone means to make them suffer in some way because they have done something wrong.

gurgle*
[gə́:rgəl]

v. (아기가) 까르륵 소리를 내다; (물이 좁은 공간을 빠르게 흐를 때 나는),
꼴꼴[콸콸] 소리 나다
If someone, especially a baby, is gurgling, they are making a sound in their throat similar to the gurgling of water.

nurture^{복습}
[nə́:rtʃər]

vt. 양육하다, 기르다; n. 양육, 양성, 교육 (nurturing n. 양육)
If you nurture something such as a young child or a young plant, you care for it while it is growing and developing.

shift**
[ʃift]

v. 옮기다, 방향을 바꾸다; n. 변화, 이동; 교대
If you shift something or if it shifts, it moves slightly.

recreate
[rékrièit]

vt. (과거에 존재하던 것을) 되살리다, 재현하다
If you recreate something, you succeed in making it exist or seem to exist in a different time or place to its original time or place.

tub^{복습}
[tʌb]

n. 목욕통, 욕조; 통
A tub is a long, usually rectangular container which you fill with water and sit in to wash your body.

damp**
[dæmp]

a. 축축한; n. 습기
Something that is damp is slightly wet.

smock^{복습}
[smɑk]

n. 겉옷, 작업복
A smock is a loose garment worn by people such as artists to protect their clothing.

chest**
[tʃest]

① n. 가슴, 흉부 ② n. 상자, 궤
Your chest is the top part of the front of your body where your ribs, lungs, and heart are.

bare^{복습}
[bɛər]

a. 발가벗은; 있는 그대로의
If a part of your body is bare, it is not covered by any clothing.

perspire*
[pərspáiər]

v. 땀을 흘리다, 발한하다
When you perspire, a liquid comes out on the surface of your skin, because you are hot or frightened.

embarrass[복습]
[imbǽrəs]

v. 당황스럽게[쑥스럽게] 만들다, 곤란하게 하다
If something or someone embarrasses you, they make you feel shy or ashamed.

convince**
[kənvíns]

vt. 설득하다; 확신시키다, 납득시키다
If someone or something convinces you to do something, they persuade you to do it.

bathe[복습]
[beið]

v. 목욕시키다, 씻다; (열·빛 등이) 뒤덮다, 감싸다
If you bathe someone, especially a child, you wash them in a bath.

murky
[mɔ́:rki]

a. 애매한, 확실치 않은; 흐린, 탁한, 어두운
If you describe something as murky, you mean that the details of it are not clear or that it is difficult to understand.

vague**
[veig]

a. 희미한, 모호한, 애매한
If something written or spoken is vague, it does not explain or express things clearly.

flood***
[flʌd]

v. (갑자기 강하게) 밀려들다; 범람하다, 넘치다; n. 홍수
If an emotion, feeling, or thought floods you, you suddenly feel it very intensely.

keep an eye on

idiom …을 주목하다, 감시하다
If you keep an eye on someone or something, you watch them or it carefully.

wiggle[복습]
[wíɡəl]

v. 꿈틀꿈틀 움직이다, (좌우·상하로) 조금씩 움직이다
If you wiggle something or if it wiggles, it moves up and down or from side to side in small quick movements.

at length

idiom 길게, 상세하게, 충분하게; 마침내, 드디어
At length means in great detail and taking a long time.

sink[복습]
[siŋk]

v. (sank–sunk) 주저앉다; 가라앉다, 침몰하다
If something sinks, it disappears below the surface of a mass of water.

puzzle**
[pʌ́zl]

v. 어리둥절하게 만들다, 곤혹스럽게 하다, 난처하게 하다
(puzzled a. 당혹스러운, 어리둥절한)
If something puzzles you, you do not understand it and feel confused.

tidy**
[táidi]

v. 치우다, 정돈하다; a. 단정한, 말쑥한, 깔끔한
When you tidy a place such as a room or cupboard, you make it neat by putting things in their proper places.

tray**
[trei]

n. 쟁반, 음식 접시
A tray is a flat piece of wood, plastic, or metal, which usually has raised edges and which is used for carrying things, especially food and drinks.

stirring*
[stɔ́:riŋ]

n. (감정·생각 등이) 시작됨, 일어남; a. 감동시키는, 고무하는
A stirring of a feeling or thought is the beginning of one.

reference**   n. 참조; 언급; 문의
[réfərəns]
A reference is a word, phrase, or idea which comes from something such as a book, poem, or play and which you use when making a point about something.

(every) now and then   idiom 가끔, 때때로, 이따금
If you do something every now and then, you do it sometimes, but not very often.

reminder^{복습}   n. 상기시키는 조언; 생각나게 하는 것
[rimáindər]
Something that serves as a reminder of another thing makes you think about the other thing.

treatment**   n. 치료, 처치; 취급, 대우
[trí:tmənt]
Treatment is medical attention given to a sick or injured person or animal.

take place   idiom (사건 등이) 일어나다
If something takes place it happens, especially after previously being arranged or planned.

ignore^{복습}   vt. 무시하다, 모르는 체하다
[ignɔ́:r]
If you ignore someone or something, you pay no attention to them.

miserable**   a. 불쌍한, 비참한, 초라한
[mízərəbəl]
If you describe a place or situation as miserable, you mean that it makes you feel unhappy or depressed.

ceremony^{복습}   n. 의식, 의례
[sérəmòuni]
A ceremony is a formal event such as a wedding.

reassure^{복습}   vt. 안심시키다 (reassuring a. 안심시키는, 용기를 돋우는)
[rì:əʃúər]
If you reassure someone, you say or do things to make them stop worrying about something.

pill**   n. 알약
[pil]
Pills are small solid round masses of medicine or vitamins that you swallow without chewing.

brighten**   v. (사람의 얼굴이) 밝아지다; 빛내다, 밝게 하다
[bráitn]
If someone brightens or their face brightens, they suddenly look happier.

groan**   v. 신음하다, 끙끙거리다; n. 신음소리
[groun]
If you groan, you make a long, low sound because you are in pain, or because you are upset or unhappy about something.

good-natured**   a. 친절한, 사람이 좋은 (good-naturedly ad. 친절하게)
[gúdnéitʃərd]
A good-natured person or animal is naturally friendly and does not get angry easily.

swallow**   v. 삼키다, 목구멍으로 넘기다; (초조해서) 마른침을 삼키다
[swálou]
If you swallow something, you cause it to go from your mouth down into your stomach.

cupboard**
[kʌ́bərd]

n. 식기장, 찬장
A cupboard is a piece of furniture that has one or two doors, usually contains shelves, and is used to store things.

dosage
[dóusidʒ]

n. 정량, 복용량
A dosage is the amount of a medicine or drug that someone takes or should take.

adjust**
[ədʒʌ́st]

v. 조절하다, 조정하다; (옷매무새 등을) 바로 하다
If you adjust something, you change it so that it is more effective or appropriate.

confide^{복습}
[kənfáid]

v. (비밀을) 털어놓다; 신임하다, 신뢰하다
If you confide in someone, you tell them a secret.

pedal^{복습}
[pédl]

v. 페달을 밟다; n. 페달, 발판
When you pedal a bicycle, you push the pedals around with your feet to make it move.

pleasurable
[pléʒərəbəl]

a. 즐거운, 유쾌한, 기쁜
Pleasurable experiences or sensations are pleasant and enjoyable.

slip***
[slip]

v. 미끄러지다; 미끄러져 사라지다; 미끄러지듯 움직이다
If you slip somewhere, you go somewhere quickly and quietly, especially without being noticed.

guilty^{복습}
[gílti]

a. 죄진 듯한, 가책을 느끼는; 유죄의 (guiltily ad. 죄진 것처럼)
If you feel guilty, you feel unhappy because you think that you have done something wrong or have failed to do something which you should have done.

chapter six

1. Four, Fives, and Sixes wore jackets that button in the back because _____.

   (A) they played with the buttons

   (B) they learned interdependence by helping each other getting dressed

   (C) they learned how to ask for help without confusing words

   (D) they could not disobey the rule against Nakedness if they could not get undressed alone

2. Why is receiving a bicycle an important event for a child in the community?

   (A) The child receives his or her Assignment with the bicycle and shows the people in the community the child is able to be independent.

   (B) The child shows that his or her hand-eye coordination is good enough to be a productive member of the community.

   (C) The child receives his or her bicycle and is then considered an adult in the community.

   (D) The bicycle symbolizes the child being able to move away from the protection of his or her family unit.

3. Why was Gabriel not at the Naming Ceremony?

   (A) The committee decided that Gabriel would be released on the day of the Naming Ceremony.

   (B) Gabriel was not sleeping soundly and did not gain the weight required to be placed with a family unit.

   (C) The committee decided to give Gabriel to Jonas's family unit until he was old enough to begin his Assignment.

   (D) Gabriel was given to a new family unit before the Naming Ceremony.

4. Which of the following was NOT true about the death of the child, Caleb?

   (A) The community performed the Ceremony of Loss when Caleb died.

   (B) The community was usually very safe, but Caleb had wandered away and fallen into the river.

   (C) The family unit had to wait a five years before getting a new child as punishment for not being responsible parents.

   (D) The community performed the Murmur-of-Replacement when the parental pair was given the new child.

5. What was special about becoming an Eight in the community?

   (A) The girls no longer had to wear ribbons in their hair.

   (B) The Eights receive their own bicycles.

   (C) The Eights were given a jacket with pockets.

   (D) The Eights were given jackets with larger buttons.

6. Which of the following is NOT true about the annual ceremony?

   (A) The Nines receive bicycles for the first time.

   (B) The Tens have their hair cut into shorter styles.

   (C) Elevens were given volunteer hours for the first time.

   (D) Twelves receive their Assignments in the community.

7. How can a citizen get a spouse in the community?

   (A) A citizen can apply for a spouse and then the Committee of Elders choose a compatible spouse the citizen.

   (B) A citizen finds his/her own spouse and then applies for the Matching of Spouses ceremony.

   (C) A citizen can apply for a spouse and waits three years for the Committee of Elders to choose a match.

   (D) A citizen must take a test which assigns them a spouse.

1분에 몇 단어를 읽는지 리딩 속도를 측정해보세요.

$$\frac{2{,}491 \text{ words}}{\text{reading time (} \qquad \text{) sec}} \times 60 = (\qquad) \text{ WPM}$$

● *Build Your Vocabulary*

fidget^{복습}
[fídʒit]

v. 꼼지락거리다, 만지작거리다, 안절부절 못하다
If you fidget, you keep moving your hands or feet slightly or changing your position slightly, for example because you are nervous, bored, or excited.

impatient^{복습}
[impéiʃənt]

a. 성급한, 조급한, 참을성 없는 (impatiently ad. 성급하게, 조바심 내며)
If you are impatient, you are annoyed because you have to wait too long for something.

straighten**
[stréitn]

v. 똑바르게 하다, 곧게 하다
If you straighten something, you make it tidy or put it in its proper position.

braid*
[breid]

n. 땋은 머리; 땋은 끈; vt. (머리 · 끈 등을) 땋다
A braid is a length of hair which has been divided into three or more lengths and then woven together.

more often than not

idiom 자주, 종종, 대개
If something happens more often than not, it usually or frequently happens.

dangle^{복습}
[dǽŋgəl]

v. (달랑달랑) 매달(리)다; n. 매달린 것
If something dangles from somewhere or if you dangle it somewhere, it hangs or swings loosely

neat^{복습}
[ni:t]

a. 산뜻한, 깔끔한 (neatly ad. 깔끔하게)
A neat place, thing, or person is tidy and smart, and has everything in the correct place.

irritable*
[írətəbəl]

a. 화를 잘 내는, 성미가 급한 (irritably ad. 성질내며, 화를 내며)
If you are irritable, you are easily annoyed.

volunteer^{복습}
[vὰləntíər]

n. 지원자, 자원 봉사자; v. 자발적으로 나서다; a. 자발적인
A volunteer is someone who offers to do a particular task or job without being forced to do it.

designate**
[dézignèit]

vt. 지명하다, 지정하다, 선정하다, 명시하다
When you designate someone or something as a particular thing, you formally give them that description or name.

fasten**
[fǽsn]

v. 매다, 묶다, 잠그다
When you fasten something, you close it by means of buttons or a strap, or some other device.

inter-dependence
[ìntərdipéndəns]

n. 상호 의존
Interdependence is the condition of a group of people or things that all depend on each other.

emblem *
[émbləm]

n. 상징, 표상; 엠블럼
An emblem is something that represents a quality or idea.

gradual **
[ɡrǽdʒuəl]

a. 점진적인, 단계적인 (gradually ad. 점진적으로)
A gradual change or process occurs in small stages over a long period of time, rather than suddenly.

protective *
[prətéktiv]

a. 보호하는, (위험에서) 지키는, 방어하는
Protective means designed or intended to protect something or someone from harm.

grin 복습
[grin]

v. (이를 드러내고) 싱긋 웃다, 활짝 웃다; n. 싱긋 웃음
When you grin, you smile broadly.

wriggle *
[ríɡəl]

v. 꿈틀거리다, 몸부림치다; n. 몸부림침, 꿈틀거림
If you wriggle or wriggle part of your body, you twist and turn with quick movements.

assign 복습
[əsáin]

v. 맡기다, 배정하다, 임명하다, 지정하다 (assignment n. 임무, 과제, 할당된 일)
If you assign a piece of work to someone, you give them the work to do.

parachute *
[pǽrəʃùːt]

n. 낙하산; v. 낙하산으로 강하하다
A parachute is a device which enables a person to jump from an aircraft and float safely to the ground.

groan 복습
[groun]

v. 신음하다, 끙끙거리다; n. 신음소리
If you groan, you make a long, low sound because you are in pain, or because you are upset or unhappy about something.

appeal 복습
[əpíːl]

n. 항소, 상소; 애원, 간청; vi. 애원하다, 호소하다
An appeal is a formal request for a decision to be changed.

tug *
[tʌg]

n. 힘껏 당김; 분투, 노력; v. (세게) 당기다, 끌다; 노력[분투]하다
A tug is a quick and usually strong pull.

pill 복습
[pil]

n. 알약
Pills are small solid round masses of medicine or vitamins that you swallow without chewing.

auditorium 복습
[ɔ̀ːditɔ́ːriəm]

n. 강당, 회관; 청중석, 관객석
An auditorium is a large room, hall, or building which is used for events such as meetings and concerts.

prod
[prad]

v. 찌르다, 쑤시다; 자극하다; n. 찌르기, 찌름
If you prod someone or something, you give them a quick push with your finger or with a pointed object.

stow
[stou]

v. (짐을) 실어 넣다, 채워 넣다
If you stow something somewhere, you carefully put it there until it is needed.

throng**
[θrɔ(:)ŋ]

n. 군중, 인파; v. 떼 지어 모이다
A throng is a large crowd of people.

glimpse복습
[glimps]

n. 흘끗 봄, 잠깐 봄; v. 흘끗 보다, 잠깐보다
If you get a glimpse of someone or something, you see them very briefly and not very well.

spot복습
[spɑt]

vt. 발견하다, 분별하다; n. 반점, 얼룩; 장소, 지점
If you spot something or someone, you notice them.

wail**
[weil]

n. 울부짖음, 통곡; v. 울부짖다, 통곡하다; (큰 소리로) 투덜거리다
A wail is a long, loud, high-pitched cry which express sorrow or pain.

howl**
[haul]

n. 울부짖는 소리; v. 울부짖다, 아우성치다; 크게 웃다
A howl is a long, loud, crying sound.

squirm
[skwə:rm]

vi. (벌레처럼) 꿈틀거리다, 몸부림치다; 우물쭈물하다
If you squirm, you move your body from side to side, usually because you are nervous or uncomfortable.

lap**
[læp]

① n. 무릎; (트랙의) 한 바퀴 ② v. (파도가) 찰싹거리다, (할짝할짝) 핥다
If you have something on your lap, it is on top of your legs and near to your body.

attentive복습
[əténtiv]

a. 주의를 기울이는, 경청하는; 배려하는, 친절한
If you are attentive, you are paying close attention to what is being said or done.

indulgent*
[indʎldʒənt]

a. 하고 싶은 대로 놔두는, 관대한 (indulgently ad. 관대하게)
If you are indulgent, you treat a person with special kindness, often in a way that is not good for them.

commotion*
[kəmóuʃən]

n. 소란, 소동, 동요
A commotion is a lot of noise, confusion, and excitement.

reprieve
[riprí:v]

n. 집행 유예; vt. 형 집행을 연기하다
A reprieve is a delay before a very unpleasant or difficult situation which may or may not take place.

committee복습
[kəmíti]

n. 위원회
A committee is a group of people who meet to make decisions or plans for a larger group or organization that they represent.

grant***
[grænt]

vt. 승인하다; 주다, 수여하다; n. 허가, 인가
If someone in authority grants you something, or if something is granted to you, you are allowed to have it.

placement*
[pléismənt]

n. 배치
The placement of something or someone is the act of putting them in a particular place or position.

plea*
[pli:]

n. 탄원, 청원; 간청, 기도
A plea is an appeal or request for something, made in an intense or emotional way.

appropriate***
[əpróupriət]

a. 적당한, 적절한, 알맞은; vt. 사용하다, 충당하다
Something that is appropriate is suitable or acceptable for a particular situation.

sleep soundly***

idiom 깊이 잠들다
If someone sleep soundly, they are sleeping very deeply.

label**
[léibəl]

vt. 분류되다; 라벨을 붙이다
If you say that someone or something is labeled as a particular thing, you mean that people generally describe them that way.

inadequate**
[inǽdikwət]

a. 부적당한, 부적절한; 불충분한
If something is inadequate, there is not enough of it or it is not good enough.

release***
[rilí:s]

vt. 놓아주다, 해방시키다, 풀어놓다; n. 석방
If a person or animal is released from somewhere where they have been looked after, they are set free or allowed to go.

pledge**
[pledʒ]

n. 맹세, 서약; vt. 맹세하다, 서약하다
When someone makes a pledge, they make a serious promise that they will do something.

attach***
[ətǽʃ]

vt. 소속시키다; 붙이다, 달다 (attached a. 소속된, 애착을 갖는)
If you are attached to someone or something, you like them very much.

temporary***
[témpərèri]

a. 일시적인, 임시의
Something that is temporary lasts for only a limited time.

relinquish*
[rilíŋkwiʃ]

vt. 포기하다, 내주다, 양도하다
If you relinquish something such as power or control, you give it up.

protest**
[próutest]

n. 항의; v. 항의하다, 이의를 제기하다; 주장하다
A protest is the act of saying or showing publicly that you object to something.

represent***
[rèprizént]

vt. 나타내다, 대표하다, 표현하다
If a sign or symbol represents something, it is accepted as meaning that thing.

hover***
[hʌ́vər]

v. 맴돌다, 서성이다, 배회하다
If you hover, you stay in one place and move slightly in a nervous way.

accompany***
[əkʌ́mpəni]

v. 동반하다, 동행하다; 수반하다
If you accompany someone, you go somewhere with them.

beam**
[bi:m]

v. 활짝 웃다; 빛나다; n. 광선, 빛남; 환한 얼굴
If you say that someone is beaming, you mean that they have a big smile on their face.

poke*
[pouk]

v. 찌르다, 쑤시다; n. 찌름, 쑤심
If you poke someone or something, you quickly push them with your finger or with a sharp object.

suspect[복습]
[səspékt]

v. 짐작하다; 의심하다, 혐의를 두다; n. 용의자
You use suspect when you are stating something that you believe is probably true, in order to make it sound less strong or direct.

exhaust**
[igzɔ́:st]

vt. 지치게 하다; 다 써버리다, 소진시키다 (exhausted a. 지칠 대로 지친)
If something exhausts you, it makes you so tired, either physically or mentally, that you have no energy left.

lively**
[láivli]

a. 생기에 넘치는, 기운찬, 활발한
You can describe someone as lively when they behave in an enthusiastic and cheerful way.

make a face

idiom 얼굴을 찌푸리다, 침울한 표정을 짓다
If you make a face, you twist your face to indicate a certain mental or emotional state.

giggle[복습]
[gígəl]

v. 낄낄 웃다; n. 낄낄 웃음
If someone giggles, they laugh in a childlike way, because they are amused, nervous, or embarrassed.

applause[복습]
[əplɔ́:z]

n. 박수(갈채); 칭찬
Applause is the noise made by a group of people clapping their hands to show approval.

enthusiastic**
[enθú:ziæ̀stik]

a. 열렬한, 열광적인
If you are enthusiastic about something, you show how much you like or enjoy it by the way that you behave and talk.

exuberant
[igzú:bərənt]

a. 열광적인, 열의가 넘치는
If you are exuberant, you are full of energy, excitement, and cheerfulness.

swell***
[swel]

n. 팽창, 증대; v. 부풀다, 팽창하다; 증가하다
A swell is an increase in sound produced by instruments.

glow***
[glou]

v. 상기되다, 발개지다, 달아오르다; 빛을 내다, 빛나다; n. 빛, 밝음
If someone glows with an emotion such as pride or pleasure, the expression on their face shows how they feel.

extraordinary**
[ikstrɔ́:rdənèri]

a. 기이한, 놀라운; 비상한, 비범한 (extraordinarily ad. 엄청나게, 유별나게)
If you describe something as extraordinary, you mean that it is very unusual or surprising.

wander[복습]
[wándər]

v. 돌아다니다, 방황하다; n. 유랑, 방랑
If you wander in a place, you walk around there in a casual way, often without intending to go in any particular direction.

somber*
[sámbər]

a. 침울한, 우울한; 어둠침침한, 거무스름한
Somber colors and places are dark and dull.

midday*
[míddèi]

n. 정오, 한낮
Midday is twelve o'clock in the middle of the day.

march***
[mɑːrtʃ]

① v. 행진하다, 당당하게 걷다; n. 행진, 행군 ② n. 3월
If you say that someone marches somewhere, you mean that they walk there quickly and in a determined way, for example because they are angry.

mature**
[mətʃúər]

a. 성숙한, 다 자란, 분별 있는
When a child or young animal matures, it becomes an adult.

keep track of

idiom …을 놓치지 않다; …의 진로를 쫓다
If you keep track of something, you remember about the number of something or the time.

belong***
[bilɔ́(:)ŋ]

vi. 속하다, 소유물이다 (belonging n. (pl.) 소유물, 재산, 소지품)
If something belongs to you, you own it.

solemn**
[sáləm]

a. 엄숙한, 근엄한 (solemnly ad. 장엄하게; 진지하게)
Someone or something that is solemn is very serious rather than cheerful or humorous.

longing**
[lɔ́(:)ŋiŋ]

a. 갈망하는, 동경하는; n. 갈망, 열망 (longingly ad. 간절히)
If you feel longing or a longing for something, you have a rather sad feeling because you want it very much.

gleam**
[gli:m]

vi. 빛나다, 반짝이다, 번득이다; n. 번득임, 어스레한 빛
If an object or a surface gleams, it reflects light because it is shiny and clean.

retrieve*
[ritrí:v]

vt. 되찾다, 회수하다
If you retrieve something, you get it back from the place where you left it.

applaud**
[əplɔ́:d]

v. 박수를 보내다, 성원하다
When a group of people applaud, they clap their hands in order to show approval, for example when they have enjoyed a play or concert.

dutiful
[djú:tifəl]

a. 의무를 다하는, 충실한 (dutifully ad. 책임감 있게)
If you say that someone is dutiful, you mean that they do everything that they are expected to do.

nametag**
[neimtæg]

n. 이름표
name (n. 이름) + tag (n. 꼬리표, 번호표)

cringe
[krindʒ]

vi. 움찔하다, 움츠리다
If you cringe at something, you feel embarrassed or disgusted, and making a slight movement.

bump**
[bʌmp]

v. 부딪치다, 충돌하다; n. 충돌
If you bump into something or someone, you accidentally hit them while you are moving.

podium
[póudiəm]

n. 연단, 연설대; 지휘대
A podium is a small platform on which someone stands in order to give a lecture or conduct an orchestra.

awkward**
[ɔ́:kwərd]

a. 어색한, 불편한, 곤란한
Someone who feels awkward behaves in a shy or embarrassed way.

summon**
[sʌ́mən]

vt. 소환하다, 호출하다
If you summon someone, you order them to come to you.

transgression^{복습}
[trænsgréʃən]

n. 위반, 범죄
Transgression is the action of going beyond or overstepping some boundary or limit.

adequate^{복습}
[ǽdikwit]

a. 적당한, 충분한; 어울리는 (adequately ad. 적당히, 충분히)
If something is adequate, there is enough of it or it is good enough to be used or accepted.

reflect**
[riflékt]

v. 반영하다, 나타내다; 비추다, 반사하다
If something reflects an attitude or situation, it shows that the attitude or situation exists or it shows what it is like.

guidance^{복습}
[gáidns]

n. 안내, 지도, 길잡이
Guidance is help and advice.

infringe*
[infríndʒ]

v. (법ㆍ계약ㆍ의무 등을) 어기다, 위반하다; 침해하다
If someone infringes a law or a rule, they break it or do something which disobeys it.

port^{복습}
[pɔ:rt]

n. 항구 (여기서는 '자전거를 세우는 곳' 이라는 의미로 사용)
A port is a harbor area where ships load and unload goods or passengers.

resettle
[ri:sétl]

v. 다시 자리에 앉다, 다시 자리잡다
re (다시) + settle (v. 정착하다, 자리 잡게 하다)

chuckle^{복습}
[tʃʌ́kl]

vi. 낄낄 웃다; n. 낄낄 웃음
When you chuckle, you laugh quietly.

invariably^{복습}
[invɛ́əriəbli]

ad. 변함없이; 늘, 반드시
If something invariably happens or is invariably true, it always happens or is always true.

violation*
[vàiəléiʃən]

n. 위반, 위배; 방해, 침해
Violation is the infringement or breach, as of a law, rule or right.

mount***
[maunt]

v. 오르다, 타다; 상승하다
If you mount a horse or cycle, you climb on to it so that you can ride it.

snip
[snip]

v. (가위로) 자르다, 싹둑 베다; n. 싹둑 자름, 가위질
If you snip something, you cut it quickly using sharp scissors.

distinguish**
[distíŋgwiʃ]

v. 구별하다, 분별하다 (distinguishing a. 특징적인, 다른 것과 구별되는)
If you can distinguish one thing from another or distinguish between two things, you can see or understand how they are different.

broom**
[bru(:)m]

n. 비, 빗자루
A broom is a kind of brush with a long handle. You use a broom for sweeping the floor.

mound**
[maund]

n. 더미, 무더기, 언덕
A mound of something is a large rounded pile of it.

discard[*]
[diskáːrd]

vt. 버리다
If you discard something, you get rid of it because you no longer want it or need it.

stir[※合]
[stəːr]

v. 휘젓다, 움직이다; n. 움직임; 휘젓기
If you stir, you move slightly, for example because you are uncomfortable or beginning to wake up.

dwelling[※合]
[dwéliŋ]

n. 거처, 주소, 사는 집
A dwelling is a place where someone lives.

hasty[**]
[héisti]

a. 급한, 성급한 (hastily ad. 급히, 허둥지둥)
A hasty movement, action, or statement is sudden, and often done in reaction to something that has just happened.

trim[※合]
[trim]

v. 다듬다, 정돈하다, 손질하다
If you trim something you cut off small amounts of it in order to make it look neater and tidier.

undergarment
[ʌndərgàːrmənt]

n. 속옷, 내의
Undergarments are items of clothing that you wear next to your skin and under your other clothes.

trousers[**]
[tráuzərz]

n. (남자용) 바지
Trousers are a piece of clothing that you wear over your body from the waist downwards, and that cover each leg separately.

calculator
[kǽlkjəlèitər]

n. 계산기
A calculator is a small electronic device that you use for making mathematical calculations.

congregate[*]
[káŋgrigèit]

v. 모이다, 군집하다; 모으다, 소집하다
When people congregate, they gather together and form a group.

merriment[*]
[mérimənt]

n. 명랑함, 흥겹게 떠듦
Merriment means laughter.

anxious[※合]
[ǽŋkʃəs]

a. 걱정하는, 염려하는; 열망하는, 간절히 바라는
(anxiously ad. 걱정스럽게, 불안해하며)
If you are anxious, you are nervous or worried about something.

gravitate[※合]
[grǽvətèit]

v. 인력에 끌리다, (사람 등이) …에 자연히 끌리다
If you gravitate towards a particular place, thing, or activity, you are attracted by it and go to it or get involved in it.

stroke[※合]
[strouk]

① vt. 쓰다듬다, 어루만지다; n. 쓰다듬기, 달램 ② n. 타격, 일격, 치기
If you stroke someone or something, you move your hand slowly and gently over them.

unaccustomed[*]
[ʌnəkʌ́stəmd]

a. 익숙지 못한
If you are unaccustomed to something, you do not know it very well or have not experienced it very often.

mutter[**]
[mʌ́tər]

v. 중얼거리다, 투덜거리다; n. 중얼거림, 불평
If you mutter, you speak very quietly so that you cannot easily be heard, often because you are complaining about something.

sanitation*
[sǽnətéiʃən]

n. 공중위생; 위생 설비
Sanitation is the process of keeping places clean and healthy, especially by providing a sewage system and a clean water supply.

boyish
[bɔ́iiʃ]

a. 소년 같은, 소년의 (boyishness n. 소년 같음)
If you describe a girl or woman as boyish, you mean that she looks like a boy.

buoyancy
[bɔ́iənsi]

n. 부력, 뜨는 성질
Buoyancy is the ability that something has to float on a liquid or in the air.

shrug^{복습}
[ʃrʌg]

v. (양 손바닥을 내보이면서 어깨를) 으쓱하다; n. 으쓱하기
If you shrug, you raise your shoulders to show that you are not interested in something or that you do not know or care about something.

meticulous
[mətíkjələs]

a. 꼼꼼한, 세심한; 정확한 (meticulously ad. 꼼꼼하게)
If you describe someone as meticulous, you mean that they do things very carefully and with great attention to detail.

spouse^{복습}
[spaus]

n. 배우자, 남편, 아내
Someone's spouse is the person they are married to.

weighty*
[wéiti]

a. 중대한; 무거운
If you describe something such as an issue or a decision as weighty, you mean that it is serious or important.

approve^{복습}
[əprú:v]

v. 찬성하다, 승인하다
If someone in a position of authority approves a plan or idea, they formally agree to it and say that it can happen.

disposition^{복습}
[dìspəzíʃən]

n. 성질, 기질, 경향; 배열, 배치
Someone's disposition is the way that they tend to behave or feel.

correspond**
[kɔ̀:rəspánd]

v. 일치하다, 부합하다; 대응하다; 서신을 주고받다
If one thing corresponds to another, there is a close similarity or connection between them.

interact
[ìntərǽkt]

vi. 상호 작용하다, 서로 영향을 끼치다
When people interact with each other, they communicate as they spend time together.

elder^{복습}
[éldər]

n. 연장자, 웃어른; a. 나이가 더 많은
A person's elder is someone who is older than them, especially someone quite a lot older.

scrupulous*
[skrú:pjələs]

a. 꼼꼼한, 세심한; 양심적인, 지조 있는 (scrupulously ad. 세밀하게)
Scrupulous means thorough, exact, and careful about details.

reenter*
[ri:éntər]

v. 다시 들어가다
re (다시) + enter (v. …에 들어가다)

suspense^{복습}
[səspéns]

n. 긴장감, 조마조마한 상태; 미결, 미정
Suspense is a state of excitement or anxiety about something that is going to happen very soon, for example about some news that you are waiting to hear.

chapter seven

1. How are the children's numbers determined?

    (A) The child's weight at the Naming Ceremony

    (B) The child's intelligence

    (C) The order in which they were born

    (D) The committee of Elders chooses each child's number

2. Which of the following is NOT true about the Ceremony of Twelve?

    (A) The Twelves are given their Assignments.

    (B) A Twelve is considered an adult in the community.

    (C) The Ceremony of Twelve is a time to honor the differences of the citizens turning Twelve.

    (D) The Chief Elder individually decides the Assignments of each Twelve at the ceremony.

3. What was explained as one of the most important tasks of small children?

    (A) Learning how to read

    (B) Learning precision of language

    (C) Learning the rules of the community

    (D) Learning to receive discipline

4. Once the Twelves received their Assignment and sat with their group, they thought about _____.

    (A) the training that came with their Assignment

    (B) the Assignments of the rest of the group

    (C) leaving their childhood behind them

    (D) the excitement of becoming an adult

5. At first, Jonas thought _____ when his number wasn't called.

    (A) the Chief Elder was joking

    (B) the Chief Elder made a mistake

    (C) the Chief Elder would announce his release

    (D) the Chief Elder forgot about him

• *Check Your Reading Speed*

1분에 몇 단어를 읽는지 리딩 속도를 측정해보세요.

$$\frac{2,165 \text{ words}}{\text{reading time } (\qquad) \text{ sec}} \times 60 = (\qquad) \text{ WPM}$$

• *Build Your Vocabulary*

irritation*
[ìrətéiʃən]

n. 짜증, 화
Irritation is a feeling of annoyance, especially when something is happening that you cannot easily stop or control.

misbehavior
[mìsbihéivjər]

n. 버릇없음, 품행 나쁨
Misbehavior is an action that is inappropriate, improper or unexpected.

mischief**
[místʃif]

n. 못된 짓, 장난
Mischief is playing harmless tricks on people or doing things you are not supposed to do.

unworthy**
[ʌnwə́:rði]

a. 가치 없는; 자격이 없는; 어울리지 않는
If you say that an action is unworthy of someone, you mean that it is not a nice thing to do and someone with their reputation or position should not do it.

chuckle
[tʃʌ́kl]

vi. 낄낄 웃다; n. 낄낄 웃음
When you chuckle, you laugh quietly.

exasperate*
[igzǽspərèit]

vt. 성나게 하다, 격분시키다 (exasperated a. 화가 치민, 짜증스러운)
If something exasperates you, they annoy you and make you feel frustrated or upset.

whine*
[hwain]

v. 징징거리다, 우는 소리를 하다; 푸념하다
If something or someone whines, they make a long, high-pitched noise, especially one which sounds sad or unpleasant.

toddler
[tádlər]

n. 아장아장 걷는 아이, 유아
A toddler is a young child who has only just learned to walk or who still walks unsteadily with small, quick steps.

maturity
[mətʃúərəti]

n. 성숙(함), 다 자란 상태
Someone's maturity is their quality of being fully developed in their personality and emotional behavior.

even out

phrasal v. 평등[동등, 평형]하게 되다
If something evens out, it becomes level or steady after a period when it has gone up and down or changed a lot.

progress***
[prágres]

vi. 진행하다, 진보하다; n. 전진, 진행; 진보, 향상
To progress means to move over a period of time to a stronger, more advanced, or more desirable state.

technically[복습]
[téknikəli]

ad. 엄밀히 말해서; 전문적으로, 기술적으로
Technically means according to an exact understanding of rules or facts.

duplication[*]
[djù:pləkéiʃən]

n. 이중, 중복; 복사, 복제
If you say that there has been duplication of something, you mean that someone has done a task unnecessarily because it has already been done before.

worrier
[wɔ́:riər]

n. 걱정이 많은 사람
If you describe someone as a worrier, you mean that they spend a lot of time thinking about problems that they have or unpleasant things that might happen.

tattletale
[tǽtltèil]

n. 수다쟁이, 고자질쟁이; a. 고자질하는, 비밀을 폭로하는
A tattletale is a person who tells tales about others.

tunic[복습]
[tʃú:nik]

n. 튜닉 (고대 그리스나 로마인들이 입던, 무릎까지 내려오는 헐렁한 가운 같은 웃옷)
A tunic is a loose piece of clothing covering the body down to the knees, usually without sleeves.

breeze[**]
[bri:z]

n. 산들바람, 미풍; vi. 산들산들 불다
A breeze is a gentle wind.

initial[**]
[iníʃəl]

a. 처음의, 최초의; n. 이니셜, 머리글자
You use initial to describe something that happens at the beginning of a process.

elect[***]
[ilékt]

vt. 선거하다, 선출하다
When people elect someone, they choose that person to represent them, by voting for them.

recollection[복습]
[rèkəlékʃən]

n. 회상, 회고
If you have a recollection of something, you remember it.

profound[**]
[prəfáund]

a. 깊이가 있는, 심오한
You use profound to emphasize that something is very great or intense.

acknowledge[복습]
[əknálidʒ]

vt. 인정하다, 알리다; 감사하다
If you acknowledge a fact or a situation, you accept or admit that it is true or that it exists.

standardize[*]
[stǽndərdàiz]

vt. 표준화하다, 표준에 맞추다
To standardize things means to change them so that they all have the same features.

curb[*]
[kəːrb]

vt. 억제하다; n. 재갈, 고삐; 구속
If you curb something, you control it and keep it within limits.

impulse[**]
[ímpʌls]

n. 충동, 욕구; 충격, 자극
An impulse is a sudden desire to do something.

determine[***]
[ditə́ːrmin]

v. 결심하다, 결정하다
If you determine something, you decide it or settle it.

aptitude ^{복습}
[ǽptitùːd]

n. 소질, 적성
Someone's aptitude for a particular kind of work or activity is their ability to learn it quickly and to do it well.

shift ^{복습}
[ʃift]

v. 옮기다, 방향을 바꾸다; n. 변화, 이동; 교대
If you shift something or if it shifts, it moves slightly.

reference ^{복습}
[réfərəns]

n. 언급; 참조; 문의
A reference is a word, phrase, or idea which comes from something such as a book, poem, or play and which you use when making a point about something.

tender ^{복습}
[téndər]

a. 부드러운, 상냥한, 다정한 (tenderness n. 친절, 다정, 애정)
Someone or something that is tender expresses gentle and caring feelings.

devise**
[diváiz]

v. 궁리하다, 고안하다
If you devise a plan, system, or machine, you have the idea for it and design it.

equipment ^{복습}
[ikwípmənt]

n. 장비, 설비
Equipment consists of the things which are used for a particular purpose, for example a hobby or job.

rehabilitation ^{복습}
[rìːhəbílətèiʃən]

n. 사회 복귀, 갱생; 복직, 복위
Rehabilitation is the process of assisting someone to improve and recover lost function after an event, illness or injury that has caused functional limitations.

tribute**
[tríbjuːt]

n. 감사[칭찬, 존경]의 표시, 헌사
A tribute is something that you say, do, or make to show your admiration and respect for someone.

observation ^{복습}
[àbzərvéiʃən]

n. 관찰, 감시
Observation is the action or process of carefully watching someone or something.

meticulous ^{복습}
[mətíkjələs]

a. 꼼꼼한, 세심한; 정확한 (meticulously ad. 꼼꼼하게)
If you describe someone as meticulous, you mean that they do things very carefully and with great attention to detail.

yawn**
[jɔːn]

vi. 하품하다; n. 하품
If you yawn, you open your mouth very wide and breathe in more air than usual, often when you are tired or when you are not interested in something.

lengthy ^{복습}
[léŋkθi]

a. 긴, 오랜; 장황한, 지루한
You use lengthy to describe an event or process which lasts for a long time.

accompany ^{복습}
[əkʌ́mpəni]

v. 동반하다, 동행하다, 수반하다
If one thing accompanies another, it happens or exists at the same time, or as a result of it.

hatchery ^{복습}
[hǽtʃəri]

n. (물고기 · 닭의) 부화장
A hatchery is a place where people control the hatching of eggs, especially fish eggs.

attendant
[əténdənt]

n. 안내원, 수행원; 참석자
An attendant is someone whose job is to serve or help people in a place such as a petrol station, a car park, or a cloakroom.

praise***
[preiz]

n. 칭찬, 찬사, 찬양; vt. 칭찬하다
If you praise someone or something, you express approval for their achievements or qualities.

nourishment*
[nə́:riʃmənt]

n. 음식물, 영양분
If something provides a person, animal, or plant with nourishment, it provides them with the food that is necessary for life, growth, and good health.

amidst**
[əmídst]

prep. (=amid) …의 한복판에, 한창 …하는 중에
If something happens amidst noises or events of some kind, it happens while the other things are happening.

designate
[dézignèit]

vt. 지명하다, 지정하다, 선정하다, 명시하다
When you designate someone or something as a particular thing, you formally give them that description or name.

pamper
[pǽmpər]

vt. 욕망을 한껏 채워주다, 응석 받아 주다
If you pamper someone, you make them feel comfortable by doing things for them or giving them expensive or luxurious things, sometimes in a way which has a bad effect on their character.

impose**
[impóuz]

v. 부과하다, 강요하다
If you impose something on people, you use your authority to force them to accept it.

discipline*
[dísəplin]

n. 훈련, 규율; vt. 훈련하다 (self-discipline n. 자기 훈련, 수양)
Discipline is the practice of making people obey rules or standards of behavior, and punishing them when they do not.

resume**
[rizú:m]

v. 다시 시작하다, 되찾다
If an activity resumes, or if you resume it, it starts again after a pause.

prestige*
[prestí:dʒ]

n. 위신, 명성; a. 명성이 있는
If a person, a country, or an organization has prestige, they are admired and respected because of the position they hold or the things they have achieved.

glance
[glæns]

v. 흘긋 보다, 잠깐 보다; n. 흘긋 봄
If you glance at something or someone, you look at them very quickly and then look away again immediately.

chastise
[tʃæstáiz]

vt. 벌하다, 꾸짖다, 혼내주다 (chastisement n. 혼내 줌, 체벌)
If you chastise someone, you speak to them angrily or punish them for something wrong that they have done.

deserve
[dizə́:rv]

vt. …을 할[받을] 만하다, …할 가치가 있다
If you say that a person or thing deserves something, you mean that they should have it or receive it because of their actions or qualities.

amuse^{중고}
[əmjúːz]

vt. 즐겁게 하다, 재미나게 하다 (amusement n. 즐거움, 재미)
If something amuses you, it makes you want to laugh or smile.

self-conscious^{중고}
[sélfkánʃəs]

a. 남의 시선을 의식하는, 자의식이 강한 (self-consciously ad. 수줍게)
Someone who is self-conscious is easily embarrassed and nervous because they feel that everyone is looking at them and judging them.

discard^{중고}
[diskáːrd]

vt. 버리다
If you discard something, you get rid of it because you no longer want it or need it.

howl^{중고}
[haul]

v. 크게 웃다; 울부짖다, 아우성치다; n. 울부짖는 소리
If you howl with laughter, you laugh very loudly.

sheepish
[ʃíːpiʃ]

a. 매우 수줍어하는; 양 같은
If you look sheepish, you look slightly embarrassed because you feel foolish or you have done something silly.

acquisition[*]
[æ̀kwəzíʃən]

n. 획득, 습득
The acquisition of a skill or a particular type of knowledge is the process of learning it or developing it.

retroactive
[rètrouǽktiv]

a. (법률 · 승급 등의 효력이) 소급하는
If a decision or action is retroactive, it is intended to take effect from a date in the past.

smack[*]
[smæk]

n. 찰싹 때리기; v. 때리다, 찰싹 치다
A smack is a sharp blow with the hand or any flat object.

rueful
[rúːfəl]

a. 애처로운, 가엾은 (ruefully ad. 가엾게, 비참하게)
If someone is rueful, they feel or express regret or sorrow in a quiet and gentle way.

regulate^{중고}
[régjəlèit]

vt. 규제하다, 단속하다; 조절하다
To regulate an activity or process means to control it, especially by means of rules.

wand[*]
[wɑnd]

n. (마술사의) 지팡이
A wand is a long thin rod.

flexible[*]
[fléksəbəl]

a. 구부리기 쉬운, 휘기 쉬운; 융통성 있는
A flexible object or material can be bent easily without breaking.

sting^{**}
[stiŋ]

vt. (stung-stung) 찌르다, 쏘다; n. 찌름, 쏨
If something stings you, a sharp part of it is pushed into your skin so that you feel a sharp pain.

wield[*]
[wiːld]

vt. (무기 · 도구 등을) 휘두르다, 사용하다, (권력을) 행사하다
If you wield a weapon, tool, or piece of equipment, you carry and use it.

bare^{중고}
[bɛər]

a. 발가벗은; 있는 그대로의
If a part of your body is bare, it is not covered by any clothing.

offense^{**}
[əféns]

n. 위반, 반칙, 범죄; 공격
An offence is a crime that breaks a particular law and requires a particular punishment.

eager^{중상}
[íːgər]

a. 열망하는, 간절히 하고 싶어 하는
If you are eager to do or have something, you want to do or have it very much.

treat***
[triːt]

n. 만족[즐거움]을 주는 것, 맛있는 간식; 대접, 환대; vt. 다루다, 대우하다
If you give someone a treat, you buy or arrange something special for them which they will enjoy.

precision*
[prisíʒən]

n. 정확, 정밀; 꼼꼼함
If you do something with precision, you do it exactly as it should be done.

whimper^{중상}
[hwímpər]

v. 훌쩍이다, 울먹이다; 낑낑거리다
If someone whimpers, they make quiet unhappy or frightened sounds, as if they are about to start crying.

cringe^{중상}
[krindʒ]

vi. 움찔하다, 움츠리다
If you cringe at something, you feel embarrassed or disgusted, and making a slight movement.

lapse**
[læps]

n. 착오, 실수; (시간의) 경과, 흐름
A lapse is a moment or instance of bad behavior by someone who usually behaves well.

escalate*
[éskəlèit]

v. 확대하다, 증가되다
If a bad situation escalates or if someone or something escalates it, it becomes greater in size, seriousness, or intensity.

lash**
[læʃ]

n. 채찍질; 가죽 끈; v. 후려치다, 채찍으로 때리다
A lash is a blow with a whip, especially a blow on someone's back as a punishment.

eventually^{중상}
[ivéntʃuəli]

ad. 결국, 마침내
Eventually means at the end of a situation or process or as the final result of it.

prompt**
[prɑmpt]

a. 신속한, 재빠른; 즉석의; v. 자극하다, 부추기다
A prompt action is done without any delay.

unfailing
[ʌnféiliŋ]

a. 한결같은; 틀림없는
If you describe someone's good qualities or behavior as unfailing, you mean that they never change.

murmur^{중상}
[mə́ːrmər]

v. 중얼거리다; 투덜거리다; n. 중얼거림
If you murmur something, you say it very quietly, so that not many people can hear what you are saying.

disposition^{중상}
[dìspəzíʃən]

n. 성질, 기질, 경향; 배열, 배치
Someone's disposition is the way that they tend to behave or feel.

beam^{중상}
[biːm]

v. 활짝 웃다; 빛나다; n. 광선, 빛남; 환한 얼굴
If you say that someone is beaming, you mean that they have a big smile on their face.

relieve^{중상}
[rilíːv]

vt. (걱정·고통 등을) 덜다, 완화하다
If something relieves an unpleasant feeling or situation, it makes it less unpleasant or causes it to disappear completely.

apprehensive ^{수능}
[ǽprihénsiv]

a. 우려하는, 염려하는
Someone who is apprehensive is afraid that something bad may happen.

finger***
[fíŋgər]

v. 손으로 만지다, 더듬다; n. 손가락
If you finger something, you touch or feel it with your fingers.

studious
[stjú:diəs]

a. 학문적인, 공부하기 좋아하는
Someone who is studious spends a lot of time reading and studying books.

justice ^{수능}
[dʒʌ́stis]

n. 사법, 재판; 정의, 공정
Justice is the legal system that a country uses in order to deal with people who break the law.

serene ^{수능}
[sirí:n]

a. 조용한, 평온한; 고요한, 잔잔한 (serenely ad. 침착하게)
Someone or something that is serene is calm and quiet.

enthusiastic ^{수능}
[enθú:ziǽstik]

a. 열렬한, 열광적인
If you are enthusiastic about something, you show how much you like or enjoy it by the way that you behave and talk.

caretaker ^{수능}
[kɛ́ərtèikər]

n. 돌보는 사람, 간호인; 관리인
A caretaker is someone who is responsible for looking after another person, for example, a person who is disabled, ill, or very young.

skip**
[skíp]

v. 건너뛰다, 생략하다; 뛰어다니다, 깡충깡충 뛰다
If you skip something that you usually do or something that most people do, you decide not to do it.

stun*
[stʌn]

vt. 어리벙벙하게 하다; 기절시키다; n. 놀라게 함
If you are stunned by something, you are extremely shocked or surprised by it and are therefore unable to speak or do anything.

hush**
[hʌʃ]

n. 침묵, 고요함; v. 잠잠하게 하다; 침묵하다
You say there is a hush in a place when everything is quiet and peaceful, or suddenly becomes quiet.

startle ^{수능}
[stá:rtl]

v. 깜짝 놀라게 하다; 움찔하다; n. 깜짝 놀람 (startled a. 놀란)
If something sudden and unexpected startles you, it surprises and frightens you slightly.

dizzy*
[dízi]

a. 현기증 나는, 아찔한
If you feel dizzy, you feel as if everything is spinning round and being unable to balance.

dim**
[dim]

a. 어둑한, 흐릿한, 희미한; v. 어둑하게 하다, 흐려지다 (dimly ad. 어렴풋이)
If you have a dim memory or understanding of something, it is difficult to remember or is unclear in your mind.

daze**
[deiz]

vt. 멍하게 하다; n. 멍한 상태 (dazed ad. 아찔해진, 멍해진)
If someone is dazed, they are confused and unable to think clearly, often because of shock or a blow to the head.

avert[*]
[əvə́ːrt]

vt. (눈 · 얼굴 따위를) 돌리다, 외면하다; 피하다

If you avert your eyes or gaze from someone or something, you look away from them.

hunch[복습]
[hʌntʃ]

v. 둥글게 구부리다; n. 예감, 직감

If you hunch forward, you raise your shoulders, put your head down, and lean forwards, often because you are cold, ill, or unhappy.

shame[**]
[ʃeim]

n. 부끄럼, 수치, 치욕; vt. 부끄러워하게 하다

Shame is an uncomfortable feeling that you get when you have done something wrong or embarrassing, or when someone close to you has.

bow[복습]
[báu]

v. (인사로 혹은 좌절 · 수치심에) 머리를 숙이다, 굽히다; n. 절, 경례; 몸을 굽힘

When you bow, you move your head or the top half of your body forwards and downwards.

chapter eight

1. How did Jonas feel after the Chief Elder announced the final assignment?

    (A) He felt excited because he wouldn't need to work.

    (B) He felt uneasy.

    (C) He felt humiliation and terror.

    (D) He felt disappointed in himself.

2. What happened when the committee failed in their last selection for the Receiver of Memory?

    (A) It caused the community terrible discomfort.

    (B) It started fights between people in the community.

    (C) The community was angry at the Chief Elder.

    (D) The committee members were released.

3. What is different about the assignment of Receiver of Memory?

    (A) The Receiver of Memory does not need any training.

    (B) The Receiver of Memory will be alone and apart from the rest of the community during training.

    (C) The Receiver of Memory will not live inside of the community during training.

    (D) The Receiver of Memory has easier training than the other citizens of the community.

4. Which of the following character traits did the Chief Elder NOT associate with Jonas?

(A) Intelligence

(B) Integrity

(C) Knowledge

(D) Wisdom

5. Which quality did the Chief Elder not understand?

(A) Strength

(B) The Capacity to See Beyond

(C) Intelligence

(D) Wisdom

6. Which of the following did Jonas NOT feel after being assigned as the new Receiver of Memory?

(A) Fear

(B) Pride

(C) Gratitude

(D) Disappointment

7. What did the audience do when the Chief Elder left the stage?

(A) They chanted his name.

(B) They stood and cheered.

(C) They clapped their hands.

(D) They went outside.

1분에 몇 단어를 읽는지 리딩 속도를 측정해보세요.

$$\frac{1,444 \text{ words}}{\text{reading time (\quad) sec}} \times 60 = (\qquad) \text{ WPM}$$

• *Build Your Vocabulary*

ill at ease

idiom 안절부절못하는, 마음이 놓이지 않는, 불편해 하는
When you feel ill at ease, you are nervous, especially in a social situation.

applaud복습
[əplɔ́:d]

v. 박수를 보내다, 성원하다
When a group of people applaud, they clap their hands in order to show approval, for example when they have enjoyed a play or concert.

piecemeal
[pí:smì:l]

a. 단편적인, 하나씩, 조금씩 하는
If you describe a change or process as piecemeal, you disapprove of it because it happens gradually, usually at irregular intervals, and is probably not satisfactory.

crescendo
[kriʃéndou]

n. [음악] 크레센도 (점점 세게, 점점 커짐)
A crescendo is a noise that gets louder and louder.

clap복습
[klæp]

v. 박수를 치다; 가볍게 치다[두드리다]
When you clap, you hit your hands together to show appreciation or attract attention.

anticipation**
[æntìsəpéiʃən]

n. 기대, 예상
Anticipation is a feeling of excitement about something pleasant or exciting that you know is going to happen.

kinship
[kínʃip]

n. 연대감, 동류의식; 친척 관계, 혈족 관계
If you feel kinship with someone, you feel close to them, because you have a similar background or similar feelings or ideas.

humiliation복습
[hju:mìliéiʃən]

n. 창피, 굴욕
Humiliation is the embarrassment and shame you feel when someone makes you appear stupid, or when you make a mistake in public.

subside*
[səbsáid]

vi. 가라앉다, 진정되다
If a feeling or noise subsides, it becomes less strong or loud.

vibrant
[váibrənt]

a. 활기찬, 생기가 넘치는; 강렬한, 선명한
Someone or something that is vibrant is full of life, energy, and enthusiasm.

gracious**
[gréiʃəs]

a. 품위 있는, 우아한, 정중한
If you describe someone, especially someone you think is superior to you, as gracious, you mean that they are very well-mannered and pleasant.

relieve ^{手令}
[rilíːv]

vt. (걱정 · 고통 등을) 덜다, 완화하다
If something relieves an unpleasant feeling or situation, it makes it less unpleasant or causes it to disappear completely.

discomfort [*]
[diskʌ́mfərt]

n. 불쾌, 불안; vt. 불쾌[불안]하게 하다
Discomfort is a painful feeling in part of your body when you have been hurt slightly or when you have been uncomfortable for a long time.

benign
[bináin]

a. 인자한, 친절한, 상냥한
You use benign to describe someone who is kind, gentle, and harmless.

anxiety ^{**}
[æŋzáiəti]

n. 걱정, 근심, 불안
Anxiety is a feeling of nervousness or worry.

apologize ^{手令}
[əpálədʒàiz]

v. 사과하다, 사죄하다
When you apologize to someone, you say that you are sorry that you have hurt them or caused trouble for them.

assemble ^{手令}
[əsémbəl]

v. 모이다, 집합하다; 모으다, 조립하다
When people assemble or when someone assembles them, they come together in a group, usually for a particular purpose such as a meeting.

apology ^{手令}
[əpálədʒi]

n. 사죄, 사과
An apology is something that you say or write in order to tell someone that you are sorry that you have hurt them or caused trouble for them.

utter ^{**}
[ʌ́tər]

① v. 발언하다, 입을 열다 ② a. 완전한, 전적인, 절대적인
If someone utters sounds or words, they say them.

anguish [*]
[ǽŋgwiʃ]

n. 괴로움, 고뇌, 번민; v. 괴로워하다, 괴롭히다
Anguish is great mental suffering or physical pain.

jaunty
[dʒɔ́ːnti]

a. 쾌활한, 의기양양한, 경쾌한
If you describe someone or something as jaunty, you mean that they are full of confidence and energy.

self-assured
[sélfəʃúərd]

a. 자신감 있는, 확신에 찬
Someone who is self-assured shows confidence in what they say and do because they are sure of their own abilities.

will ^{***}
[wil]

v. 의지를 발동하다; 뜻하다; n. 의지; 유언장
If you will something to happen, you try to make it happen by using mental effort rather than physical effort.

weighted
[wéitid]

a. (슬픔 등을) 짊어진, 무거워진; 치우친, 편중된
If something is weighted, it becomes heavier by adding something to it.

clumsy ^{手令}
[klʌ́mzi]

a. 꼴사나운, 어색한, 서투른
A clumsy person moves or handles things in a careless, awkward way, often so that things are knocked over or broken.

reassure[표意]
[riːəʃúər]
vt. 안심시키다 (reassuringly ad. 안심시키듯이)
If you reassure someone, you say or do things to make them stop worrying about something.

sink[표意]
[siŋk]
v. (sank-sunk) 가라앉다, 침몰하다; 주저앉다
If your heart or your spirits sink, you become depressed or lose hope.

blink[표意]
[bliŋk]
v. 눈을 깜박거리다; (등불 · 별 등이) 깜박이다; n. 깜박거림
When you blink or when you blink your eyes, you shut your eyes and very quickly open them again.

collective[*]
[kəléktiv]
a. 집단적인, 단체의
Collective actions, situations, or feelings involve or are shared by every member of a group of people.

questioning
[kwéstʃəniŋ]
a. 따지는, 캐묻는; n. 의문, 질문
If someone has a questioning expression on their face, they look as if they want to know the answer to a question.

puzzle[표意]
[pʌzl]
v. 어리둥절하게 만들다, 곤혹스럽게 하다, 난처하게 하다
(puzzled a. 당혹스러운, 어리둥절한)
If something puzzles you, you do not understand it and feel confused.

gasp[**]
[gæsp]
n. 헐떡거림; v. (놀람 따위로) 숨이 막히다, 헐떡거리다
A gasp is a short quick breath of air that you take in through your mouth, especially when you are surprised, shocked, or in pain.

intake[*]
[íntèik]
n. 빨아들임, 흡입; 받아들이는 곳
Your intake of a particular kind of food, drink, or air is the amount that you eat, drink, or breathe in.

astonish[**]
[əstániʃ]
vt. 깜짝 놀라게 하다 (astonishment n. 놀람, 경악)
If something or someone astonishes you, they surprise you very much.

awe[표意]
[ɔː]
n. 경외, 외경심; vt. 경외심을 갖게 하다
Awe is the feeling of respect and amazement that you have when you are faced with something wonderful and often rather frightening.

rare[표意]
[rɛər]
a. 드문, 진귀한
Something that is rare is not common and is therefore interesting or valuable.

successor[**]
[səksésər]
n. 후임자, 후계자
Someone's successor is the person who takes their job after they have left.

beard[**]
[biərd]
n. 턱수염 (bearded a. 수염이 있는, 수염이 난)
A bearded man has a beard.

intent[**]
[intént]
① a. 집중된, 열심인, 여념이 없는 (intently ad. 골똘하게) ② n. 의지, 의향
If someone does something in an intent way, they pay great attention to what they are doing.

toddler[중급]
[tádlər]

n. 아장아장 걷는 아이, 유아
A toddler is a young child who has only just learned to walk or who still walks unsteadily with small, quick steps.

dwell**
[dwel]

vi. 살다, 거주하다
(dwell on phrasal v. …을 자세히 설명하다, …을 깊이 생각하다)
If you dwell on something, especially something unpleasant, you think, speak, or write about it a lot or for quite a long time.

hasty[중급]
[héisti]

a. 급한, 성급한
A hasty movement, action, or statement is sudden, and often done in reaction to something that has just happened.

tension*
[ténʃən]

n. 긴장, 불안
Tension is a feeling of worry and anxiety which makes it difficult for you to relax.

painstaking*
[péinztèikiŋ]

a. 공들인, 노고를 아끼지 않는, 고생스러운
A painstaking search, examination, or investigation is done extremely carefully and thoroughly.

observation[중급]
[àbzərvéiʃən]

n. 관찰, 감시
Observation is the action or process of carefully watching someone or something.

attribute**
[ətríbjuːt]

n. 속성, 특성; vt. …에 귀착시키다, (…을 …의) 결과로 보다
An attribute is a quality or feature that someone or something has.

observe[중급]
[əbzə́ːrv]

vt. 관찰하다, 목격하다
If you observe a person or thing, you watch them carefully, especially in order to learn something about them.

patient[중급]
[péiʃənt]

a. 인내심[참을성] 있는; n. 환자 (patience n. 인내, 참을성)
If you are patient, you stay calm and do not get annoyed, for example when something takes a long time, or when someone is not doing what you want them to do.

nurture[중급]
[nə́ːrtʃər]

vt. 양육하다, 기르다; n. 양육, 양성, 교육 (nurturer n. 양육자)
If you nurture something such as a young child or a young plant, you care for it while it is growing and developing.

reveal***
[riví:l]

vt. 드러내다, 폭로하다, 밝히다
If you reveal something that has been out of sight, you uncover it so that people can see it.

indolence
[índələns]

n. 게으름, 나태
Indolence means laziness.

modify**
[mádəfài]

v. 변경하다, 수정하다
If you modify something, you change it slightly, usually in order to improve it.

unanimous*
[juːnǽnəməs]

a. 만장일치의, 이의 없는
When a group of people are unanimous , they all agree about something or all vote for the same thing.

fleeting[*]
[flí:tiŋ]

a. 순식간의, 잠깐 동안의; 어느덧 지나가는
Fleeting is used to describe something which lasts only for a very short time.

candidate[**]
[kǽndədèit]

n. 지원자, 후보자
A candidate is someone who is being considered for a position, for example someone who is running in an election or applying for a job.

integrity[*]
[intégrəti]

n. 진실성, 온전함, 고결, 성실
If you have integrity, you are honest and firm in your moral principles.

prompt[복습]
[prampt]

a. 신속한, 재빠른; 즉석의; v. 자극하다, 부추기다 (promptly ad. 재빨리)
A prompt action is done without any delay.

rigorous[*]
[rígərəs]

a. 엄한, 엄격한
A test, system, or procedure that is rigorous is very thorough and strict.

involve[**]
[inválv]

vt. 수반하다, 포함하다, 관련시키다
If a situation or activity involves something, that thing is a necessary part or consequence of it.

flutter[**]
[flʌ́tər]

v. (깃발 등이) 펄럭이다; (새 등이) 날갯짓하다; n. 펄럭임
If something thin or light flutters, or if you flutter it, it moves up and down or from side to side with a lot of quick, light movements.

scrape[**]
[skreip]

v. 스쳐서 상처를 내다; 긁다, 긁어내다, 문지르다
If you scrape a part of your body, you accidentally rub it against something hard and rough, and damage it slightly.

crush[**]
[krʌʃ]

v. 으스러뜨리다, 짓밟다, 눌러 부수다
If you are crushed against someone or something, you are pushed or pressed against them.

recall[복습]
[rikɔ́:l]

vt. 생각해내다, 상기하다, 소환하다; n. 회상, 상기
When you recall something, you remember it and tell others about it.

incident[복습]
[ínsədənt]

n. 일어난 일, 작은 사건
An incident is something that happens, often something that is unpleasant.

accompany[복습]
[əkʌ́mpəni]

v. 동반하다, 동행하다; 수반하다 (accompanying a. 수반하는, 함께한)
If one thing accompanies another, it happens or exists at the same time, or as a result of it.

misery[**]
[mízəri]

n. 고통, 괴로움, 비탄
Misery is great unhappiness.

magnitude[*]
[mǽgnətjù:d]

n. 거대함, 큼, (엄청난) 규모
If you talk about the magnitude of something, you are talking about its great size, scale, or importance.

comprehend[**]
[kàmprihénd]

vt. 이해하다, 파악하다
If you cannot comprehend something, you cannot understand it.

immense[**]
[iméns]
a. 막대한, 무한한, 강대한
If you describe something as immense, you mean that it is extremely large or great.

acquire[적습]
[əkwáiər]
vt. 습득하다, 배우다; 얻다, 획득하다
If you acquire something such as a skill or a habit, you learn it, or develop it through your daily life or experience.

acquisition[복습]
[ækwəzíʃən]
n. 획득, 습득
The acquisition of a skill or a particular type of knowledge is the process of learning it or developing it.

convince[복습]
[kənvíns]
vt. 확신시키다, 납득시키다; 설득하다
If someone or something convinces you of something, they make you believe that it is true or that it exists.

capacity[복습]
[kəpǽsəti]
n. 능력, 역량; 수용력, 용량
Your capacity for something is your ability to do it, or the amount of it that you are able to do.

freeze[**]
[fri:z]
v. (froze-frozen) 얼다, 얼어붙다; 얼게 하다; n. 결빙
If someone who is moving freezes, they suddenly stop and become completely still and quiet.

consume[**]
[kənsú:m]
v. …의 마음을 빼앗다, 사로잡다; 소비하다, 소모하다
If a feeling or idea consumes you, it affects you very strongly indeed.

confess[복습]
[kənfés]
v. 자백하다, 고백하다; 인정하다
If someone confesses to doing something wrong, they admit that they did it.

mercy[**]
[mə́:rsi]
n. 자비, 연민
If you refer to an event or situation as a mercy, you mean that it makes you feel happy or relieved, usually because it stops something unpleasant happening.

straighten[복습]
[stréitn]
v. 똑바르게 하다, 곧게 하다
If you straighten something, you make it tidy or put it in its proper position.

sliver
[slívər]
n. 찢어진 조각, 가느다란 조각; vt. 세로로 길게 베다[찢다]
A sliver of something is a small thin piece or amount of it.

spontaneous[*]
[spɑntéiniəs]
a. 자연히 일어나는, 자연적인
Spontaneous acts are not planned or arranged, but are done because someone suddenly wants to do them.

hush[복습]
[hʌʃ]
v. 잠잠하게 하다; 침묵하다 n. 침묵, 고요함 (hushed a. 조용해진, 고요한)
A hushed voice or hushed conversation is very quiet.

barely[복습]
[béərli]
ad. 간신히, 가까스로; 거의 …않다
You use barely to say that something is only just true or only just the case.

audible[*]
[ɔ́:dəbl]
a. 들리는, 들을 수 있는
A sound that is audible is loud enough to be heard.

chant^{복습}
[tʃænt]

n. (규칙적으로 반복되는) 구호, 문구; 노래; v. 노래를 부르다; 일제히 외치다
A chant is a word or group of words that is repeated over and over again.

swell^{복습}
[swel]

v. 부풀다, 팽창하다; 증가하다; n. 팽창, 증대
If the amount or size of something swells or if something swells it, it becomes larger than it was before.

gratitude**
[grǽtətjùːd]

n. 감사, 고마움
Gratitude is the state of feeling grateful.

chapter nine

1. How did Jonas feel after leaving the auditorium?

   (A) He felt more respected than he ever had before.

   (B) He felt separate and different from the other people in the community.

   (C) He felt excitement because the people in the community were talking about him.

   (D) He felt scared about going home.

2. What changed between Jonas and Asher?

   (A) Jonas felt that his friendship with Asher had changed slightly.

   (B) Asher was jealous of Jonas.

   (C) Asher was rude to Jonas.

   (D) Jonas and Asher realized they could no longer be friends.

3. What indicated the highest degree of disgrace in the community?

   (A) Being released after committing three transgressions.

   (B) Having one's name designated as a name Not-to-Be-Spoken.

   (C) Being publicly shunned by the Chief Elder.

   (D) To not be given an assignment at the ceremony.

4. Jonas's new schedule left no time for

_____.

(A) recreation
(B) schooling
(C) spending time in his own dwelling
(D) intense training

5. Which of the following rules did Jonas feel no reaction to?

(A) The prohibition of dream telling.
(B) The restriction of medication.
(C) The restriction of applying for release.
(D) Exemption from rudeness.

6. What frightened Jonas about the permission to lie?

(A) He thought a person would never have a reason to lie.
(B) Others might have been given the same permission to lie, so he
would never know if they were telling him the truth.
(C) He was scared about the repercussions of lying to others because of
his negative experience as a Four.
(D) He was concerned about the rules regarding precision of speech.

1분에 몇 단어를 읽는지 리딩 속도를 측정해보세요.

$$\frac{1,578 \text{ words}}{\text{reading time (}\qquad\text{) sec}} \times 60 = (\qquad) \text{ WPM}$$

• *Build Your Vocabulary*

elder^{복습}
[éldər]

n. 연장자, 웃어른; a. 나이가 더 많은
A person's elder is someone who is older than them, especially someone quite a lot older.

auditorium^{복습}
[ɔ̀:ditɔ́:riəm]

n. 강당, 회관; 청중석, 관객석
An auditorium is a large room, hall, or building which is used for events such as meetings and concerts.

throng^{복습}
[θrɔ(:)ŋ]

n. 군중, 인파; v. 떼 지어 모이다
A throng is a large crowd of people.

spot^{복습}
[spɑt]

vt. 발견하다, 분별하다; n. 반점, 얼룩; 장소, 지점
If you spot something or someone, you notice them.

hesitation^{**}
[hèzətéiʃən]

n. 주저, 망설임
Hesitation is an unwillingness to do something, or a delay in doing it, because you are uncertain, worried, or embarrassed about it.

smack^{복습}
[smæk]

n. 찰싹 때리기; v. 때리다, 찰싹 치다
A smack is a sharp blow with the hand or any flat object.

applause^{복습}
[əplɔ́:z]

n. 박수(갈채); 칭찬
Applause is the noise made by a group of people clapping their hands to show approval.

cluster^{**}
[klʌ́stər]

v. 밀집하다; n. 떼, 무리, 집단
If people cluster together, they gather together in a small group.

dwelling^{복습}
[dwéliŋ]

n. 거처, 주소, 사는 집
A dwelling is a place where someone lives.

memorize^{**}
[méməràiz]

vt. 기억하다, 암기하다
If you memorize something, you learn it so that you can remember it exactly.

yawn^{복습}
[jɔ:n]

vi. 하품하다; n. 하품
If you yawn, you open your mouth very wide and breathe in more air than usual, often when you are tired or when you are not interested in something.

boredom
[bɔ́:rdəm]

n. 지루함, 권태
Boredom is the state of being bored.

strap^{복습}
[stræp]

vt. 끈으로 묶다, 잡아매다; n. 가죽 끈, 혁대
If you strap something somewhere, you fasten it there with a narrow piece of leather or cloth.

solemn^{복습}
[sáləm]

a. 엄숙한, 근엄한
Someone or something that is solemn is very serious rather than cheerful or humorous.

remark***
[rimá:rk]

n. 의견, 발언; v. 말하다, 언급하다
If you make a remark about something, you say something about it.

dismount*
[dismáunt]

vt. (말·자전거 따위에서) 내리다
If you dismount from a horse or a bicycle, you get down from it.

chatter^{복습}
[tʃǽtər]

v. 수다를 떨다, 재잘거리다; 지저귀다; n. 재잘거림, 수다
If you chatter, you talk quickly and continuously, usually about things which are not important.

volunteer^{복습}
[vàləntíər]

n. 지원자, 자원 봉사자; v. 자발적으로 나서다; a. 자발적인
A volunteer is someone who offers to do a particular task or job without being forced to do it.

expert**
[ékspə:rt]

n. 전문가, 숙련가; a. 숙련된, 노련한
An expert is a person who is very skilled at doing something or who knows a lot about a particular subject.

mutter^{복습}
[mʌ́tər]

v. 중얼거리다, 투덜거리다; n. 중얼거림, 불평
If you mutter, you speak very quietly so that you cannot easily be heard, often because you are complaining about something.

assign^{복습}
[əsáin]

v. 맡기다, 배정하다, 임명하다, 지정하다 (assignment n. 임무, 과제, 할당된 일)
If you assign a piece of work to someone, you give them the work to do.

hesitate**
[hézətèit]

v. 주저하다, 머뭇거리다, 망설이다
If you hesitate, you do not speak or act for a short time, usually because you are uncertain, embarrassed, or worried about what you are going to say or do.

suspense^{복습}
[səspéns]

n. 긴장감, 조마조마한 상태; 미결, 미정
Suspense is a state of excitement or anxiety about something that is going to happen very soon, for example about some news that you are waiting to hear.

single out

phrasal v. 추려내다, 선발하다
If you single out someone or something, you choose them from among a group for special comment or treatment.

indicate***
[índikèit]

vt. 가리키다, 지시하다, 나타내다
If one thing indicates another, the first thing shows that the second is true or exists.

disgrace^{복습}
[disgréis]

n. 불명예, 치욕, 창피; vt. 수치가 되다; 욕보이다
You say that someone is a disgrace to someone else when you want to emphasize that their behavior causes the other person to feel ashamed.

blank^{복습}
[blæŋk]

a. 멍한, 얼빠진; 공허한, 공백의; n. 공백
If you look blank, your face shows no feeling, understanding, or interest.

relish[*]
[réliʃ]

n. 흥미, 의욕; 맛, 풍미; v. 즐기다; 기쁘게 생각하다
Relish is a strong appreciation or liking of something.

annex[*]
[ənéks]

n. 별관, 별채; 부속물; vt. 부가하다; 합병하다
An annex is a building that is an addition to another building.

exempt[*]
[igzémpt]

vt. (의무 등을) 면제하다; a. 면제된
To exempt a person or thing from a particular rule, duty, or obligation means to state officially that they are not bound or affected by it.

govern^{복습}
[gʌ́vərn]

v. 다스리다, 통치하다
To govern a place such as a country, or its people, means to be officially in charge of the place, and to have responsibility for making laws, managing the economy, and controlling public services.

prohibit^{**}
[prouhíbit]

vt. 금하다, 금지하다
If a law or someone in authority prohibits something, they forbid it or make it illegal.

injury^{**}
[índʒəri]

n. 부상, 상처, 손상
An injury is damage done to a person's or an animal's body.

medication
[mèdəkéiʃən]

n. 투약, 약물 치료; 약제, 약물
Medication is medicine that is used to treat and cure illness.

permit^{복습}
[pəːrmít]

v. 허가하다, 허락하다; n. 허가(증)
If someone permits something, they allow it to happen.

release^{복습}
[rilíːs]

n. 석방; vt. 놓아주다, 해방시키다, 풀어놓다
If a person or animal is released from somewhere where they have been looked after, they are set free or allowed to go.

stun^{복습}
[stʌn]

vt. 어리벙벙하게 하다; 기절시키다; n. 놀라게 함
If you are stunned by something, you are extremely shocked or surprised by it and are therefore unable to speak or do anything.

vital^{복습}
[váitl]

a. 극히 중대한, 필수적인; 생명 유지와 연관된
If you say that something is vital, you mean that it is necessary or very important.

logistic
[loudʒístik]

a. 논리적인, 논리주의의; n. 기호(記號) 논리학
Logistic means relating to the organization of something complicated.

dismay[*]
[disméi]

vt. 낙담[실망]하게 하다; n. 실망, 낙담, 경악
If you are dismayed by something, it makes you feel afraid, worried, or sad.

apparent^{**}
[əpǽrənt]

a. 또렷한; 명백한; 외관상의 (apparently ad. 보아하니, 명백히)
If something is apparent to you, it is clear and obvious to you.

compel^{***}
[kəmpél]

v. 강요하다, 억지로 …을 시키다
If a situation, a rule, or a person compels you to do something, they force you to do it.

thorough[**]
[θə́ːrou]
a. 철저한, 완전한; 절대적인 (thoroughly ad. 완전히, 철저히)
Thorough is used to emphasize the great degree or extent of something.

accustom[**]
[əkʌ́stəm]
v. 익히다, 익숙해지다 (accustomed a. 익숙해진)
If you accustom yourself or another person to something, you make yourself or them become used to it.

courtesy[**]
[kə́ːrtəsi]
n. 공손함, 정중함
Courtesy is politeness, respect, and consideration for others.

intimate[**]
[íntəmit]
a. 사적인, 은밀한; 친밀한, 친숙한
An intimate conversation or detail, for example, is very personal and private.

awkward[복습]
[ɔ́ːkwərd]
a. 어색한, 불편한, 곤란한 (awkwardness n. 어색함)
Someone who feels awkward behaves in a shy or embarrassed way.

unnerve
[ʌnnə́ːrv]
vt. 기운을 빼앗다, 용기를 잃게 하다, 낙담시키다
If you say that something unnerves you, you mean that it worries or troubles you.

prohibition[**]
[pròuhəbíʃən]
n. 금지
A prohibition is a law or rule forbidding something.

restriction[*]
[ristríkʃən]
n. 제한, 제약
A restriction is an official rule that limits what you can do or that limits the amount or size of something.

crush[복습]
[krʌʃ]
v. 으스러뜨리다, 짓밟다, 눌러 부수다
If you are crushed against someone or something, you are pushed or pressed against them.

gasp[복습]
[gæsp]
v. (놀람 따위로) 숨이 막히다, 헐떡거리다; n. 헐떡거림
When you gasp, you take a short quick breath through your mouth, especially when you are surprised, shocked, or in pain.

notify[**]
[nóutəfài]
vt. 알리다, 통보하다
If you notify someone of something, you officially inform them about it.

hasty[복습]
[héisti]
a. 급한, 성급한 (hastily ad. 급히, 허둥지둥)
A hasty movement, action, or statement is sudden, and often done in reaction to something that has just happened.

requisition
[rèkwəzíʃən]
vt. 요구하다; n. 요구, 청구
If people in authority requisition a vehicle, building, or food, they formally demand it and take it for official use.

prompt[복습]
[prɑmpt]
a. 신속한, 재빠른; 즉석의; v. 자극하다, 부추기다 (promptly ad. 재빨리)
A prompt action is done without any delay.

excruciating
[ikskrúːʃièitiŋ]
a. 극심한 고통을 주는; 맹렬한, 극심한
If you describe something as excruciating, you are emphasizing that it is extremely painful, either physically or emotionally.

diminish**
[dəmíniʃ]

v. 줄(이)다, 감소시키다
When something diminishes, or when something diminishes it, it becomes reduced in size, importance, or intensity.

throb*
[θrɑb]

n. 고동, 맥박; vi. (심장이) 고동치다, 맥이 뛰다
Throb is a beat or pulsation that you feel from part of your body.

pill복습
[pil]

n. 알약
Pills are small solid round masses of medicine or vitamins that you swallow without chewing.

indescribable*
[ìndiskráibəbəl]

a. 형언할 수 없는, 말로 표현할 수 없는
You use indescribable to emphasize that a quality or condition is very intense or extreme, and therefore cannot be properly described.

swallow복습
[swálou]

v. 삼키다, 목구멍으로 넘기다; (초조해서) 마른침을 삼키다
If you swallow, you make a movement in your throat as if you are swallowing something, often because you are nervous or frightened.

steel***
[sti:l]

vt. (마음을) 단단히 하다; 강철을 입히다, 견고하게 하다; n. 강철
If you steel yourself, you prepare to deal with something unpleasant.

integral*
[íntigrəl]

a. 필수적인, 없어서는 안 될; 내장된, 완전한
Something that is an integral part of something is an essential part of that thing.

precise**
[prisáis]

a. 정확한, 정밀한; 명확한
You use precise to emphasize that you are referring to an exact thing, rather than something vague.

starve**
[stɑ:rv]

v. 굶주리다, 굶어죽다
If people starve, they suffer greatly from lack of food which sometimes leads to their death.

precision복습
[prisíʒən]

n. 정확, 정밀; 꼼꼼함
If you do something with precision, you do it exactly as it should be done.

unintentioned
[inténʃənd]

a. 의도하지 않은, 고의가 아닌 (unintentional a. 고의가 아닌, 무심코 한)
un (부정, 반대의 접두사) + intentioned (a. 의도한, …할 작정의)

ensure*
[enʃúər]

vt. 보장하다, 확실하게 하다
To ensure something, or to ensure that something happens, means to make certain that it happens.

utter복습
[ʌ́tər]

① v. 발언하다, 입을 열다 ② a. 완전한, 전적인, 절대적인
If someone utters sounds or words, they say them.

tempt**
[tempt]

vt. 유혹하다, 부추기다
Something that tempts you attracts you and makes you want it, even though it may be wrong or harmful.

frighten^{복습}
[fráitn]

v. 놀라게 하나, 심뜩하게 히다; 기겁하다 (frightening a. 깜짝 놀라게 하는)
If something or someone frightens you, they cause you to suddenly feel afraid, anxious, or nervous.

terrify**
[térəfài]

vt. 무섭게[겁나게] 하다, 놀래다 (terrifying a. 겁나게 하는, 무서운)
If something terrifies you, it makes you feel extremely frightened.

reel
[riːl]

① v. (마음이) 어지럽다, 동요하다; 비틀거리다; n. 현기증
② n. 릴, 물레; v. (실을) 감다
If you are reeling from a shock, you are feeling extremely surprised or upset because of it.

empower*
[empáuər]

vt. 권한을 주다, 자율권을 주다
If someone is empowered to do something, they have the authority or power to do it.

utmost**
[ʌtmòust]

a. 극도의, 최대의; n. 최대한도
You can use utmost to emphasize the importance or seriousness of something or to emphasize the way that it is done.

conceivable*
[kənsíːvəbəl]

a. 생각할 수 있는, 상상할 수 있는 (conceivably ad. 생각할 수 있는 바로는)
If something is conceivable, you can imagine it or believe it.

chapter ten

1. What surprised Jonas about the woman at the Annex?

   (A) She stood when he entered the room.

   (B) She called him Receiver of Memory.

   (C) She didn't ask him any questions.

   (D) She worked in a small lobby with only a desk inside.

2. What made Jonas uncomfortable before entering the Receiver of Memory's room?

   (A) The woman addressed Jonas as the Receiver of Memory.

   (B) He found out that the Receiver of Memory did not like to be kept waiting.

   (C) The door to the Receiver of Memory's room was locked.

   (D) The woman told Jonas a joke.

3. What was different about the Receiver of Memory's room?

   (A) The room was very dark.

   (B) There were hundreds of books inside of the room.

   (C) The room was very practical.

   (D) The room was more like an office than a living area.

4. How did Jonas know that the Receiver of Memory has been the Receiver for a long time?

   (A) He was wrinkled and his eyes looked tired.

   (B) He seemed separate from the rest of the elders at the ceremony.

   (C) He did not give the standard accepting-of-apology response to Jonas.

   (D) He told Jonas that he deserved the highest respect.

5. Why did the Receiver of Memory tell Jonas to ask him questions about the training process?

    (A) He wasn't allowed to tell Jonas about the training, so he wanted Jonas to ask him questions.
    (B) He didn't have experience describing the process because it was forbidden to talk about it.
    (C) He was too tired to tell Jonas about the process and he didn't want Jonas to ask too many questions.
    (D) He wanted to tell Jonas about the story of his life but didn't know where to start.

6. What would the Receiver of Memory be transmitting to Jonas?

    (A) Memories of his own childhood in the community
    (B) Memories of the whole world before the present time
    (C) Wisdom of the people in the community
    (D) Memories of the people currently living Elsewhere

7. Which of the following was NOT true about Jonas?

    (A) He didn't understand that there was a world and life before the present time.
    (B) He was amazed that there was an "off" switch for the speaker in The Giver's room.
    (C) At first, he had problems understanding the role of The Receiver of Memory.
    (D) He knew what a sled and snow were.

• *Check Your Reading Speed*

1분에 몇 단어를 읽는지 리딩 속도를 측정해보세요.

$$\frac{2{,}006 \text{ words}}{\text{reading time ( ) sec}} \times 60 = (\quad) \text{ WPM}$$

• *Build Your Vocabulary*

designate^{복습}
[dézignèit]

vt. 지명하다, 지정하다, 선정하다, 명시하다
When you designate someone or something as a particular thing, you formally give them that description or name.

indicate^{복습}
[índikèit]

vt. 가리키다, 지시하다, 나타내다
If one thing indicates another, the first thing shows that the second is true or exists.

annex^{복습}
[ənéks]

n. 별관, 별채; 부속물; vt. 부가하다; 합병하다
An annex is a building that is an addition to another building.

attach^{복습}
[ətǽtʃ]

vt. 붙이다, 달다; 소속시키다 (attached a. 붙여진)
If you attach something to an object, you join it or fasten it to the object.

ordinary***
[ɔ́:rdənèri]

a. 보통의, 평범한
Ordinary people or things are normal and not special or different in any way.

remarkable^{복습}
[rimá:rkəbəl]

a. 비범한, 뛰어난; 주목할 만한 (unremarkable a. 주의를 끌지 않는, 평범한)
Someone or something that is remarkable is unusual or special in a way that makes people notice them and be surprised or impressed.

buzzer
[bʌ́zər]

n. 버저, 사이렌 (buzz v. 버저를 누르다; 윙윙거리다)
A buzzer is an electrical device that is used to make a buzzing sound for example, to attract someone's attention.

click*
[klik]

n. 딸깍[찰깍]하는 소리; v. 딸깍 소리를 내다
A click is a short, sharp sound.

unlatch
[ʌnlǽtʃ]

v. (문의) 빗장을 끄르다; (문이) 열리다
If you unlatch a door, you remove the latch from it.

attendant^{복습}
[əténdənt]

n. 안내원, 수행원; 참석자
An attendant is someone whose job is to serve or help people in a place such as a petrol station, a car park, or a cloakroom.

acknowledge^{복습}
[əknálidʒ]

vt. 인정하다, 알리다; 감사하다
If you acknowledge someone, for example by moving your head or smiling, you show that you have seen and recognized them.

respectful*
[rispéktfəl]

a. 경의를 표하는, 공손한, 정중한 (respectfully ad. 공손하게, 정중하게)
If you are respectful, you show respect for someone.

discomfort [복습]
[diskʌ́mfərt]

n. 불쾌, 불안; vt. 불쾌[불안]하게 하다
Discomfort is a painful feeling in part of your body when you have been hurt slightly or when you have been uncomfortable for a long time.

insure **
[inʃúər]

v. 보증하다, 안전하게 하다; 보험에 들다
If you insure yourself against something unpleasant that might happen in the future, you do something to protect yourself in case it happens, or to prevent it happening.

concentration *
[kànsəntréiʃən]

n. 집중, 전념
Concentration on something involves giving all your attention to it.

wander [복습]
[wándər]

v. 돌아다니다, 방황하다; n. 유랑, 방랑
If you wander in a place, you walk around there in a casual way, often without intending to go in any particular direction.

relocate
[ri:lóukeit]

v. (주거 · 공장 · 주민 등을) 다시 배치하다, 이전시키다
If people or businesses relocate or if someone relocates them, they move to a different place.

glance [복습]
[glæns]

v. 흘긋 보다, 잠깐 보다; n. 흘긋 봄
If you glance at something or someone, you look at them very quickly and then look away again immediately.

furnish [복습]
[fə́:rniʃ]

v. 갖추다, 비치하다; 공급하다, 제공하다
If you furnish a room or building, you put furniture and furnishings into it.

practical ***
[prǽktikəl]

a. 실용적인; 실제의, 실제적인
Practical ideas and methods are likely to be effective or successful in a real situation.

sturdy *
[stə́:rdi]

a. 억센, 튼튼한; 힘센
Someone or something that is sturdy looks strong and is unlikely to be easily injured or damaged.

spacious *
[spéiʃəs]

a. 넓은, 훤히 트인
A spacious room or other place is large in size or area, so that you can move around freely in it.

fabric **
[fǽbrik]

n. 직물, 천
Fabric is cloth or other material produced by weaving together cotton, nylon, wool, silk, or other threads.

upholster
[ʌphóulstər]

vt. (의자 등에) 커버를 씌우다, 겉 천을 대다
(upholstered a. (의자 등에) 천을 씌운)
Upholstered chairs and seats have a soft covering that makes them comfortable to sit on.

luxurious **
[lʌgʒúəriəs]

a. 사치스러운, 호화로운
If you describe something as luxurious, you mean that it is very comfortable and expensive.

slender **
[sléndər]

a. 호리호리한, 가느다란, 날씬한
A slender person is attractively thin and graceful.

carve**
[kɑːrv]

vt. 새기다, 조각하다 (carved a. 조각된, 새겨진)
If you carve an object, you make it by cutting it out of a substance such as wood or stone.

decoration**
[dèkəréiʃən]

n. 장식, 장식품
Decorations are features that are added to something in order to make it look more attractive.

alcove
[ǽlkouv]

n. 골방, 방 안의 벽면을 우묵하게 들어가게 해서 만든 공간
An alcove is a small area of a room which is formed by one part of a wall being built further back than the rest of the wall.

drape*
[dreip]

vt. 우아하게 걸치다, 주름을 잡아 예쁘게 덮다; n. 드리워진 모양, 드레이프
If you drape a piece of cloth somewhere, you place it there so that it hangs down in a casual and graceful way.

splendid***
[spléndid]

a. 멋진, 화려한
If you say that something is splendid, you mean that it is very good.

embroider*
[embrɔ́idər]

v. 자수하다, 수를 놓다, 장식하다
If something such as clothing or cloth is embroidered with a design, the design is stitched into it.

intricate*
[íntrəkit]

a. 얽힌, 복잡한; 난해한
You use intricate to describe something that has many small parts or details.

conspicuous**
[kənspíkjuəs]

a. 눈에 띄는, 잘 보이는, 뚜렷한
If someone or something is conspicuous, people can see or notice them very easily.

reference^{수능}
[réfərəns]

n. 참조; 언급; 문의
A reference is a word, phrase, or idea which comes from something such as a book, poem, or play and which you use when making a point about something.

committee^{수능}
[kəmíti]

n. 위원회
A committee is a group of people who meet to make decisions or plans for a larger group or organization that they represent.

bookcase**
[búkkèis]

n. 책장, 책꽂이, 서가
A bookcase is a piece of furniture with shelves that you keep books on.

emboss*
[embɔ́s]

vt. 돋을새김(글자나 그림 따위를 도드라지게 새기는 것)을 하다
(embossed a. 돋을새김을 한)
If a surface such as paper or wood is embossed with a design, the design stands up slightly from the surface.

bow^{수능}
[báu]

v. (인사로 혹은 좌절 · 수치심에) 머리를 숙이다, 굽히다; n. 절, 경례; 몸을 굽힘
When you bow, you move your head or the top half of your body forwards and downwards.

ceremony^{수능}
[sérəmòuni]

n. 의식, 의례
A ceremony is a formal event such as a wedding.

self-conscious 복습
[sélfkánʃəs]

a. 남의 시선을 의식하는, 자의식이 강한 (self-consciously ad. 수줍게)
Someone who is self-conscious is easily embarrassed and nervous because they feel that everyone is looking at them and judging them.

curiosity **
[kjùəriásəti]

n. 호기심
Curiosity is a desire to know about something.

sympathy **
[símpəθi]

n. 동정, 연민; 공감, 동감
If you have sympathy for someone who is in a bad situation, you are sorry for them, and show this in the way you behave towards them.

wrinkle **
[ríŋkəl]

v. 주름이 지게 하다, 구겨지다; n. 주름, 잔주름
(wrinkled a. 주름이 있는, 쭈글쭈글한)
When you wrinkle your nose or forehead, or when it wrinkles, you tighten the muscles in your face so that the skin folds.

piercing ***
[píərsiŋ]

a. (눈이) 날카로운, 통찰력 있는; 꿰뚫는; n. 피어싱 (장식으로 몸에 구멍을 뚫는 것)
If someone has piercing eyes or a piercing stare, they seem to look at you very intensely.

flesh ***
[fleʃ]

n. 살, 살집, 고기; 피부
Flesh is the soft part of a person's or animal's body between the bones and the skin.

sag
[sæg]

v. 가라앉다, 꺼지다; 축 늘어지게 하다; n. 늘어짐, 처짐
When part of someone's body begins to sag, it starts to become less firm and hang down.

amuse 복습
[əmjúːz]

vt. 즐겁게 하다, 재미나게 하다 (amusement n. 즐거움, 재미)
If something amuses you, it makes you want to laugh or smile.

diminish 복습
[dəmíniʃ]

v. 줄(이)다, 감소시키다
When something diminishes, or when something diminishes it, it becomes reduced in size, importance, or intensity.

cushion 복습
[kúʃən]

vt. 쿠션으로 받치다, 충격을 완화하다; n. 쿠션; 완충물
If you cushion something, you cover or hide it with or like a cushion.

peer 복습
[piər]

vi. 응시하다, 자세히 보다
If you peer at something, you look at it very hard.

forbidden 복습
[fərbídn]

a. 금지된
If something is forbidden, you are not allowed to do it or have it.

neglect **
[niglékt]

vt. 무시하다, 등한시하다; n. 태만, 소홀
If you neglect someone or something, you fail to look after them properly.

chuckle 복습
[tʃʌ́kl]

vi. 낄낄 웃다; n. 낄낄 웃음
When you chuckle, you laugh quietly.

enormous **
[inɔ́ːrməs]

a. 엄청난, 거대한, 막대한
You can use enormous to emphasize the great degree or extent of something.

successor^{四급}
[səksésər]

n. 후임자, 후계자
Someone's successor is the person who takes their job after they have left.

transmit[*]
[trænsmít]

v. 보내다, 전달하다
If you transmit an idea or feeling to someone else, you make them understand and share the idea or feeling.

tentative[*]
[téntətiv]

a. 머뭇거리는, 주저하는; 잠정적인, 임시의
(tentatively ad. 조심스럽게, 주저하며)
If someone is tentative, they are cautious and not very confident because they are uncertain or afraid.

impatient^{수능}
[impéiʃənt]

a. 성급한, 조급한, 참을성 없는 (impatiently ad. 성급하게, 조바심 내며)
If you are impatient, you are annoyed because you have to wait too long for something.

frown^{편입}
[fraun]

vi. 얼굴을 찡그리다, 눈살을 찌푸리다; n. 찌푸린 얼굴
When someone frowns, their eyebrows become drawn together, because they are annoyed or puzzled.

grasp^{편입}
[græsp]

v. 붙잡다, 움켜쥐다; n. 움켜잡기
If you grasp something, you take it in your hand and hold it very firmly.

weighted^{편입}
[wéitid]

a. (슬픔 등을) 짊어진, 무거워진; 치우친, 편중된
If something is weighted, it becomes heavier by adding something to it.

sled[*]
[sled]

n. 썰매
A sled is an object used for travelling over snow.

exhilarating
[igzílərèitiŋ]

a. 기분을 돋우는, 아주 신나는, 상쾌한
If you describe an experience or feeling as exhilarating, you mean that it makes you feel very happy and excited.

accumulate^{**}
[əkjú:mjəlèit]

v. (서서히) 모으다, 축적하다
When you accumulate things or when they accumulate, they collect or are gathered over a period of time.

tunic^{편입}
[tʃú:nik]

n. 튜닉 (고대 그리스나 로마인들이 입던, 무릎까지 내려오는 헐렁한 가운 같은 웃옷)
A tunic is a loose piece of clothing covering the body down to the knees, usually without sleeves.

apprehensive^{편입}
[æprihénsiv]

a. 우려하는, 염려하는 (apprehensively ad. 염려하여, 걱정스럽게)
Someone who is apprehensive is afraid that something bad may happen.

bare^{수능}
[bɛər]

a. 발가벗은; 있는 그대로의
If a part of your body is bare, it is not covered by any clothing.

magnificent^{**}
[mægnífəsənt]

a. 웅장한, 장엄한, 훌륭한
If you say that something or someone is magnificent, you mean that you think they are extremely good, beautiful, or impressive.

deft
[deft]

a. 손재주 있는, 솜씨 좋은 (deftly ad. 솜씨 좋게, 교묘히)
A deft action is skilful and often quick.

snap**
[snæp]

v. 홱 잡다, 짤깍 소리 내다; 날카롭게[느닷없이] 말하다; n. 툭 소리 냄
If something snaps or if you snap it, it breaks suddenly, usually with a sharp cracking noise.

astonish^{복습}
[əstániʃ]

vt. 깜짝 놀라게 하다 (astonishing a. 놀라운)
If something or someone astonishes you, they surprise you very much.

encourage**
[enkə́ːridʒ]

vt. 용기를 북돋우다, 장려하다
If you encourage someone, you give them confidence, hope, or support.

betray**
[bitréi]

vt. 무심코 드러내다; 배반하다, 누설하다
If you betray a feeling or quality, you show it without intending to.

chapter eleven

1. What was the first entirely new sensation that Jonas felt?

   (A) The coldness of the air
   (B) Seeing his breath in the air
   (C) Snowflakes
   (D) The motion of going downhill

2. How did Jonas know the describing words and the words for objects in the memory?

   (A) He remembered the words that the Receiver of Memory had told him about the experience.
   (B) His new consciousness told him the words.
   (C) The Receiver of Memory verbally described the memory to Jonas as he transmitted it.
   (D) Jonas learned the vocabulary from textbooks at school.

3. What did Jonas experience in the memory?

   (A) Going down a snowy hill on a sled
   (B) Sitting on top of a hill on a snowy day
   (C) Running down a snowy hill pulling a sled
   (D) Skiing down a snowy hill

4. What happens when a memory is transmitted to Jonas?

(A) The people in the community also experience the memory.

(B) The Receiver of Memory feels like a weight is lifted off of him.

(C) Jonas is frightened of the new experience and resists receiving the memory.

(D) The Receiver of Memory can still experience the memory after he has transmitted it to Jonas.

5. Why had Jonas never experienced snow before?

(A) The community had a naturally warm climate.

(B) Children were forbidden to go outside when it was snowing.

(C) The community controlled the climate.

(D) Everywhere on Earth became too warm so snow was naturally impossible.

6. How did the Receiver of Memory look different by the time Jonas left?

(A) He looked a little sad and drained.

(B) He looked better than when he first met him.

(C) He looked annoyed.

(D) He looked angry.

7. How does the Receiver of Memory transmit memories to Jonas?

(A) He places his hands on Jonas's shoulders.

(B) He places his hands on Jonas's bare back.

(C) He holds Jonas's hands.

(D) He places one hand on Jonas's forehead.

1분에 몇 단어를 읽는지 리딩 속도를 측정해보세요.

$$\frac{1,946 \text{ words}}{\text{reading time (\hspace{1cm}) sec}} \times 60 = (\hspace{1cm}) \text{ WPM}$$

• *Build Your Vocabulary*

even***
[í:vən]

a. 규칙적인, 한결같은; 떡[꼭] 맞는; ad. 한층, 더욱
(evenly ad. 차분하게, 고르게)
If your voice is even, you are speaking in a very controlled way which makes it difficult for people to tell what your feelings are.

disgrace^{빈출}
[disgréis]

vt. 수치가 되다; 욕보이다; n. 불명예, 치욕, 창피
If you say that someone disgraces someone else, you are emphasizing that their behavior causes the other person to feel ashamed.

shiver^{빈출}
[ʃívər]

v. (추위·공포로) 후들후들 떨다; 전율하다; n. 떨림, 전율
When you shiver, your body shakes slightly because you are cold or frightened.

lick**
[lik]

vt. 핥다; (불길이 혀처럼) 날름거리다, 넘실거리다; n. 핥기
When people or animals lick something, they move their tongue across its surface.

chill*
[tʃil]

v. 춥게 하다; 오싹하게 하다; a. 차가운; n. 냉기 (chilled a. 차갑게 한, 오싹한)
When you chill something or when it chills, you lower its temperature so that it becomes colder.

startle^{빈출}
[stá:rtl]

v. 깜짝 놀라게 하다; 움찔하다; n. 깜짝 놀람
(startling a. 깜짝 놀라게 하는, 놀라운)
If something sudden and unexpected startles you, it surprises and frightens you slightly.

intake^{빈출}
[íntèik]

n. 빨아들임, 흡입; 받아들이는 곳
Your intake of a particular kind of food, drink, or air is the amount that you eat, drink, or breathe in.

frigid*
[frídʒid]

a. 몹시 추운; 싸늘한, 냉랭한
Frigid means extremely cold.

swirl*
[swə:rl]

vi. 소용돌이치다, 빙빙 돌다
If liquid or flowing swirls, it moves round and round quickly.

pinprick
[pínprìk]

n. 바늘로 콕 찌름; 성가신 일; vt. 콕콕 찌르다
A pinprick is a prick caused by a pin.

pepper***
[pépər]

vt. 흩어 뿌리다, 후추를 치다; n. 후추
If something is peppered with things, it has a lot of those things in it or on it.

upright^{필수}
[ʌ́práit]

a. 똑바른, 꼿꼿한, 수직으로 선
If you are sitting or standing upright, you are sitting or standing with your back straight, rather than bending or lying down.

decorate**
[dékərèit]

vt. 장식하다, 꾸미다 (decorated a. 장식된, 훌륭하게 꾸민)
If you decorate something, you make it more attractive by adding things to it.

damp^{필수}
[dæmp]

a. 축축한; n. 습기
Something that is damp is slightly wet.

whirl**
[hwəːrl]

v. 빙글 돌다, 선회하다
If something or someone whirls around or if you whirl them around, they move around or turn around very quickly.

torrent**
[tɔ́ːrənt]

n. 급류; 마구 쏟아짐, 빗발침
A torrent is a lot of water falling or flowing rapidly or violently.

fur***
[fəːr]

n. 부드러운 털; 모피
Fur is the thick and usually soft hair that grows on the bodies of many mammals.

perceive**
[pərsíːv]

vt. 지각하다, 감지하다
If you perceive something, you see, notice, or realize it, especially when it is not obvious.

furry
[fə́ːri]

a. 털 같은, 털로 덮인
If you describe something as furry, you mean that it has a soft rough texture like fur.

sled^{빈출}
[sled]

n. 썰매
A sled is an object used for travelling over snow.

abrupt*
[əbrʌ́pt]

a. 갑작스러운, 뜻밖의; 퉁명스러운 (abruptly ad. 갑자기)
An abrupt change or action is very sudden, often in a way which is unpleasant.

poise*
[pɔiz]

vt. (어떤 자세를) 취하다; 균형 잡히게 하다; n. 균형, 평형
If you poise, you hold something steady in a particular position, especially above something else.

extend***
[iksténd]

v. 넓히다, 확장하다; (손·발 등을) 뻗다, 늘이다 (extended a. 넓은, 광대한)
If you say that something, usually something large, extends for a particular distance or extends from one place to another, you are indicating its size or position.

mound^{빈출}
[maund]

n. 더미, 무더기, 언덕
A mound of something is a large rounded pile of it.

descent**
[disént]

n. 내려오기, 하강; 가계, 혈통
A descent is a movement from a higher to a lower level or position.

vehicle^{빈출}
[víːikəl]

n. 탈것, 차량
A vehicle is a machine such as a car, bus, or truck which has an engine and is used to carry people from place to place.

propel[*]
[prəpél]

vt. 추진하다, 나아가게 하다
To propel something in a particular direction means to cause it to move in that direction.

comprehend[복습]
[kὰmprihénd]

vt. 이해하다, 파악하다
If you cannot comprehend something, you cannot understand it.

breathless[복습]
[bréθlis]

a. 숨도 못 쉴 정도의, 숨 가쁜
If you are breathless, you have difficulty in breathing properly, for example because you have been running or because you are afraid or excited.

glee[*]
[gli:]

n. 기쁨, 즐거움
Glee is a feeling of happiness and excitement.

overwhelm[복습]
[òuvərhwélm]

vt. 압도하다, 제압하다; 질리게 하다
If you are overwhelmed by a feeling or event, it affects you very strongly, and you do not know how to deal with it.

incline[**]
[inkláin]

n. 경사, 기울기; v. 기울다, 경사지게 하다
An incline is land that slopes at an angle.

exhilarating[복습]
[igzílərèitiŋ]

a. 기분을 돋우는, 아주 신나는, 상쾌한
If you describe an experience or feeling as exhilarating, you mean that it makes you feel very happy and excited.

obstruction[*]
[əbstrʌ́kʃən]

n. 방해(물), 장애(물)
An obstruction is something that blocks a road or path.

pant[**]
[pænt]

vi. 헐떡거리다, 숨차다; n. 헐떡거림, 숨 가쁨
If you pant, you breathe quickly and loudly with your mouth open, because you have been doing something energetic.

tentative[복습]
[téntətiv]

a. 머뭇거리는, 주저하는; 잠정적인, 임시의 (tentatively ad. 조심스럽게, 주저하며)
If someone is tentative, they are cautious and not very confident because they are uncertain or afraid.

ordinary[복습]
[ɔ́:rdənèri]

a. 보통의, 평범한
Ordinary people or things are normal and not special or different in any way.

wipe[**]
[waip]

vt. 닦다, 닦아 내다; n. 닦기
If you wipe something, you rub its surface to remove dirt or liquid from it.

forehead[**]
[fɔ́:rhèd]

n. 이마
Your forehead is the area at the front of your head between your eyebrows and your hair.

sleeve[**]
[sli:v]

n. (옷의) 소매
The sleeves of a coat, shirt, or other item of clothing are the parts that cover your arms.

exhaust[복습]
[igzɔ́:st]

vt. 지치게 하다; 다 써버리다, 소진시키다 (exhausting a. 피로하게 하는)
If something exhausts you, it makes you so tired, either physically or mentally, that you have no energy left.

transmit^{최상}
[trænsmít]

v. 보내다, 전달하다
If you transmit an idea or feeling to someone else, you make them understand and share the idea or feeling.

encourage^{최상}
[enkə́:ridʒ]

vt. 용기를 북돋우다, 장려하다
If you encourage someone, you give them confidence, hope, or support.

steer^{최상}
[stiər]

v. 조종하다, 이끌다, 나아가다
When you steer a car, boat, or plane, you control it so that it goes in the direction that you want.

treat^{최상}
[tri:t]

n. 만족[즐거움]을 주는 것, 맛있는 간식: 대접, 환대: vt. 다루다, 대우하다
If you give someone a treat, you buy or arrange something special for them which they will enjoy.

businesslike*
[bíznislàik]

a. 사무적인, 업무에 충실한
If you describe someone as businesslike, you mean that they deal with things in an efficient way without wasting time.

eager^{최상}
[í:gər]

a. 열망하는, 간절히 하고 싶어 하는
If you are eager to do or have something, you want to do or have it very much.

shrug^{최상}
[ʃrʌg]

v. (양 손바닥을 내보이면서 어깨를) 으쓱하다: n. 으쓱하기
If you shrug, you raise your shoulders to show that you are not interested in something or that you do not know or care about something.

tug^{최상}
[tʌg]

v. (세게) 당기다, 끌다: 노력[분투]하다: n. 힘껏 당김: 분투, 노력
If you tug something or tug at it, you give it a quick and usually strong pull.

agricultural**
[ǽgrikʌ́ltʃərəl]

a. 농업의, 농사의
Agricultural means involving or relating to farming and the methods that are used to raise and look after crops and animals.

predictable
[pridíktəbl]

a. 예상[예측, 예언]할 수 있는 (unpredictable a. 예상할 수 없는)
If you say that an event is predictable, you mean that it is obvious in advance that it will happen.

practical^{최상}
[prǽktikəl]

a. 실용적인: 실제의, 실제적인
Practical ideas and methods are likely to be effective or successful in a real situation.

obsolete*
[àbsəlí:t]

a. 쓸모없게 된, 안 쓰이는: vt. 쇠퇴시키다
Something that is obsolete is no longer needed because something better has been invented.

conveyance*
[kənvéiəns]

n. 운반, 수송
The conveyance of something is the process of carrying or transporting it from one place to another.

unwieldy
[ʌnwí:ldi]

a. (크기·무게 때문에) 다루기 힘든, 통제하기 힘든
If you describe an object as unwieldy, you mean that it is difficult to move or carry because it is so big or heavy.

(every) now and then 복습

idiom 가끔, 때때로, 이따금
If you do something every now and then, you do it sometimes, but not very often.

moisten *
[mɔ́isən]

v. 젖다, 축축해지다; 적시다
To moisten something means to make it slightly wet.

posture *
[pɑ́stʃər]

n. 자세; 태도, 마음가짐; v. 자세[태도]를 취하다
Your posture is the position in which you stand or sit.

pleasurable 복습
[pléʒərəbəl]

a. 즐거운, 유쾌한, 기쁜
Pleasurable experiences or sensations are pleasant and enjoyable.

quizzical
[kwízikəl]

a. 미심쩍어하는; 약간 놀란 듯한 (quizzically ad. 의아한 듯이)
If you give someone a quizzical look or smile, you look at them in a way that shows that you are surprised or amused by their behavior.

transmission *
[trænsmíʃən]

n. 전달, 전송
The transmission of something is the passing or sending of it to a different person or place.

obey 복습
[oʊbéi]

v. …에 복종하다, …에 따르다
If you obey a person, a command, or an instruction, you do what you are told to do.

bask *
[bæsk]

vi. (햇볕·불 등을) 쬐다
If you bask in the sunshine, you lie somewhere sunny and enjoy the heat.

sting 복습
[stiŋ]

vt. 찌르다, 쏘다; n. 찌름, 쏨
If something stings you, a sharp part of it is pushed into your skin so that you feel a sharp pain.

restless **
[réstlis]

a. 침착하지 못한; 가만히 못 있는; 쉬지 못하는, 불안한
(restlessly ad. 침착하지 못하게)
If you are restless, you are bored, impatient, or dissatisfied, and you want to do something else.

crease
[kri:s]

n. 접은 자국, 주름; v. 주름을 잡다, 구겨지다
Creases in someone's skin are lines which form where their skin folds when they move.

shift 복습
[ʃift]

v. 옮기다, 방향을 바꾸다; n. 변화, 이동; 교대
If you shift something or if it shifts, it moves slightly.

wince *
[wins]

vi. (아픔·무서움 때문에) 주춤하다, 움츠리다; n. 위축
If you wince, the muscles of your face tighten suddenly because you have felt a pain or because you have just seen, heard, or remembered something unpleasant.

sunburn *
[sʌ́nbə̀:rn]

n. 햇볕에 탐, 햇볕으로 입은 화상
If someone has sunburn, their skin is bright pink and sore because they have spent too much time in hot sunshine.

drain**
[drein]

v. 빼내 가다, 소모시키다; 배수하다, 비우다; n. 배수로, 하수구
(drained a. 진이 빠진, 녹초가 된)
If something drains you, it leaves you feeling physically and emotionally exhausted.

upholster^{복습}
[ʌphóulstər]

vt. (의자 등에) 커버를 씌우다, 겉 천을 대다
(upholstered a. (의자 등에) 천을 씌운)
Upholstered chairs and seats have a soft covering that makes them comfortable to sit on.

weary**
[wíəri]

a. 피로한, 지친
If you are weary, you are very tired.

chapter twelve

1. Jonas was forbidden to share his training experience, and _____.

   (A) he was embarrassed because his training was nothing like the other Twelves
   (B) he didn't like his training
   (C) his friends wouldn't understand his experience
   (D) he wasn't interested in listening to his friends' training experiences

2. How did Jonas experience the sled ride again?

   (A) The Giver gave him the memory of the sled again.
   (B) The Giver helped Jonas remember the sled by putting his hands on Jonas's back.
   (C) Jonas recalled the memory himself.
   (D) The Giver took the memory from Jonas and gave it back again.

3. Which of the following was NOT something that Jonas saw change color during his first experiences of seeing beyond?

   (A) Fiona's hair
   (B) An apple
   (C) Snow
   (D) A sled

4. Why did the community no longer experience colors?

(A) Genetic scientists made a mistake and children could no longer see colors.

(B) A disease from long ago stopped the people of the community from seeing colors.

(C) Genetic scientists wanted to stop the people in the community from seeing colors.

(D) The community suffered from a genetic illness that stopped most of the people from seeing colors.

5. How does The Giver help Jonas understand different colors?

(A) He was able to explain what all the colors looked like.

(B) He gave Jonas another memory of a ride on a sled.

(C) He explained the different colors by using examples from the community.

(D) He is going to give Jonas a memory of a rainbow.

6. Which of the following is true about the community?

(A) The people chose Sameness a long time ago.

(B) There are people with different skin colors.

(C) The people of the community are able to see colors.

(D) There is sunshine in the community.

1분에 몇 단어를 읽는지 리딩 속도를 측정해보세요.

$$\frac{2,159 \text{ words}}{\text{reading time (} \qquad \text{) sec}} \times 60 = (\qquad) \text{ WPM}$$

• *Build Your Vocabulary*

sleep soundly複습
idiom 깊이 잠들다
If someone sleep soundly, they are sleeping very deeply.

fist複습
[fist]
n. (쥔) 주먹
Your hand is referred to as your fist when you have bent your fingers in towards the palm in order to hit someone, to make an angry gesture, or to hold something.

hippo複습
[hípou]
n. (= hippopotamus) [동물] 하마
A hippo is a very large African animal with short legs and thick, hairless skin.

blank複습
[blæŋk]
a. 멍한, 얼빠진; 공허한, 공백의; n. 공백
If you look blank, your face shows no feeling, understanding, or interest.

fretful*
[frétfəl]
a. 안달하는, 보채는, 조바심 내는
If someone is fretful, they behave in a way that shows that they worried or unhappy about something.

destination**
[dèstənéiʃən]
n. 목적지, 행선지
The destination of someone or something is the place to which they are going or being sent.

significant**
[signífikənt]
a. 중요한, 의미 있는
A significant action or gesture is intended to have a special meaning.

shed**
[ʃed]
① v. 없애다, 버리다 ② n. 오두막, 헛간
To shed something means to get rid of it.

leftover
[léftòuvər]
a. 나머지의, 남은; n. (pl.) 나머지, 찌꺼기
You use leftover to describe an amount of something that remains after the rest of it has been used or eaten.

commerce**
[kámə:rs]
n. 상업, 거래
Commerce is the activities and procedures involved in buying and selling things.

procedure複습
[prəsí:dʒər]
n. 순서, 차례; 절차
A procedure is a way of doing something, especially the usual or correct way.

govern^{복습}
[gʌ́vərn]

v. 다스리다, 통치하다 (government n. 정부, 정권; 통치[정치] 체제)
To govern a place such as a country, or its people, means to be officially in charge of the place, and to have responsibility for making laws, managing the economy, and controlling public services.

abuzz
[əbʌ́z]

a. 윙윙거리는, 떠들썩한; 활기에 넘치는
If someone says that a place is abuzz, it is noisy like the sound of a bee.

hasty^{복습}
[héisti]

a. 급한, 성급한 (hastily ad. 급히, 허둥지둥)
A hasty movement, action, or statement is sudden, and often done in reaction to something that has just happened.

apology^{복습}
[əpɑ́lədʒi]

n. 사죄, 사과
An apology is something that you say or write in order to tell someone that you are sorry that you have hurt them or caused trouble for them.

admonition
[æ̀dməníʃən]

n. 훈계, 권고, 충고
An admonition is a warning or criticism about someone's behavior.

feathery
[féðəri]

a. 깃털 같은, 가벼운
Feathery is used to describe things that are soft and light.

precision^{복습}
[prisíʒən]

n. 정확, 정밀; 꼼꼼함
If you do something with precision, you do it exactly as it should be done.

pedal^{복습}
[pédl]

v. 페달을 밟다; n. 페달, 발판
When you pedal a bicycle, you push the pedals around with your feet to make it move.

volunteer^{복습}
[vɑ̀ləntíər]

n. 지원자, 자원 봉사자; v. 자발적으로 나서다; a. 자발적인
A volunteer is someone who offers to do a particular task or job without being forced to do it.

administrative*
[ædmínəstrèitiv]

a. 행정상의, 관리의, 경영상의
Administrative work involves organizing and supervising an organization or institution.

dietary
[dáiətèri]

a. 음식의, 식이 요법의
You can use dietary to describe anything that concerns the food that you eat and drink regularly.

punish^{복습}
[pʌ́niʃ]

v. 벌하다, 응징하다, 처벌하다 (punishment n. 처벌, 징계)
To punish someone means to make them suffer in some way because they have done something wrong.

disobedience*
[dìsəbí:diəns]

n. 불복종, 반항; 위반, 반칙
Disobedience is deliberately not doing what someone tells you to do, or what a rule or law says that you should do.

discipline^{복습}
[dísəplin]

n. 훈련, 규율; vt. 훈련하다
Discipline is the practice of making people obey rules or standards of behavior, and punishing them when they do not.

wand^{수능}
[wɑnd]

n. (마술사의) 지팡이, 막대기
A wand is a long thin rod.

occupational*
[ɑ̀kjəpéiʃənəl]

a. 직업의, 직업상의
Occupational means relating to a person's job or profession.

therapy*
[θérəpi]

n. 치료, 요법
Therapy is the treatment of someone with mental or physical illness without the use of drugs or operations.

medication^{수능}
[mèdəkéiʃən]

n. 투약, 약물 치료; 약제, 약물
Medication is medicine that is used to treat and cure illness.

confess^{평가원}
[kənfés]

v. 자백하다, 고백하다, 인정하다
If someone confesses to doing something wrong, they admit that they did it.

fleeting^{수능}
[flíːtiŋ]

a. 순식간의, 잠깐 동안의; 어느덧 지나가는
Fleeting is used to describe something which lasts only for a very short time.

indescribable^{수능}
[ìndiskráibəbəl]

a. 형언할 수 없는, 말로 표현할 수 없는
You use indescribable to emphasize that a quality or condition is very intense or extreme, and therefore cannot be properly described.

entirety
[entáiərti]

n. 완전함, 온전한 상태
If something is used or affected in its entirety, the whole of it is used or affected.

flicker*
[flíkər]

v. (등불·희망·빛 등이) 깜빡이다; n. 깜박임 (flickering a. 깜박거리는)
If a light or flame flickers, it shines unsteadily.

auditorium^{수능}
[ɔ̀ːditɔ́ːriəm]

n. 강당, 회관; 청중석, 관객석
An auditorium is a large room, hall, or building which is used for events such as meetings and concerts.

energetic*
[ènərdʒétik]

a. 활기에 찬, 원기 왕성한
An energetic person is very active and does not feel at all tired.

fluster
[flʌ́stər]

v. 허둥지둥하게 만들다, 어리둥절하게 만들다; n. 허둥거림, 혼란
(flustered a. 허둥대는, 어리둥절한)
If you fluster someone, you make them feel nervous and confused by rushing them and preventing them from concentrating on what they are doing.

phenomenon*
[finámənàn]

n. 현상
A phenomenon is something that is observed to happen or exist.

frustrate*
[frʌ́streit]

v. 좌절시키다, 불만스럽게 만들다; 방해하다 (frustrated a. 실망한, 좌절한)
If something frustrates you, it upsets or angers you because you are unable to do anything about the problems it creates.

questioning^{수능}
[kwéstʃəniŋ]

a. 따지는, 캐묻는; n. 의문, 질문 (questioningly ad. 질문조로, 미심쩍게)
If someone has a questioning expression on their face, they look as if they want to know the answer to a question.

observe^{복습}
[əbzə́:rv]

vt. 관찰하다, 목격하다
If you observe a person or thing, you watch them carefully, especially in order to learn something about them.

perceive^{복습}
[pərsí:v]

vt. 지각하다, 감지하다
If you perceive something, you see, notice, or realize it, especially when it is not obvious.

capacity^{복습}
[kəpǽsəti]

n. 능력, 역량; 수용력, 용량
Your capacity for something is your ability to do it, or the amount of it that you are able to do.

puzzle^{복습}
[pʌ́zl]

v. 어리둥절하게 만들다, 곤혹스럽게 하다, 난처하게 하다
(puzzled a. 당혹스러운, 어리둥절한)
If something puzzles you, you do not understand it and feel confused.

concentrate^{**}
[kánsəntrèit]

v. 집중하다, 전념하다
If you concentrate on something, you give all your attention to it.

sought^{**}
[sɔ:t]

SEEK(v. 찾다; 구하다)의 과거 · 과거분사
Sought is the past tense and past participle of seek.

whirl^{복습}
[hwə:rl]

v. 빙글 돌다, 선회하다
If something or someone whirls around or if you whirl them around, they move around or turn around very quickly.

snowflake[*]
[snóuflèik]

n. 눈송이
A snowflake is one of the soft, white bits of frozen water that fall as snow.

grin^{복습}
[grin]

v. (이를 드러내고) 싱긋 웃다, 활짝 웃다; n. 싱긋 웃음
When you grin, you smile broadly.

fur^{복습}
[fə:r]

v. 털처럼 뒤덮이다; 털로 덮다; n. 부드러운 털 (furred a. 털로 덮인)
If something is furred, it is made of, lined with, or covered in fur.

glimpse^{복습}
[glimps]

n. 흘끗 봄, 잠깐 봄; v. 흘끗 보다, 잠깐보다
If you get a glimpse of someone or something, you see them very briefly and not very well.

dumbfounded
[dʌ̀mfáundid]

a. (놀라서) 말문이 막힌, 어안이 벙벙한
If you are dumbfounded, you are extremely surprised by something.

impression^{**}
[impréʃən]

n. 인상, 감명, 느낌
Your impression of a person or thing is what you think they are like, usually after having seen or heard them.

blink^{복습}
[bliŋk]

v. 눈을 깜박거리다; (등불 · 별 등이) 깜박이다; n. 깜박거림
When you blink or when you blink your eyes, you shut your eyes and very quickly open them again.

bookcase^{복습}
[búkkèis]

n. 책장, 책꽂이, 서가
A bookcase is a piece of furniture with shelves that you keep books on.

shelf복습
[ʃelf]

n. 선반
A shelf is a flat piece which is attached to a wall or to the sides of a cupboard for keeping things on.

slip복습
[slip]

v. 미끄러지다; 미끄러져 사라지다; 미끄러지듯 움직이다
If you slip somewhere, you go somewhere quickly and quietly, especially without being noticed.

distinctive＊
[distíŋktiv]

a. 특유의, 특이한, 특색 있는
Something that is distinctive has a special quality or feature which makes it easily recognizable and different from other things of the same type.

clue＊
[klu:]

n. 단서, 실마리
A clue is a sign or some information which helps you to find the answer to a problem.

flesh복습
[fleʃ]

n. 살, 살집, 고기; 피부
Flesh is the soft part of a person's or animal's body between the bones and the skin.

vibrant복습
[váibrənt]

a. 강렬한, 선명한; 활기찬, 생기가 넘치는
Someone or something that is vibrant is full of life, energy, and enthusiasm.

chuckle복습
[tʃʌkl]

vi. 낄낄 웃다; n. 낄낄 웃음
When you chuckle, you laugh quietly.

genetic
[dʒinétik]

a. 유전의, 유전학적인
You use genetic to describe something that is concerned with genetics or with genes.

work out

phrasal v. (문제를) 풀다; (계획 등이) 잘되어 가다
If you work out something, you make it happen in a particular way, especially in a successful way.

kink
[kiŋk]

n. (실 · 밧줄 등의) 꼬임, 비틀림; v. 꼬이(게 하)다, 비틀리(게 하)다
A kink is a curve or twist in something which is otherwise or normally straight.

drive someone crazy

idiom ⋯를 미치게 하다
If something drives someone crazy, it makes them more and more angry or irritated, especially over a long period of time.

comprehend복습
[kàmprihénd]

vt. 이해하다, 파악하다
If you cannot comprehend something, you cannot understand it.

precise복습
[prisáis]

a. 정확한, 정밀한; 명확한
You use precise to emphasize that you are referring to an exact thing, rather than something vague.

fascinate복습
[fǽsənèit]

v. 매혹하다, 반하게 하다
If something fascinates you, it interests and delights you so much that your thoughts tend to concentrate on it.

relinquish^{應용}
[rilíŋkwiʃ]

vt. 포기하다, 내주다, 양도하다
If you relinquish something such as power or control, you give it up.

fierce**
[fiərs]

a. 사나운; 격렬한, 지독한 (fiercely ad. 사납게)
A fierce animal or person is very aggressive or angry.

wry*
[rai]

a. 빈정대는, 비꼬는, 풍자적인 (wryly ad. 빈정대면서)
If someone has a wry expression, it shows that they find a bad situation or a change in a situation slightly amusing.

chapter thirteen

1. At first, Jonas thought that not seeing color was unfair because
_____.

  (A) it was safer for citizens to make their own choices
  (B) there were not any choices
  (C) he thought all people should see colors instead of only a few
  (D) he thought that the community should be able to make the wrong
  choices

2. What did Jonas find frightening about citizens making their
own choices?

  (A) The community would be less organized.
  (B) The community would be less safe.
  (C) The community would not want to make their own choices.
  (D) The community would be less interesting.

3. How did Jonas feel after the conversation about Sameness?

  (A) He felt frustration he didn't understand.
  (B) He felt he was better than the other people in the community.
  (C) He was angry at The Giver.
  (D) He was thankful for sameness.

4. Why did Jonas hurt Lily?

    (A) He hit Lily because she didn't believe that elephants existed in the past.

    (B) He accidentally hurt Lily when he tried to transmit a part of a memory to her.

    (C) He intentionally hurt Lily when he tried to share a memory of pain with her.

    (D) He hit Lily's back because she couldn't receive memories.

5. Which would be true if Jonas had a spouse in the future?

    (A) He would not be allowed to walk around the community.

    (B) He would be allowed to talk about his work with his spouse.

    (C) His living arrangements would be the same as the other family units.

    (D) He would be allowed to share books with his spouse.

6. What happened to the community when the new Receiver failed?

    (A) The memories that were given to the new Receiver were lost forever.

    (B) The community felt nothing but it took a long time to find a new candidate for the job.

    (C) The memories were given back to The Giver.

    (D) The community experienced the memories that were given to the new Receiver.

7. What did Jonas know about the world outside his own community?

    (A) He had never experienced the world outside his own community.

    (B) He knew there were hills and mountains in the nearby communities.

    (C) He knew about a few nearby communities but he didn't know what was beyond them.

    (D) He knew that the rest of the world was completely different from his own community.

1분에 몇 단어를 읽는지 리딩 속도를 측정해보세요.

$$\frac{2{,}820 \text{ words}}{\text{reading time (\quad) sec}} \times 60 = (\qquad) \text{ WPM}$$

• *Build Your Vocabulary*

lawn**
[lɔːn]

n. 잔디, 잔디밭
A lawn is an area of grass that is kept cut short and is usually part of someone's garden or backyard, or part of a park.

riverbank^{복습}
[rívərbæ̀ŋk]

n. 강둑, 강기슭
A riverbank is the land along the edge of a river.

truck*
[trʌk]

v. 트럭에 싣다, 나르다; n. 트럭, 화물 자동차
When something or someone is trucked somewhere, they are driven there in a truck.

agricultural^{복습}
[æ̀grikʌ́ltʃərəl]

a. 농업의, 농사의
Agricultural means involving or relating to farming and the methods that are used to raise and look after crops and animals.

boundary**
[báundəri]

n. 경계(선)
The boundary of an area of land is an imaginary line that separates it from other areas.

flash***
[flæʃ]

n. 번쩍임, 번쩍하는 빛; v. 번쩍 비추다; 휙 지나가다
A flash is a sudden burst of light or of something shiny or bright.

brilliant**
[bríljənt]

a. 빛나는, 찬란한; 훌륭한, 멋진
A brilliant color is extremely bright.

hueless
[hjúːlis]

a. 빛깔 없는, 색조 없는
hue (n. 색조, 빛깔) + less (a. …없는)

tunic^{복습}
[tjúːnik]

n. 튜닉 (고대 그리스나 로마인들이 입던, 무릎까지 내려오는 헐렁한 가운 같은 웃옷)
A tunic is a loose piece of clothing covering the body down to the knees, usually without sleeves.

fabric^{복습}
[fǽbrik]

n. 직물, 천
Fabric is cloth or other material produced by weaving together cotton, nylon, wool, silk, or other threads.

inaccurate
[inǽkjərit]

a. 부정확한, 정밀하지 않은; 틀린
If a statement or measurement is inaccurate, it is not accurate or correct.

muscle**
[mʌ́səl]

n. 근육
A muscle is a piece of tissue inside your body which connects two bones and which you use when you make a movement.

definite*
[défənit]

a. 확정된, 확실한, 명확한 (definitely ad. 확실히, 명확히)
If something such as a decision or an arrangement is definite, it is firm and clear, and unlikely to be changed.

absurd*
[əbsə́:rd]

a. 터무니없는; 불합리한, 부조리한 (absurdity n. 어리석은 일)
If you say that something is absurd, you are criticizing it because you think that it is ridiculous or that it does not make sense.

frighten복습
[fráitn]

v. 놀라게 하다, 섬뜩하게 하다; 기겁하다 (frightening a. 깜짝 놀라게 하는)
If something or someone frightens you, they cause you to suddenly feel afraid, anxious, or nervous.

chuckle복습
[tʃʌ́kl]

vi. 낄낄 웃다; n. 낄낄 웃음
When you chuckle, you laugh quietly.

frustration복습
[frʌstréiʃən]

n. 좌절, 실패; 낙담, 좌절감
Frustration is the feeling of being annoyed or angry because you cannot do or achieve what you want.

irrational*
[iráʃənəl]

a. 이성을 잃은, 분별이 없는; 불합리한 (irrationally ad. 이성을 잃고)
If you say that something is absurd, you are criticizing it because you think that it is ridiculous or that it does not make sense.

vibrant복습
[váibrənt]

a. 떠는, 진동하는; 활기에 넘치는, 활발한 (vibrance n. 떨림, 진동)
Something that is vibrant moves continuously and rapidly.

concentrate복습
[kánsəntrèit]

v. 집중하다, 전념하다
If you concentrate on something, you give all your attention to it.

petal*
[pétl]

n. 꽃잎
The petals of a flower are the thin colored or white parts which together form the flower.

wilt*
[wilt]

v. 풀이 죽(게 하)다; 시들(게 하)다
If someone wilts, they become weak or tired, or lose confidence.

weighted복습
[wéitid]

a. (슬픔 등을) 짊어진, 무거워진; 치우친, 편중된
If something is weighted, it becomes heavier by adding something to it.

disturb**
[distə́:rb]

v. 방해하다, 어지럽히다
If you disturb someone, you interrupt what they are doing and upset them.

alien*
[éiljən]

a. 이질적인, 낯설고 익숙하지 않은; 외국의; n. 이방인, 외계인
You use alien to describe something that seems strange and perhaps frightening, because it is not part of your normal experience.

tuft*
[tʌft]

n. (머리칼 · 깃털 · 실 따위의) 술, 타래, 한 움큼
A tuft of something such as hair or grass is a small amount of it which is growing together in one place or is held together at the bottom.

sparse*
[spɑ:rs]

a. 희박한, 드문드문한
Something that is sparse is small in number or amount and spread out over an area.

vegetation
[vèdʒətéiʃən]

n. 초목, 식물
Plants, trees, and flowers can be referred to as vegetation.

immense
[iméns]

a. 막대한, 무한한, 광대한
If you describe something as immense, you mean that it is extremely large or great.

thud*
[θʌd]

n. 쿵, 털썩, 덜컥 (무거운 물건이 떨어지는 소리)
A thud is a dull sound, such as that which a heavy object makes when it hits something soft.

peer
[piər]

vi. 응시하다, 자세히 보다
If you peer at something, you look at it very hard.

shrubbery
[ʃrʌ́bəri]

n. 관목 숲, 관목을 심은 길
You can refer to a lot of shrubs or to shrubs in general as shrubbery.

hack*
[hæk]

v. 마구 자르다; (흙을) 파 뒤집다, 경작하다
If you hack your way through an area such as a jungle or hack a path through it, you move forward, cutting back the trees or plants that are in your way.

tusk
[tʌsk]

n. (코끼리의) 상아; (삽 등의) 뾰족한 끝
The tusks of an elephant, wild boar, or walrus are its two very long, curved, pointed teeth.

haul**
[hɔ:l]

v. 끌고 가다, 연행하다; 세게 잡아당기다
If you haul something which is heavy or difficult to move, you move it using a lot of effort.

spatter*
[spǽtər]

v. (액체 방울 등이) 흩어지다, 후두둑 떨어지다, 튀(기)다
If a liquid spatters a surface or you spatter a liquid over a surface, drops of the liquid fall on an area of the surface.

overwhelm
[òuvərhwélm]

vt. 압도하다, 제압하다; 질리게 하다
If you are overwhelmed by a feeling or event, it affects you very strongly, and you do not know how to deal with it.

horizon**
[həráizən]

n. 지평선, 수평선
The horizon is the line in the far distance where the sky seems to meet the land or the sea.

spit**
[spit]

v. 뱉다, 내뿜다
If you spit liquid or food somewhere, you force a small amount of it out of your mouth.

pebble**
[pébəl]

n. 조약돌, 자갈
A pebble is a small, smooth, round stone which is found on beaches and at the bottom of rivers.

whirl
[hwə:rl]

v. 빙글 돌다, 선회하다
If something or someone whirls around or if you whirl them around, they move around or turn around very quickly.

forehead
[fɔ́:rhèd]

n. 이마
Your forehead is the area at the front of your head between your eyebrows and your hair.

sting^{복습}
[stiŋ]

vt. (stung-stung) 찌르다, 쏘다; n. 찌름, 쏨
If something stings you, a sharp part of it is pushed into your skin so that you feel a sharp pain.

emerge**
[imə́:rdʒ]

vi. 나오다, 나타나다
To emerge means to come out from an enclosed or dark space.

mutilate*
[mjú:təlèit]

vt. 훼손하다, 불구로 만들다, 망쳐 놓다
If a person or animal is mutilated, their body is severely damaged, usually by someone who physically attacks them.

sinuous
[sínjuəs]

a. 물결 모양의, 꾸불꾸불한
Something that is sinuous moves with smooth twists and turns.

trunk***
[trʌŋk]

n. 코끼리 코; 여행 가방; (나무의) 줄기, 몸뚱이
An elephant's trunk is its very long nose that it uses to lift food and water to its mouth.

stroke^{복습}
[strouk]

① vt. 쓰다듬다, 어루만지다; n. 쓰다듬기, 달램 ② n. 타격, 일격, 치기
If you stroke someone or something, you move your hand slowly and gently over them.

corpse*
[kɔːrps]

n. 시체
A corpse is a dead body, especially the body of a human being.

leafy*
[líːfi]

a. 잎이 많은, 잎이 무성한
Leafy trees and plants have lots of leaves on them.

snap^{복습}
[snæp]

n. 툭 소리 냄; v. 홱 잡다, 짤깍 소리 내다; 날카롭게[느닷없이] 말하다
A snap is a sharp cracking noise.

drape^{복습}
[dreip]

vt. 우아하게 걸치다, 주름을 잡아 예쁘게 덮다; n. 드리워진 모양, 드레이프
If you drape a piece of cloth somewhere, you place it there so that it hangs down in a casual and graceful way.

tilt*
[tilt]

v. 기울(이)다; n. 경사, 기울기
If you tilt an object or if it tilts, it moves into a sloping position with one end or side higher than the other.

roar***
[rɔːr]

vi. 으르렁거리다, 포효하다; n. 으르렁거리는 소리
If something roars, it makes a very loud noise.

rage**
[reidʒ]

n. 격노, 분노; 열광; v. 격노하다
Rage is strong anger that is difficult to control.

grief**
[griːf]

n. 슬픔, 비탄
Grief is a feeling of extreme sadness.

anguish^{복습}
[ǽŋgwiʃ]

v. 괴로워하다, 괴롭히다; n. 괴로움, 고뇌, 번민 (anguished a. 번민의, 고뇌에 찬)
Anguished means showing or feeling great mental suffering or physical pain.

pedal^{복습}
[pédl]

v. 페달을 밟다; n. 페달, 발판
When you pedal a bicycle, you push the pedals around with your feet to make it move.

shelf^{수능}
[ʃelf]

n. 선반
A shelf is a flat piece which is attached to a wall or to the sides of a cupboard for keeping things on.

glance^{수능}
[glæns]

v. 흘긋 보다, 잠깐 보다; n. 흘긋 봄
If you glance at something or someone, you look at them very quickly and then look away again immediately.

ragged**
[rǽgid]

a. 누더기가 된, 해어진; 남루한, 초라한
Ragged clothes are old and torn.

skeptical*
[sképtikəl]

a. 의심 많은, 회의적인 (skeptically ad. 회의적으로)
If you are skeptical about something, you have doubts about it.

comb***
[koum]

v. (머리카락 · 털 등을) 빗질하다, 빗다; n. 빗
When you comb your hair, you tidy it using a comb.

torture**
[tɔ́ːrtʃər]

vt. 고문하다, 고통을 주다; n. 고문, 고뇌
To torture someone means to cause them to suffer mental pain or anxiety.

tower***
[táuər]

vi. 솟다, …보다 높다; n. 탑 (towering a. 우뚝 솟은)
Someone or something that towers over surrounding people or things is a lot taller than they are.

meticulous^{수능}
[mətíkjələs]

a. 꼼꼼한, 세심한; 정확한
If you describe someone as meticulous, you mean that they do things very carefully and with great attention to detail.

tend**
[tend]

① v. 돌보다, 간호하다 ② vi. 향하다, 경향이 있다
If you tend someone or something, you do what is necessary to keep them in a good condition or to improve their condition.

impatient^{수능}
[impéiʃənt]

a. 성급한, 조급한, 참을성 없는
If you are impatient, you are annoyed because you have to wait too long for something.

wiggle^{수능}
[wígəl]

v. 꿈틀꿈틀 움직이다, (좌우 · 상하로) 조금씩 움직이다
If you wiggle something or if it wiggles, it moves up and down or from side to side in small quick movements.

apologize^{수능}
[əpálədʒàiz]

v. 사과하다, 사죄하다
When you apologize to someone, you say that you are sorry that you have hurt them or caused trouble for them.

mumble*
[mʌ́mbəl]

v. 중얼거리다, 웅얼거리다; n. 중얼거림
If you mumble, you speak very quietly and not at all clearly with the result that the words are difficult to understand.

indifferent**
[indífərənt]

a. 무관심한, 개의치 않는; 중요치 않은, 관계없는 (indifferently ad. 무관심하게)
If you accuse someone of being indifferent to something, you mean that they have a complete lack of interest in it.

spouse^{수능}
[spaus]

n. 배우자, 남편, 아내
Someone's spouse is the person they are married to.

exempt
[igzémpt]

vt. (의무 등을) 면제하다; a. 면제된
To exempt a person or thing from a particular rule, duty, or obligation means to state officially that they are not bound or affected by it.

encourage
[enkə́:ridʒ]

vt. 용기를 북돋우다, 장려하다
If you encourage someone, you give them confidence, hope, or support.

embarrass
[imbǽrəs]

v. 당황스럽게[쑥스럽게] 만들다, 곤란하게 하다
If something or someone embarrasses you, they make you feel shy or ashamed.

offend**
[əfénd]

v. 불쾌하게 하다, 성나게 하다; 죄를 범하다
If you offend someone, you say or do something rude which upsets or embarrasses them.

forbidden
[fərbídn]

a. 금지된
If something is forbidden, you are not allowed to do it or have it.

astonish
[əstániʃ]

vt. 깜짝 놀라게 하다 (astonishing a. 놀라운)
If something or someone astonishes you, they surprise you very much.

array*
[əréi]

n. 정렬; vt. 정렬시키다, 배열하다
An array of objects is a collection of them that is displayed or arranged in a particular way.

**from time
to time**

idiom 가끔, 이따금
If something happens from time to time, it happens occasionally.

consume
[kənsúːm]

v. …의 마음을 빼앗다, 사로잡다; 소비하다, 소모하다
If a feeling or idea consumes you, it affects you very strongly indeed.

transmission
[trænsmíʃən]

n. 전달, 전송
The transmission of something is the passing or sending of it to a different person or place.

belong
[bilɔ́(ː)ŋ]

vi. 속하다, 소유물이다
If something belongs to you, you own it.

permit
[pəːrmít]

v. 허가하다, 허락하다; n. 허가(증)
If someone permits something, they allow it to happen.

frustrate
[frʌ́streit]

v. 좌절시키다, 불만스럽게 만들다; 방해하다 (frustrating a. 좌절감을 일으키는)
If something frustrates you, it upsets or angers you because you are unable to do anything about the problems it creates.

obey
[oubéi]

v. …에 복종하다, …에 따르다
If you obey a person, a command, or an instruction, you do what you are told to do.

committee
[kəmíti]

n. 위원회
A committee is a group of people who meet to make decisions or plans for a larger group or organization that they represent.

elder 복습
[éldər]

n. 연장자, 웃어른; a. 나이가 더 많은
A person's elder is someone who is older than them, especially someone quite a lot older.

counsel **
[káunsəl]

n. 조언, 충고, 상담; v. 상담을 하다
Counsel is advice.

rare 복습
[rɛər]

a. 드문, 진귀한 (rarely ad. 드물게, 좀처럼 …하지 않는)
Something that is rare is not common and is therefore interesting or valuable.

seldom ***
[séldəm]

ad. 드물게, 거의 …없는
If something seldom happens, it happens only occasionally.

predictable 복습
[pridíktəbəl]

a. 예상[예측, 예언]할 수 있는
If you say that an event is predictable, you mean that it is obvious in advance that it will happen.

successor 복습
[səksésər]

n. 후임자, 후계자
Someone's successor is the person who takes their job after they have left.

grim 복습
[grim]

a. 암울한, 음산한; 엄한, 엄격한 (grimly ad. 암울하게, 음울하게)
If you say that something is grim, you think that it is very bad, ugly, or depressing.

release 복습
[rilí:s]

vt. 놓아주다, 해방시키다, 풀어놓다; n. 석방
If a person or animal is released from somewhere where they have been looked after, they are set free or allowed to go.

struggle ***
[strʌ́gəl]

v. 고심하다, 분투하다; 발버둥치다, 몸부림치다; n. 투쟁, 분투
If you struggle to do something, you try hard to do it, even though other people or things may be making it difficult for you to succeed.

vague 복습
[veig]

a. 희미한, 모호한, 애매한 (vaguely ad. 모호하게, 막연하게)
If something written or spoken is vague, it does not explain or express things clearly.

apparent 복습
[əpǽrənt]

a. 또렷한; 명백한; 외관상의 (apparently ad. 보아하니; 명백히)
If something is apparent to you, it is clear and obvious to you.

subside 복습
[səbsáid]

vi. 가라앉다, 진정되다
If a feeling or noise subsides, it becomes less strong or loud.

assimilate *
[əsíməlèit]

v. 동화되다, 완전히 이해하다, 자기 것으로 흡수하다
If you assimilate new ideas, techniques, or information, you learn them or adopt them.

chest 복습
[tʃest]

① n. 가슴, 흉부 ② n. 상자, 궤
Your chest is the top part of the front of your body where your ribs, lungs, and heart are.

electrical **
[iléktrikəl]

a. 전기에 관한, 전기의
Electrical energy is energy in the form of electricity.

impulse^{복습}
[ímpʌls]

n. 충격, 자극; 충동, 욕구
An impulse is a short electrical signal that is sent along a wire or nerve or through the air, usually as one of a series.

stimulate**
[stímjəlèit]

v. 자극하다, 고무하다, 활성화시키다
If something stimulates a part of a person's body, it causes it to move or start working.

electrode
[iléktroud]

n. [전기] 전극(電極)
An electrode is a small piece of metal or other substance that is used to take an electric current to or from a source of power, a piece of equipment, or a living body.

bitter***
[bítər]

a. 쓴, 쓰라린; 지독한, 혹독한 (bitterly ad. 씁쓸하게; 지독하게)
You can use bitter to emphasize feelings of disappointment.

annex^{복습}
[ənéks]

n. 별관, 별채; 부속물; vt. 부가하다; 합병하다
An annex is a building that is an addition to another building.

disregard*
[dìsrigá:rd]

vt. 무시하다, 경시하다; n. 무시, 경시
If you disregard something, you ignore it or do not take account of it.

accusation*
[æ̀kjuzéiʃən]

n. 고발, 고소; 비난
An accusation is a statement or claim by a witness or someone in authority that a particular person has committed a crime, although this has not yet been proved.

terrify^{복습}
[térəfài]

vt. 무섭게[겁나게] 하다, 놀래다 (terrified a. 무서워하는, 겁먹은)
If something terrifies you, it makes you feel extremely frightened.

session**
[séʃən]

n. (어느 활동을 위한) 기간; 모임, 회의
A session of a particular activity is a period of that activity.

flick*
[flik]

vt. 가볍게 치다, 튀기다; n. 가볍게 치기
If you flick something away, or off something else, you remove it with a quick movement of your hand or finger.

burden***
[bə́:rdn]

n. 짐, 부담; vt. 짐을 지우다, 부담시키다
If you describe a problem or a responsibility as a burden, you mean that it causes someone a lot of difficulty, worry, or hard work.

phrase^{복습}
[freiz]

n. 구절, 관용구
A phrase is a short group of words that people often use as a way of saying something.

harsh**
[hɑ:rʃ]

a. 냉혹한, 가혹한; 거친, (소리 따위가) 귀에 거슬리는
Harsh actions or speech are unkind and show no understanding or sympathy.

ceremony^{복습}
[sérəmòuni]

n. 의식, 의례
A ceremony is a formal event such as a wedding.

hunch^{복습}
[hʌntʃ]

v. 둥글게 구부리다; n. 예감, 직감
If you hunch forward, you raise your shoulders, put your head down, and lean forwards, often because you are cold, ill, or unhappy.

tense^{복습}
[tens]

a. 긴장한, 긴박한; 팽팽한; v. 팽팽하게 하다 (tensely ad. 긴장한 채, 긴박하게)
A tense situation or period of time is one that makes people anxious, because they do not know what is going to happen next.

embed
[imbéd]

vt. 깊숙이 박다, 끼워 넣다
If an object embeds itself in a substance or thing, it becomes fixed there firmly and deeply.

flicker^{복습}
[flíkər]

v. (등불 · 희망 · 빛 등이) 깜박이다; n. 깜박임 (flickering a. 깜박거리는)
If something flickers, it makes very slight, quick movements.

span**
[spæn]

v. 걸치다, 가로지르다; n. 한 뼘; 기간
A bridge or other structure that spans something such as a river or a valley stretches right across it.

outlying
[áutlàiiŋ]

a. 외딴, 외진, 바깥에 있는
Outlying places are far away from the main cities of a country.

agriculture**
[ǽgrikʌ̀ltʃər]

n. 농업
Agriculture is farming and the methods that are used to raise and look after crops and animals.

alter*
[ɔ́:ltər]

v. 변경하다, 바꾸다; 달라지다
If something alters or if you alter it, it changes.

dwelling^{복습}
[dwéliŋ]

n. 거처, 주소, 사는 집
A dwelling is a place where someone lives.

sunburn^{복습}
[sʌ́nbə̀:rn]

n. 햇볕에 탐, 햇볕으로 입은 화상
If someone has sunburn, their skin is bright pink and sore because they have spent too much time in hot sunshine.

shield**
[ʃi:ld]

v. 보호하다, 지키다; n. 방패
If something or someone shields you from a danger or risk, they protect you from it.

eventually^{복습}
[ivéntʃuəli]

ad. 결국, 마침내
Eventually means at the end of a situation or process or as the final result of it.

fearful**
[fíərfəl]

a. 두려워하는, 겁내는; 무서운
If you are fearful of something, you are afraid of it.

chapter fourteen

1. How was the hill in the second sled memory different than the first?

    (A) The hill was coated with ice.

    (B) The hill was not as steep but it was longer than the first hill.

    (C) Jonas was frightened of the hill before he began to go down it.

    (D) The snow that fell was thicker.

2. What happened to Jonas in the memory?

    (A) He broke his arm.

    (B) He broke his leg.

    (C) He cracked his ribs.

    (D) His leg caught on fire.

3. Jonas felt lonely because his family had never known

    _____.

    (A) adventure

    (B) history

    (C) pain

    (D) how to ride a sled

4. What does the Receiver of Memory do with the wisdom he gains from the memories?

    (A) He gives advice to the entire community during town meetings.

    (B) He writes down his memories and puts them in the Hall of Open Records.

    (C) He advises the Committee of Elders on problems or issues they have not faced before.

    (D) He tells the Committee of Elders details about the memories from the past.

5. Why does the community have a Receiver of Memory?

    (A) The people of the community are not smart enough to receive memories.

    (B) Long ago, the community decided that it didn't want everyone burdened and pained with memories.

    (C) The Committee of Elders wants the Receiver of Memory to give the memories to the citizens.

    (D) The people of the community refuse to receive memories.

1분에 몇 단어를 읽는지 리딩 속도를 측정해보세요.

$$\frac{2,449 \text{ words}}{\text{reading time (\quad) sec}} \times 60 = (\qquad) \text{ WPM}$$

• *Build Your Vocabulary*

steep**
[sti:p]
① a. 가파른, 험한; 급격한 ② v. 적시다, 담그다; 열중하다
A steep slope rises at a very sharp angle and is difficult to go up.

coat***
[kout]
vt. 덮다, 입히다, 칠하다; n. 외투, 코트
If you coat something with a substance or in a substance, you cover it with a thin layer of the substance.

bluish*
[blú:iʃ]
a. 푸르스름한, 푸른빛을 띤
Something that is bluish is slightly blue in color.

breathtaking*
[bréθtèikiŋ]
a. 숨이 막히는, (너무 아름답거나 놀라서) 숨이 멎는 듯한
If you say that something is breathtaking, you are emphasizing that it is extremely beautiful or amazing.

invigorate
[invígərèit]
vt. 기운 나게 하다, 활기를 띠게 하다 (invigorating a. 기운 나게 하는, 상쾌한)
If something invigorates you, it makes you feel more energetic.

freeze^{복습}
[fri:z]
v. (froze–frozen) 얼다, 얼어붙다; 얼게 하다; n. 결빙
If a liquid or a substance containing a liquid freezes, or if something freezes it, it becomes solid because of low temperatures.

expanse*
[ikspǽns]
n. 넓게 퍼진 지역; 팽창, 확장
An expanse of something, usually sea, sky, or land, is a very large amount of it.

cushion^{복습}
[kúʃən]
vt. 쿠션으로 받치다, 충격을 완화하다; n. 쿠션; 완충물
If you cushion something, you cover or hide it with or like a cushion.

skitter
[skítər]
v. 경쾌하게 나아가(게 하)다
If something skitters, it moves about very lightly and quickly.

steer^{복습}
[stiər]
v. 조종하다, 이끌다, 나아가다
When you steer a car, boat, or plane, you control it so that it goes in the direction that you want.

mercy^{복습}
[má:rsi]
n. 자비, 연민
If you refer to an event or situation as a mercy, you mean that it makes you feel happy or relieved, usually because it stops something unpleasant happening.

acceleration
[æksèləréiʃən]
n. 가속, 가속도; 촉진
The acceleration of a process or change is the fact that it is getting faster and faster.

sled^{수능}
[sled]

n. 썰매
A sled is an object used for travelling over snow.

bump^{수능}
[bʌmp]

n. 튀어나온 부분, 요철; 혹, 타박상; 충돌; v. 부딪치다, 충돌하다
A bump on a road is a raised, uneven part.

jar^{**}
[dʒɑːr]

① v. 덜컹덜컹 흔들리다, 진동하다; 삐걱거리다; n. 삐걱거리는 소리, 잡음
② n. 병, 단지
If an object jars, or if something jars it, the object moves with a fairly hard shaking movement.

scrape^{수능}
[skreip]

v. 스쳐서 상처를 내다; 긁다, 긁어내다, 문지르다
If you scrape a part of your body, you accidentally rub it against something hard and rough, and damage it slightly.

jagged[*]
[dʒǽgid]

a. 삐죽삐죽한, 들쭉날쭉한
Something that is jagged has a rough, uneven shape or edge with lots of sharp points.

gasp^{수능}
[gæsp]

v. (놀람 따위로) 숨이 막히다, 헐떡거리다; n. 헐떡거림
When you gasp, you take a short quick breath through your mouth, especially when you are surprised, shocked, or in pain.

hatchet[*]
[hǽtʃit]

n. 손도끼
A hatchet is a small axe that you can hold in one hand.

lodge^{**}
[lɑdʒ]

v. 박히다, 꽂히다; 숙박하다, 묵다; n. 오두막
If an object lodges somewhere, it becomes stuck there.

nerve^{**}
[nəːrv]

n. 신경; 용기, 대담성
Nerves are long thin fibers that transmit messages between your brain and other parts of your body.

blade^{**}
[bleid]

n. 칼날; 잎, 잎사귀
The blade of a knife, axe, or saw is the edge, which is used for cutting.

agony
[ǽgəni]

n. 고뇌, 고통, 번민
Agony is great physical or mental pain.

lick^{수능}
[lik]

vt. (불길이 혀처럼) 날름거리다, 넘실거리다; 핥다; n. 핥기
If a flame, wave, or breeze licks, it moves lightly and quickly like a tongue.

sob^{**}
[sɑb]

v. 흐느껴 울다; n. 흐느낌, 오열
When someone sobs, they cry in a noisy way, breathing in short breaths.

vomit[*]
[vɑ́mit]

v. 토하다, 게우다; n. 토함, 게움
If you vomit, food and drink comes back up from your stomach and out through your mouth.

drip^{**}
[drip]

v. 물방울이 떨어지다, 뚝뚝 흐르다
When something drips, drops of liquid fall from it.

writhe[*]
[raið]

v. (고통으로) 몸부림치다, 몸을 뒤틀다
If you writhe, your body twists and turns violently backwards and forwards, usually because you are in great pain or discomfort.

brutal[**]
[brú:tl]

a. 잔인한, 혹독한, 악랄한
A brutal act or person is cruel and violent.

bruise[복습]
[bru:z]

n. 타박상, 멍; v. 멍들게 하다, 타박상을 입히다
A bruise is an injury which appears as a purple mark on your body, although the skin is not broken.

wound[**]
[wu:nd]

n. 상처, 부상, 상해; vt. 상처를 입히다
A wound is damage to part of your body, especially a cut or a hole in your flesh, which is caused by a gun, knife, or other weapon.

mash[*]
[mæʃ]

vt. 으깨다, 짓찧다, 짓이기다
If you mash something, you crush it so that it forms a soft mass.

skin[***]
[skin]

v. 생채기 내다, 스쳐서 상처를 입히다; 껍질을 벗기다; n. 피부; 가죽
If one's knee or elbow is skinned, it is injured by scraping.

daub
[dɔ:b]

n. 바르기, 칠함; 도료; v. 흠뻑 칠하다, 바르다
A daub of something such as mud or paint is a spread of it.

anesthetic
[æ̀nəsθétik]

a. 마취의; 무감각한; n. 마취제
Anesthetic is a substance that doctors use to stop you feeling pain during an operation, either in the whole of your body when you are unconscious, or in a part of your body when you are awake.

ointment
[ɔ́intmənt]

n. 연고, 고약(膏藥)
An ointment is a smooth thick substance that is put on sore skin or a wound to help it heal.

pill[복습]
[pil]

n. 알약
Pills are small solid round masses of medicine or vitamins that you swallow without chewing.

injection[*]
[indʒékʃən]

n. 주사, 주입
If you have an injection, a doctor or nurse puts a medicine into your body using a device with a needle called a syringe.

instantaneous[*]
[ìnstəntéiniəs]

a. 즉시의, 순간의; 동시에 일어나는, 동시적인
Something that is instantaneous happens immediately and very quickly.

deliverance[*]
[dilívərəns]

n. 구출, 구조, 해방
Deliverance is rescue from imprisonment, danger, or evil.

limp[**]
[limp]

① vi. 절뚝거리다; n. 절뚝거리기 ② a. 약한, 기운이 없는
If a person or animal limps, they walk with difficulty or in an uneven way because one of their legs or feet is hurt.

sunburn[복습]
[sʌ́nbə̀:rn]

n. 햇볕에 탐, 햇볕으로 입은 화상
If someone has sunburn, their skin is bright pink and sore because they have spent too much time in hot sunshine.

comparison** n. 비교, 대조
[kəmpǽrisən] When you make a comparison, you consider two or more things and discover the differences between them.

linger** vi. 남아 있다, 계속되다, 오래 머물다
[líŋgər] When something lingers, it continues to exist for a long time, often much longer than expected.

unendurable a. 참을 수 없는, 견디기 힘든
[ʌnindʒúərəbəl] If you describe a bad situation as unendurable, you mean that it is so extremely unpleasant that you have to end it.

medication복습 n. 투약, 약물 치료; 약제, 약물
[mèdəkéiʃən] Medication is medicine that is used to treat and cure illness.

desperate복습 a. 자포자기의, 절망적인; 필사적인 (desperately ad. 절망적으로)
[déspərit] If you are desperate, you are in such a bad situation that you are willing to try anything to change it.

throb복습 vi. (심장이) 고동치다, 맥이 뛰다; n. 고동, 맥박
[θrab] If part of your body throbs, you feel a series of strong and usually painful beats there.

isolate** vt. 고립시키다, 격리시키다 (isolation n. 격리, 분리)
[áisəlèit] To isolate a person or organization means to cause them to lose their friends or supporters.

forsaken* a. 버림받은, 고독한; FORSAKE(버리다, 그만두다)의 과거분사
[fərséikən] A forsaken place is not lived in, used, or looked after.

fracture* v. (뼈를) 부러뜨리다, 부수다; n. 골절, 균열
[frǽktʃər] If something such as a bone is fractured or fractures, it gets a slight crack or break in it.

discomfort복습 n. 불쾌, 불안; vt. 불쾌[불안]하게 하다
[diskʌ́mfərt] Discomfort is a painful feeling in part of your body when you have been hurt slightly or when you have been uncomfortable for a long time.

brisk** a. 활발한, 활기찬, 기운찬; v. 활기를 띠(게 하)다
[brisk] A brisk activity or action is done quickly and in an energetic way.

sail*** n. 항해, 보트타기; 배의 돛; v. 항해하다
[seil] A sail is a trip in a boat or ship.

meadow** n. 목초지, 초원
[médou] A meadow is a field which has grass and flowers growing in it.

assuage vt. (고통·노여움·불안 등을) 완화하다, 진정시키다
[əswéidʒ] If you assuage an unpleasant feeling that someone has, you make them feel it less strongly.

torturous a. 고문의, 고통스러운; 일그러진
[tɔ́ːrtʃərəs] Something that is torturous is extremely painful and causes great suffering.

neglect^{최상}
[niglékt]

vt. 무시하다, 등한시하다; n. 태만, 소홀

If you neglect someone or something, you fail to look after them properly.

unfed
[ʌnféd]

a. 음식을 공급받지 못한, 굶주린

un (부정, 반대의 접두사) + fed ('FEED v. 먹이를 주다'의 과거분사형: 양육된, 먹이를 준)

excruciating^{최상}
[ikskrúːʃièitiŋ]

a. 극심한 고통을 주는; 맹렬한, 극심한

If you describe something as excruciating, you are emphasizing that it is extremely painful, either physically or emotionally.

spasm
[spǽzəm]

n. 경련, 발작

A spasm is a sudden tightening of your muscles, which you cannot control.

distend
[disténd]

v. 팽창시키다, 넓히다, 넓어지다 (distended a. 팽창한; 확대한)

If a part of your body is distended, or if it distends, it becomes swollen and unnaturally large.

fulfill**
[fulfíl]

vt. 달성하다, 이행하다

If you fulfill something such as a promise, dream, or hope, you do what you said or hoped you would do.

groan^{최상}
[groun]

v. 신음하다, 끙끙거리다; n. 신음소리

If you groan, you make a long, low sound because you are in pain, or because you are upset or unhappy about something.

petition**
[pitíʃən]

v. 청원하다, 탄원하다; n. 청원, 탄원

If you petition someone in authority, you make a formal request to them.

assign^{최상}
[əsáin]

v. 맡기다, 배정하다, 임명하다, 지정하다

If you assign a piece of work to someone, you give them the work to do.

**accommo-
date****
[əkámədèit]

vt. 숙박시키다, 수용하다; 편의를 도모하다

To accommodate someone means to provide them with a place to live or stay.

sought^{최상}
[sɔːt]

SEEK(v. 찾다; 구하다)의 과거 · 과거분사

Sought is the past tense and past participle of seek.

starvation*
[stɑːrvéiʃən]

n. 굶주림, 기아

Starvation is extreme suffering or death, caused by lack of food.

warfare*
[wɔ́ːrfɛ̀ər]

n. 전쟁, 교전, 전투

Warfare is the activity of fighting a war.

unconscious**
[ʌnkánʃəs]

a. 무의식적인, 알아채지 못하는; 의식이 없는 (unconsciously ad. 무의식적으로)

Someone who is unconscious is in a state similar to sleep, usually as the result of a serious injury or a lack of oxygen.

abdomen*
[ǽbdəmən]

n. 배, 복부

Your abdomen is the part of your body below your chest where your stomach and intestines are.

recall^{高島}
[rikɔ́ːl]

vt. 생각해내다, 상기하다, 소환하다; n. 회상, 상기
When you recall something, you remember it and tell others about it.

unfulfilled
[ʌnfulfíld]

a. 이루어지지 않은, 채워지지 않은
If you use unfulfilled to describe something such as a promise, ambition, or need, you mean that what was promised, hoped for, or needed has not happened.

destruction**
[distrʌ́kʃən]

n. 파괴; 멸망, 파멸
Destruction is the act of destroying something, or the state of being destroyed.

burden^{高島}
[bə́ːrdn]

vt. 짐을 지우다, 부담시키다; n. 짐, 부담
If someone burdens you with something that is likely to worry you, for example a problem or a difficult decision, they tell you about it.

vital^{高島}
[váitl]

a. 극히 중대한, 필수적인; 생명 유지와 연관된
If you say that something is vital, you mean that it is necessary or very important.

eager^{高島}
[íːgər]

a. 열망하는, 간절히 하고 싶어 하는 (eagerly ad. 열심히, 열망하여)
If you are eager to do or have something, you want to do or have it very much.

wry^{高島}
[rai]

a. 빈정대는, 비꼬는, 풍자적인
If someone has a wry expression, it shows that they find a bad situation or a change in a situation slightly amusing.

chuckle^{高島}
[tʃʌ́kl]

vi. 낄낄 웃다; n. 낄낄 웃음
When you chuckle, you laugh quietly.

reluctant^{高島}
[rilʌ́ktənt]

a. 마음이 내키지 않는, 마지못해 하는 (reluctantly ad. 마지못해서)
If you are reluctant to do something, you are unwilling to do it and hesitate before doing it, or do it slowly and without enthusiasm.

meaningful^{高島}
[míːniŋfəl]

a. 의미심장한; 의미 있는, 중요한
A meaningful look or gesture is one that is intended to express something, usually to a particular person, without anything being said.

ominous*
[ámənəs]

a. 불길한, 나쁜 징조의
If you describe something as ominous, you mean that it worries you because it makes you think that something unpleasant is going to happen.

maturity^{高島}
[mətʃúərəti]

n. 성숙(함), 다 자란 상태
Someone's maturity is their quality of being fully developed in their personality and emotional behavior.

nurture^{高島}
[nə́ːrtʃər]

vt. 양육하다, 기르다; n. 양육, 양성, 교육 (nurturer n. 양육자)
If you nurture something such as a young child or a young plant, you care for it while it is growing and developing.

grasp^{高島}
[græsp]

v. 붙잡다, 움켜쥐다; n. 움켜잡기
If you grasp something, you take it in your hand and hold it very firmly.

fretful^{최신}
[frétfəl]

a. 안달하는, 보채는, 조바심 내는
If someone is fretful, they behave in a way that shows that they worried or unhappy about something.

whimper^{최신}
[hwímpər]

v. 훌쩍이다, 울먹이다; 낑낑거리다
If someone whimpers, they make quiet unhappy or frightened sounds, as if they are about to start crying.

bathe^{최신}
[beið]

v. 목욕시키다, 씻다; (열·빛 등이) 뒤덮다, 감싸다
If you bathe someone, especially a child, you wash them in a bath.

hippo^{최신}
[hípou]

n. (= hippopotamus) [동물] 하마
A hippo is a very large African animal with short legs and thick, hairless skin.

placid[*]
[plǽsid]

a. 평온한, 조용한 (placidly ad. 평온하게)
A placid place, area of water, or life is calm and peaceful.

crib[*]
[krib]

n. 유아용 침대; 여물통; 곳간, 헛간
A crib is a bed for a small baby.

kneel^{최신}
[ni:l]

vi. 무릎 꿇다
When you kneel, you bend your legs so that your knees are touching the ground.

dismay^{최신}
[disméi]

n. 실망, 낙담, 경악; vt. 낙담[실망]하게 하다
Dismay is a strong feeling of fear, worry, or sadness that is caused by something unpleasant and unexpected.

ruffle[*]
[rʌ́fəl]

v. 구기다, 헝클다; (마음을) 흐트러뜨리다
If you ruffle someone's hair, you move your hand backwards and forwards through it as a way of showing your affection towards them.

status[*]
[stéitəs]

n. 지위, 신분; 상황, 상태
The status of something is its state of affairs at a particular time.

identical^{**}
[aidéntikəl]

a. 동일한, 꼭 같은
Things that are identical are exactly the same.

flutter^{최신}
[flʌ́tər]

v. (깃발 등이) 펄럭이다, (새 등이) 날갯짓하다; n. 펄럭임
If something thin or light flutters, or if you flutter it, it moves up and down or from side to side with a lot of quick, light movements.

sparkle^{**}
[spá:rkəl]

v. 반짝이다; 생기 넘치다; n. 반짝거림, 광채
If something sparkles, it is clear and bright and shines with a lot of very small points of light.

serene^{최신}
[sirí:n]

a. 조용한, 평온한; 고요한, 잔잔한
Someone or something that is serene is calm and quiet.

befit[*]
[bifít]

vt. 걸맞다, 적합하다
If something befits a person or thing, it is suitable or appropriate for them.

restless^{복습}
[réstlis]

a. 가만히 못 있는, 침착하지 못한; 쉬지 못하는, 불안한
(restlessness n. 불안함, 동요)
If you are restless, you are bored, impatient, or dissatisfied, and you want to do something else.

tend^{복습}
[tend]

① v. 돌보다, 간호하다 ② vi. 향하다, 경향이 있다
If you tend someone or something, you do what is necessary to keep them in a good condition or to improve their condition.

from time to time^{복습}

idiom 가끔, 이따금
If something happens from time to time, it happens occasionally.

undisturbed
[ʌndistə́:rbd]

a. 동요하지 않는, 편안한, 방해받지 않은
un (부정, 반대의 접두사) + disturbed a. 불안한, 동요하는

flail
[fleil]

v. 마구 움직이다, 마구 흔들다
If your arms or legs flail or if you flail them about, they wave about in an energetic but uncontrolled way.

lull**
[lʌl]

vt. 달래다, 어르다; n. 진정, 잠잠함
If someone or something lulls you, they cause you to feel calm or sleepy.

squirm^{복습}
[skwə:rm]

vi. 꿈틀거리다, 몸부림치다
If you squirm, you move your body from side to side, usually because you are nervous or uncomfortable.

breezy*
[brí:zi]

a. 산들바람이 부는, 상쾌한
When the weather is breezy, there is a fairly strong but pleasant wind blowing.

billow*
[bílou]

vi. (바람에) 부풀어 오르다; (연기·구름이) 피어오르다
When smoke or cloud billows, it moves slowly upwards or across the sky.

dim^{복습}
[dim]

a. 어둑한, 흐릿한, 희미한; v. 어둑하게 하다, 흐려지다
If you have a dim memory or understanding of something, it is difficult to remember or is unclear in your mind.

startle^{복습}
[stá:rtl]

v. 깜짝 놀라게 하다; 움찔하다; n. 깜짝 놀람 (startled a. 놀란)
If something sudden and unexpected startles you, it surprises and frightens you slightly.

murky^{복습}
[mə́:rki]

a. 흐린, 탁한, 어두운; 애매한, 확실치 않은
Murky water or fog is so dark and dirty that you cannot see through it.

cloud^{복습}
[klaud]

v. 흐리다, 흐려지다, 어둡게 하다; n. 구름 (clouded a. 흐린, 흐릿한)
If you say that something clouds a situation, you mean that it makes it unpleasant.

soothing^{복습}
[sú:ðiŋ]

a. 달래는, 위로하는, 진정시키는
Something that is soothing has a calming, assuaging, or relieving effect.

dawn***
[dɔ:n]

n. 새벽, 동틀 녘; vi. 날이 새다, 밝아지다; 나타나기 시작하다
Dawn is the time of day when light first appears in the sky, just before the sun rises.

deliberate
[dilíbərèit]

a. 신중한, 계획적인 (deliberately ad. 신중하게, 계획적으로)
If you do something that is deliberate, you planned to do it beforehand, and so it happens on purpose.

wisp
[wisp]

n. 가닥, 줄기, 작은 묶음
A wisp of something such as smoke or cloud is an amount of it in a long thin shape.

acquire
[əkwáiər]

vt. 습득하다, 배우다; 얻다, 획득하다
If you acquire something such as a skill or a habit, you learn it, or develop it through your daily life or experience.

chapter fifteen

1. Why did Jonas offer to help The Giver?

   (A) He didn't want to go home.

   (B) He wanted to know what pain felt like.

   (C) He thought he should relieve some of The Giver's pain.

   (D) He didn't want The Giver to be selfish and keep the memories.

2. Where was Jonas in the memory?

   (A) A field

   (B) A dense forest

   (C) The mountains

   (D) A desert

3. The boy next to Jonas asked for _____.

   (A) help

   (B) his parents

   (C) food

   (D) water

4. What injury did Jonas have in the memory?

   (A) He had a broken leg.

   (B) He had a broken arm.

   (C) He was shot in the stomach.

   (D) He had a cut on his arm.

5. What happened to the boy after Jonas gave him what he wanted?

    (A) He died.

    (B) He fell asleep.

    (C) He was able to stand up.

    (D) He fell over.

6. Which of the following did Jonas NOT hear in the dream?

    (A) Cannons in the distance

    (B) Cries of wounded men

    (C) Shrieks of dying horses

    (D) Enemy soldiers yelling

7. How did the memory end?

    (A) Jonas stopped The Giver from giving him the end of the memory.

    (B) Jonas welcomed death himself.

    (C) Jonas was saved by the men around him.

    (D) Jonas fell asleep in the memory.

1분에 몇 단어를 읽는지 리딩 속도를 측정해보세요.

$$\frac{583 \text{ words}}{\text{reading time (}\quad\text{) sec}} \times 60 = (\qquad) \text{ WPM}$$

• *Build Your Vocabulary*

rigid*
[rídʒid]

a. 단단한, 고정된; 완고한, 융통성 없는
A rigid substance or object is stiff and does not bend, stretch, or twist easily.

hesitate^{복습}
[hézətèit]

v. 주저하다, 머뭇거리다, 망설이다
If you hesitate, you do not speak or act for a short time, usually because you are uncertain, embarrassed, or worried about what you are going to say or do.

contort
[kəntɔ́:rt]

v. (얼굴 등이) 일그러지다, 뒤틀리다
If someone's face or body contorts or is contorted, it moves into an unnatural and unattractive shape or position.

gasp^{복습}
[gæsp]

v. (놀람 따위로) 숨이 막히다, 헐떡거리다; n. 헐떡거림
When you gasp, you take a short quick breath through your mouth, especially when you are surprised, shocked, or in pain.

brace*
[breis]

v. 대비하다; 버팀대로 받치다; n. 버팀대
If you brace yourself for something unpleasant or difficult, you prepare yourself for it.

torture^{복습}
[tɔ́:rtʃər]

vt. 고문하다, 고통을 주다; n. 고문, 고뇌
To torture someone means to cause them to suffer mental pain or anxiety.

foul**
[faul]

a. 더러운, 불결한, 악취 나는; 비열한, 못된 (foul-smelling a. 악취가 나는)
If you describe something as foul, you mean it is dirty and smells or tastes unpleasant.

expanse^{복습}
[ikspǽns]

n. 넓게 퍼진 지역; 팽창, 확장
An expanse of something, usually sea, sky, or land, is a very large amount of it.

dangle^{복습}
[dǽŋgəl]

v. (달랑달랑) 매달(리)다; n. 매달린 것
If something dangles from somewhere or if you dangle it somewhere, it hangs or swings loosely.

trot*
[trɑt]

v. 빠른 걸음으로 가다, 종종걸음을 걷다; n. 빠른 걸음
If you trot somewhere, you move fairly fast at a speed between walking and running, taking small quick step.

frantic*
[frǽntik]

a. 광란의, 극도로 흥분한 (frantically ad. 미친 듯이)
If you are frantic, you are behaving in a wild and uncontrolled way because you are frightened or worried.

mound^{복습}
[maund]

n. 더미, 무더기, 언덕
A mound of something is a large rounded pile of it.

toss^{복습}
[tɔːs]

v. (머리 등을) 갑자기 쳐들다; 던지다, 내던지다
If you toss your head or toss your hair, you move your head backwards, quickly and suddenly.

whinny
[hwíni]

v. (말이) 울다, 히힝 하는 소리를 내다
When a horse whinnies, it makes a series of high-pitched sounds, usually not very loudly.

stumble^{복습}
[stʌ́mbəl]

v. 비틀거리며 걷다, 발부리가 걸리다; n. 비틀거림
If you stumble, you put your foot down awkwardly while you are walking or running and nearly fall over.

parch[*]
[pɑːrtʃ]

v. 바싹 마르게 하다, (사람을) 목 타게 하다 (parched a. 목 타는)
If your mouth, throat, or lips are parched, they are unpleasantly dry.

croak[*]
[krouk]

v. 까악까악[개굴개굴] 울다; 쉰 목소리를 내다
When a frog or bird croaks, it makes a harsh, low sound.

streak^{복습}
[striːk]

v. 질주하다; 줄을 긋다, 기다란 흔적을 내다 n. 경향, 기미; 줄
If something streaks a surface, it makes long stripes or marks on the surface.

matted
[mǽtid]

a. 텁수룩한, 헝클어진; 매트를 깐
If you describe someone's hair as matted, you mean that it has become a thick untidy mass, often because it is wet or dirty.

sprawl[*]
[sprɔːl]

v. (팔다리 등을) 쭉 펴다, 큰 대자로 눕다; 퍼져 나가다 (sprawled a. 대자로 뻗은)
If you sprawl somewhere, you sit or lie down with your legs and arms spread out in a careless way.

glisten[*]
[glísn]

vi. 반짝이다, 반짝반짝 빛나다; n. 반짝임
If something glistens, it shines, usually because it is wet or oily.

carnage
[kɑ́ːrnidʒ]

n. 살육, 대학살
Carnage is the violent killing of large numbers of people, especially in a war.

grotesque[*]
[groutésk]

a. 괴상한, 그로테스크한, 기괴한 (grotesquely ad. 괴상하게)
You say that something is grotesque when it is so unnatural, unpleasant, and exaggerated that it upsets or shocks you.

crimson[*]
[krímzən]

a. 진홍색의; n. 진홍색
Something that is crimson is deep red in color.

fabric^{복습}
[fǽbrik]

n. 직물, 천
Fabric is cloth or other material produced by weaving together cotton, nylon, wool, silk, or other threads.

rip[*]
[rip]

v. 째다, 찢다, 잡아 찢다; 벗겨내다
When something rips or when you rip it, you tear it forcefully with your hands or with a tool such as a knife.

shred* [ʃred]	n. 조각, 파편; v. 조각조각으로 찢다, 갈가리 찢다 If there is not a shred of something, there is not even a small amount of it.
spurt* [spəːrt]	n. 분출, 뿜어져 나옴; v. 쏟아져 나오다, 내뿜다 A spurt of liquid is a stream of it which comes out of something very forcefully.
drench** [drentʃ]	vt. 흠뻑 젖게 하다 To drench something or someone means to make them completely wet.
coarse** [kɔːrs]	a. 결이 거친; 조잡한, 조악한 Coarse things have a rough texture because they consist of thick threads or large pieces.
sleeve^{복습} [sliːv]	n. (옷의) 소매 The sleeves of a coat, shirt, or other item of clothing are the parts that cover your arms.
immobilize [imóubəlàiz]	vt. 움직이지 못하게 하다, 고정시키다 To immobilize something or someone means to stop them from moving or operating.
ragged^{복습} [rǽgid]	a. 누더기가 된, 해어진; 남루한, 초라한 Ragged clothes are old and torn.
flesh^{복습} [fleʃ]	n. 살, 살집, 고기; 피부 Flesh is the soft part of a person's or animal's body between the bones and the skin.
splintery [splíntəri]	a. 파편의; 찢어[쪼개]지기 쉬운 Something that is splintery resembles or consists long slender fragments of wood having sharp points.
(every) now and then^{복습}	idiom 가끔, 때때로, 이따금 If you do something every now and then, you do it sometimes, but not very often.
surge* [səːrdʒ]	v. 쇄도하다, 밀어닥치다; n. 쇄도, 돌진 If something surges, it increases suddenly and greatly, after being steady or developing only slowly.
extend^{복습} [iksténd]	v. (손·발 등을) 뻗다, 늘이다; 연장하다 If an object extends from a surface or place, it sticks out from it.
trickle* [tríkəl]	vi. 똑똑 떨어지다, 졸졸 흐르다; (비밀 따위가) 조금씩 새어 나가다; n. 물방울, 실개울 If liquid trickles somewhere, it flows slowly and without force in a thin line.
implore** [implɔ́ːr]	vt. 애원하다, 탄원하다 (imploring a. 탄원하는, 애원하는) If you implore someone to do something, you ask them to do it in a forceful, emotional way.
grimy [gráimi]	a. 때 묻은, 더러워진 Something that is grimy is very dirty.

blank^{복습}
[blæŋk]

a. 멍한, 얼빠진; 공허한, 공백의; n. 공백 (blankness n. 공허함)
If you look blank, your face shows no feeling, understanding, or interest.

wound^{복습}
[wu:nd]

vt. 상처를 입히다; n. 상처, 부상, 상해 (wounded a. 부상한, 다친)
If a weapon or something sharp wounds you, it damages your body.

shriek^{**}
[ʃri:k]

v. 새된 소리를 지르다, 비명을 지르다; n. 비명
When someone shrieks, they make a short, very loud cry.

stab^{**}
[stæb]

v. (칼 따위로) 찌르다; n. 찌름; 찌르는 듯한 통증
If someone stabs you, they push a knife or sharp object into your body.

hoof
[huf]

n. (pl. hooves) 발굽, 발굽 소리
The hooves of an animal such as a horse are the hard lower parts of its feet.

thud^{복습}
[θʌd]

n. 쿵, 털썩, 덜컥 (무거운 물건이 떨어지는 소리)
A thud is a dull sound, such as that which a heavy object makes when it hits something soft.

cannon^{**}
[kǽnən]

n. 대포; v. 대포를 쏘다, 포격하다
A cannon is a large gun, usually on wheels, which used to be used in battles.

overwhelm^{복습}
[òuvərhwélm]

vt. 압도하다, 제압하다; 질리게 하다
If you are overwhelmed by a feeling or event, it affects you very strongly, and you do not know how to deal with it.

fearsome
[fíərsəm]

a. 무시무시한, 오싹한
Fearsome is used to describe things that are frightening, for example because of their large size or extreme nature.

stench
[stentʃ]

n. 불쾌한 냄새, 악취
A stench is a strong and very unpleasant smell.

warfare^{복습}
[wɔ́:rfɛ̀ər]

n. 전쟁, 교전, 전투
Warfare is the activity of fighting a war.

chapter sixteen

1. How did Jonas feel after the memory of warfare?

    (A) He was happy to be honored with the important job of protecting the community.

    (B) He felt proud to be receiving memories.

    (C) He didn't want to go back to his job but he did not have a choice.

    (D) He was too scared to go back to his job so he spent his time playing ball games and bicycling.

2. What memory taught Jonas about individuality?

    (A) Warfare

    (B) A trip to a museum

    (C) Riding a horse

    (D) Having a birthday party

3. Which of the following did Jonas NOT learn in this chapter?

    (A) Courage

    (B) The bond between human and animal

    (C) The joy of solitude

    (D) Love

4. Which holiday did Jonas learn about in this chapter?

    (A) New Year's Day

    (B) Halloween

    (C) Thanksgiving Day

    (D) Christmas

5. Where do people who are working and contributing to the community live after their children receive their own dwellings?

   (A) They live at the House of the Old.
   (B) They live with the other childless adults.
   (C) They are released.
   (D) They continue living in the same dwelling.

6. What will happen on the day one of Jonas's parents is released?

   (A) He will not know about the release of the parent because he will be too busy with his own life.
   (B) He will attend the release ceremony at the House of the Old.
   (C) He will not know about the release of the parent because the community keeps all of the releases a secret.
   (D) He will know about the release but will be too busy with his own job to attend.

7. Why did Jonas lie to his parents?

   (A) He didn't understand why his parents were proud of him.
   (B) He understood why the word "love" was obsolete and no longer used.
   (C) He understood why his parents said they enjoyed him but not proud of him.
   (D) He didn't understand why it was inappropriate to use the word "love."

1분에 몇 단어를 읽는지 리딩 속도를 측정해보세요.

$$\frac{1,989 \text{ words}}{\text{reading time (\quad) sec}} \times 60 = (\qquad) \text{ WPM}$$

• *Build Your Vocabulary*

dwelling
[dwéliŋ]
n. 거처, 주소, 사는 집
A dwelling is a place where someone lives.

ordinary
[ɔ́:rdənèri]
a. 보통의, 평범한
Ordinary people or things are normal and not special or different in any way.

anguish
[ǽŋgwiʃ]
n. 괴로움, 고뇌, 번민; v. 괴로워하다, 괴롭히다
Anguish is great mental suffering or physical pain.

annex
[ənéks]
n. 별관, 별채; 부속물; vt. 부가하다; 합병하다
An annex is a building that is an addition to another building.

countless
[káuntlis]
a. 셀 수 없는, 무수한
Countless means very many.

celebrate
[séləbrèit]
v. 기념하다, 축하하다
If you celebrate, you do something enjoyable because of a special occasion.

individual
[ìndəvídʒuəl]
n. 개인; a. 개개의; 개인의
An individual is a person.

ecstatic
[ekstǽtik]
a. 황홀한, 무아지경의
If you are ecstatic, you feel very happy and full of excitement.

gleam
[gli:m]
vi. 빛나다, 반짝이다, 번득이다; n. 번득임, 어스레한 빛
If an object or a surface gleams, it reflects light because it is shiny and clean.

damp
[dæmp]
a. 축축한; n. 습기
Something that is damp is slightly wet.

dismount
[dismáunt]
vt. (말·자전거 따위에서) 내리다
If you dismount from a horse or a bicycle, you get down from it.

nudge
[nʌdʒ]
vt. (주의를 끌기 위해 팔꿈치로) 슬쩍 찌르다; 주의를 환기시키다
If you nudge someone, you push them gently, usually with your elbow, in order to draw their attention to something.

affectionate
[əfékʃənit]
a. 다정한, 애정 어린 (affectionately ad. 애정을 담아서)
If you are affectionate, you show your love or fondness for another person in the way that you behave towards them.

perceive[쌍수]
[pərsíːv]
vt. 지각하다, 감지하다
If you perceive something, you see, notice, or realize it, especially when it is not obvious.

solitude**
[sálitʃùːd]
n. 고독, 외로움
Solitude is the state of being alone, especially when this is peaceful and pleasant.

get one's bearings
idiom 환경에 익숙해지다; 향방을 알다
If you get your bearings, you find out where you are or what you should do next.

pervade**
[pərvéid]
vt. 배어들다, 침투하다, 스며들다
If something pervades a place or thing, it is a noticeable feature throughout it.

glow[쌍수]
[glou]
v. 빛을 내다, 빛나다; 상기되다, 발개지다, 달아오르다; n. 빛, 밝음
If something glows, it produces a dull, steady light.

hearth**
[hɑːrθ]
n. 벽난로, 노(爐)
The hearth is the floor of a fireplace, which sometimes extends into the room.

polish**
[páliʃ]
v. 닦다, 윤내다; n. 광택; 세련 (polished a. 닦은, 광택 있는)
If you polish something, you rub it with a cloth to make it shine.

flicker[쌍수]
[flíkər]
v. (등불 · 희망 · 빛 등이) 깜박이다; n. 깜박임 (flickering a. 깜박거리는)
If a light or flame flickers, it shines unsteadily.

couch**
[kautʃ]
n. 소파, 긴 의자
A couch is a long, comfortable seat for two or three people.

reveal[쌍수]
[rivíːl]
vt. 드러내다, 폭로하다, 밝히다
If you reveal something that has been out of sight, you uncover it so that people can see it.

lap[복쌍]
[læp]
① n. 무릎; (트랙의) 한 바퀴 ② v. (파도가) 찰싹거리다, (할짝할짝) 핥다
If you have something on your lap, it is on top of your legs and near to your body.

rock**
[rɑk]
① v. (앞뒤 · 좌우로 살살) 흔들다, 움직이다; n. 록 음악; 흔들림, 진동
② n. 바위, 암석
When something rocks or when you rock it, it moves slowly and regularly backwards and forwards or from side to side.

contented*
[kənténtid]
a. 만족한 (contentedly ad. 만족해서, 느긋하게)
If you are contented, you are satisfied with your life or the situation you are in.

luxuriate
[lʌgʒúərièit]
vi. 사치스럽게 지내다, 호사하다
If you luxuriate in something, you relax in it and enjoy it very much, especially because you find it comfortable and luxurious.

treasure***
[tréʒər]
vt. 소중히 하다, 잘 간수하다; n. 보물, 보배
If you treasure something that you have, you keep it or care for it carefully because it gives you great pleasure and you think it is very special.

celebration^{복습}
[sèləbréiʃən]

n. 축하, 축전, 기념행사
The celebration of something is praise and appreciation which is given to it.

puzzle^{복습}
[pʌzl]

v. 어리둥절하게 만들다, 곤혹스럽게 하다, 난처하게 하다
If something puzzles you, you do not understand it and feel confused.

frown^{복습}
[fraun]

vi. 얼굴을 찡그리다, 눈살을 찌푸리다; n. 찌푸린 얼굴
When someone frowns, their eyebrows become drawn together, because they are annoyed or puzzled.

spouse^{복습}
[spaus]

n. 배우자, 남편, 아내
Someone's spouse is the person they are married to.

contribute^{복습}
[kəntríbjut]

v. 기여[공헌]하다; 기부[기증]하다
If you contribute to something, you say or do things to help to make it successful.

release^{복습}
[rilí:s]

vt. 놓아주다, 해방시키다, 풀어놓다; n. 석방
If a person or animal is released from somewhere where they have been looked after, they are set free or allowed to go.

vague^{복습}
[veig]

a. 희미한, 모호한, 애매한
If something written or spoken is vague, it does not explain or express things clearly.

wisp^{복습}
[wisp]

n. 단편, 조각; 한 줌, 작은 묶음
A wisp of something such as smoke or cloud is an amount of it in a long thin shape.

blurt
[blə:rt]

vt. 불쑥 말하다; 무심결에 누설하다
If someone blurts something, they say it suddenly, after trying hard to keep quiet or to keep it secret.

practical^{복습}
[prǽktikəl]

a. 실용적인; 실제의, 실제적인
Practical ideas and methods are likely to be effective or successful in a real situation.

falter*
[fɔ́:ltər]

vi. 더듬거리다, 머뭇거리다; 불안정해지다, 흔들리다
If you falter, you lose your confidence and stop doing something or start making mistakes.

confess^{복습}
[kənfés]

v. 자백하다, 고백하다, 인정하다
If someone confesses to doing something wrong, they admit that they did it.

glance^{복습}
[glæns]

v. 흘긋 보다, 잠깐 보다; n. 흘긋 봄
If you glance at something or someone, you look at them very quickly and then look away again immediately.

reassure^{복습}
[rì:əʃúər]

vt. 안심시키다
If you reassure someone, you say or do things to make them stop worrying about something.

involve^{복습}
[inválv]

vt. 수반하다, 포함하다, 관련시키다 (involved a. 관련된; 열심인, 몰두하는)
If a situation or activity involves something, that thing is a necessary part or consequence of it.

outlaw
[áutlɔ̀ː]

vt. 불법화하다, 금지하다; n. 범법자
When something is outlawed, it is made illegal.

tentative^{복습}
[téntətiv]

a. 머뭇거리는, 주저하는; 잠정적인, 임시의 (tentatively ad. 조심스럽게, 주저하며)
If someone is tentative, they are cautious and not very confident because they are uncertain or afraid.

flush***
[flʌʃ]

v. (얼굴 등을) 붉히다; (물이) 왈칵 흘러나오다; n. (볼 등의) 홍조
If you flush, your face goes red because you are hot or ill, or because you are feeling a strong emotion such as embarrassment or anger.

embarrass^{복습}
[imbǽrəs]

v. 당황스럽게[쑥스럽게] 만들다, 곤란하게 하다 (embarrassment n. 난처함, 당황)
If something or someone embarrasses you, they make you feel shy or ashamed.

rehearse*
[rihə́ːrs]

v. 예행연습을 하다, 리허설을 하다
If you rehearse something that you are going to say or do, you silently practice it by imagining that you are saying or doing it.

awkward^{복습}
[ɔ́ːkwərd]

a. 어색한, 불편한, 곤란한
Someone who feels awkward behaves in a shy or embarrassed way.

precision^{복습}
[prisíʒən]

n. 정확, 정밀; 꼼꼼함
If you do something with precision, you do it exactly as it should be done.

amuse^{복습}
[əmjúːz]

vt. 즐겁게 하다, 재미나게 하다 (amusement n. 즐거움, 재미)
If something amuses you, it makes you want to laugh or smile.

anticipate**
[æntísəpèit]

vt. 예상하다, 기대하다
If you anticipate an event, you realize in advance that it may happen and you are prepared for it.

obsolete^{복습}
[àbsəlíːt]

a. 쓸모없게 된, 안 쓰이는; vt. 쇠퇴시키다
Something that is obsolete is no longer needed because something better has been invented.

meaningful^{복습}
[míːniŋfəl]

a. 의미 있는, 중요한, 의미심장한
If you describe something as meaningful, you mean that it is serious, important, or useful in some way.

precise^{복습}
[prisáis]

a. 정확한, 정밀한; 명확한
You use precise to emphasize that you are referring to an exact thing, rather than something vague.

accomplish^{복습}
[əkámpliʃ]

vt. 이루다, 성취하다, 완수하다 (accomplishment n. 성취, 업적)
If you accomplish something, you succeed in doing it.

wholehearted*
[hóulhá:rtid]

a. 전심전력의; 성의 있는, 진심의 (wholeheartedly ad. 진심으로)
If you support or agree to something in a wholehearted way, you support or agree to it enthusiastically and completely.

inappropriate
[ìnəpróupriit]

a. 부적절한, 부적합한
Something that is inappropriate is not useful or suitable for a particular situation or purpose.

crib복습
[krib]

n. 유아용 침대; 여물통; 곳간, 헛간
A crib is a bed for a small baby.

sleep soundly복습

idiom 깊이 잠들다
If someone sleep soundly, they are sleeping very deeply.

pronounce**
[prənáuns]

v. 선언하다; 발음하다
If you pronounce something to be true, you state that it is the case.

crawl
[krɔ:l]

vi. 기어가다, 느릿느릿 가다; n. 기어감; 서행
When you crawl, you move forward on your hands and knees.

giggle복습
[gígəl]

v. 낄낄 웃다; n. 낄낄 웃음
If someone giggles, they laugh in a childlike way, because they are amused, nervous, or embarrassed.

optimistic*
[ὰptəmístik]

a. 낙천적인, 낙천주의의
Someone who is optimistic is hopeful about the future or the success of something in particular.

sould asleep

idiom 깊이 잠들다
If someone sleep soundly, they are sleeping very deeply.

dim복습
[dim]

a. 어둑한, 흐릿한, 희미한; v. 어둑하게 하다, 흐려지다
(dimness n. 어둑어둑함, 어스름)
If you have a dim memory or understanding of something, it is difficult to remember or is unclear in your mind.

even복습
[í:vən]

a. 규칙적인, 한결같은; 떡꼭 맞는; ad. 한층, 더욱
An even measurement or rate stays at about the same level.

guilty복습
[gílti]

a. 죄진 듯한, 가책을 느끼는; 유죄의
If you feel guilty, you feel unhappy because you think that you have done something wrong or have failed to do something which you should have done.

windowpane*
[wíndoupèin]

n. 창유리
A windowpane is a piece of glass in the window of a building.

bare복습
[bɛər]

a. 발가벗은; 있는 그대로의 (barefoot a. 맨발의)
If a part of your body is bare, it is not covered by any clothing.

lawn복습
[lɔ:n]

n. 잔디, 잔디밭
A lawn is an area of grass that is kept cut short and is usually part of someone's garden or backyard, or part of a park.

stir^{복습}
[stə:r]

v. 휘젓다, 움직이다; n. 움직임; 휘젓기
If you stir, you move slightly, for example because you are uncomfortable or beginning to wake up.

chapter seventeen

1. Why didn't Jonas take his pills?

    (A) The pills helped him sleep at night with fewer dreams.

    (B) The pills made him feel sick to his stomach.

    (C) He enjoyed heightened feelings he had when he didn't take the pills.

    (D) He didn't think the pills did anything to him.

2. Which of the following was NOT true about Jonas's life?

    (A) He could see all of the colors all of the time.

    (B) He felt more depth in his feelings.

    (C) He knew that other citizens did not experience and understand feelings like he did.

    (D) He found it hard to understand the other citizens' feelings.

3. What happened when Jonas realized the children were playing a war game?

    (A) He yelled at the children and told them not to play the game.

    (B) He found it difficult to breathe.

    (C) He played the game with his friends.

    (D) He told his friends his memory of warfare.

4. What did Jonas feel after Asher and Fiona left him?

   (A) Loss
   (B) Happiness
   (C) Independence
   (D) Wisdom

5. Jonas's father says the smaller twin will
   _____.

   (A) go to Elsewhere
   (B) be given to a family unit
   (C) be sent to a nearby community
   (D) go to the nurturing center

1분에 몇 단어를 읽는지 리딩 속도를 측정해보세요.

$$\frac{2{,}126 \text{ words}}{\text{reading time (\quad) sec}} \times 60 = (\qquad) \text{ WPM}$$

• *Build Your Vocabulary*

declare***
[dikléər]

v. 선언하다, 공표하다
If you declare something, you state officially and formally that it exists or is the case.

unscheduled
[ʌnskédʒu(:)ld]

a. 계획에 없는, 예정 밖의
An unscheduled event was not planned to happen, but happens unexpectedly or because someone changes their plans at a late stage.

rare복습
[rɛər]

a. 드문, 진귀한 (rarely ad. 드물게, 좀처럼 …하지 않는)
Something that is rare is not common and is therefore interesting or valuable.

treat복습
[triːt]

n. 만족[즐거움]을 주는 것, 맛있는 간식; 대접, 환대; vt. 다루다, 대우하다
If you give someone a treat, you buy or arrange something special for them which they will enjoy.

exempt복습
[igzémpt]

vt. (의무 등을) 면제하다; a. 면제된
To exempt a person or thing from a particular rule, duty, or obligation means to state officially that they are not bound or affected by it.

volunteer복습
[vàləntíər]

n. 지원자, 자원 봉사자; v. 자발적으로 나서다; a. 자발적인
A volunteer is someone who offers to do a particular task or job without being forced to do it.

substitute**
[sʌ́bstitjùːt]

a. 대체하는, 대용의; n. 대리인, 대체물; v. 대신하다, 대체하다
A substitute is something that you have or use instead of something else.

nurture복습
[nə́ːrtʃər]

vt. 양육하다, 기르다; n. 양육, 양성, 교육 (nurturing n. 양육)
If you nurture something such as a young child or a young plant, you care for it while it is growing and developing.

memorize복습
[méməràiz]

vt. 기억하다, 암기하다
If you memorize something, you learn it so that you can remember it exactly.

pill복습
[pil]

n. 알약
Pills are small solid round masses of medicine or vitamins that you swallow without chewing.

stirring복습
[stə́ːriŋ]

n. (감정 · 생각 등이) 시작됨, 일어남; a. 감동시키는, 고무하는
A stirring of a feeling or thought is the beginning of one.

guilty^{복습}
[gílti]

a. 죄진 듯한, 가책을 느끼는; 유죄의
If you feel guilty, you feel unhappy because you think that you have done something wrong or have failed to do something which you should have done.

embarrass^{복습}
[imbǽrəs]

v. 당황스럽게[쑥스럽게] 만들다, 곤란하게 하다
If something or someone embarrasses you, they make you feel shy or ashamed.

pleasurable^{복습}
[pléʒərəbəl]

a. 즐거운, 유쾌한, 기쁜
Pleasurable experiences or sensations are pleasant and enjoyable.

heighten**
[háitn]

vt. 증가시키다, 강화하다, 높이다, 고조되다
If something heightens a feeling or if the feeling heightens, the feeling increases in degree or intensity.

permeate
[pə́:rmièit]

v. 스며들다, 침투하다, 퍼지다
If something permeates a place, it spreads throughout it.

realm**
[relm]

n. 범위, 영역
You can use realm to refer to any area of activity, interest, or thought.

rosy**
[róuzi]

a. 장밋빛의, 발그레한; 희망적인
If you say that someone has a rosy face, you mean that they have pink cheeks and look very healthy.

gurgle^{복습}
[gə́:rgəl]

v. (물이 좁은 공간을 빠르게 흐를 때 나는) 꼴꼴[콸콸] 소리 나다;
(아기가) 까르륵 소리를 내다
If water is gurgling, it is making the sound that it makes when it flows quickly and unevenly through a narrow space.

precision^{복습}
[prisíʒən]

n. 정확, 정밀; 꼼꼼함
If you do something with precision, you do it exactly as it should be done.

depth^{복습}
[depθ]

n. 깊이; 깊은 곳, 깊음
The depth of something such as a river or hole is the distance downwards from its top surface, or between its upper and lower surfaces.

analyze**
[ǽnəlàiz]

vt. 분석하다
If you analyze something, you consider it carefully or use statistical methods in order to fully understand it.

fist^{복습}
[fist]

n. (쥔) 주먹
Your hand is referred to as your fist when you have bent your fingers in towards the palm in order to hit someone, to make an angry gesture, or to hold something.

indicate^{복습}
[índikèit]

vt. 가리키다, 지시하다, 나타내다
If one thing indicates another, the first thing shows that the second is true or exists.

fury**
[fjúəri]

n. 격노, 격분
Fury is violent or very strong anger.

patient^{복습}
[péiʃənt]

a. 인내심[참을성] 있는; n. 환자 (patience n. 인내, 참을성)
If you are patient, you stay calm and do not get annoyed, for example when something takes a long time, or when someone is not doing what you want them to do.

shallow**
[ʃǽlou]

a. 얕은, 얄팍한
If you describe a person, piece of work, or idea as shallow, you disapprove of them because they do not show or involve any serious or careful thought.

impatient^{복습}
[impéiʃənt]

a. 성급한, 조급한, 참을성 없는 (impatience n. 성급함, 조바심)
If you are impatient, you are annoyed because you have to wait too long for something.

exasperation
[igzæspəréiʃən]

n. 격분, 격노, 분통
Exasperation is the state of being annoyed and frustrated.

injustice**
[indʒʌ́stis]

n. 불법, 부정, 불공평
Injustice is a lack of fairness in a situation.

cruel**
[krú:əl]

a. 잔혹한, 잔인한, 무자비한 (cruelty n. 잔혹, 무자비)
A situation or event that is cruel is very harsh and causes people distress.

rage^{복습}
[reidʒ]

n. 격노, 분노; 열광; v. 격노하다
Rage is strong anger that is difficult to control.

well up

phrasal v. 솟아나다, 넘쳐 나오다
If an emotion wells up, you start to feel it very strongly.

passionate**
[pǽʃənit]

a. 열정적인, 열렬한, 격정적인 (passionately ad. 열정적으로)
A passionate person has very strong feelings about something or a strong belief in something.

unthinkable
[ʌnθíŋkəbəl]

a. 상상할 수 없는, 감히 생각도 할 수 없는
un (부정, 반대의 접두사) + think (v. 생각하다) + able (a. …할 수 있는)

grief^{복습}
[gri:f]

n. 슬픔, 비탄
Grief is a feeling of extreme sadness.

strew*
[stru:]

vt. (strewed–strewn) 온통 뒤덮다; 뿌리다, 흩뿌리다
If a place is strewn with things, they are lying scattered there.

disregard^{복습}
[dìsrigá:rd]

vt. 무시하다, 경시하다; n. 무시, 경시
If you disregard something, you ignore it or do not take account of it.

skid
[skid]

v. 미끄러지다; n. 미끄러짐
If a vehicle skids, it slides sideways or forwards while moving, for example when you are trying to stop it suddenly on a wet road.

stagger**
[stǽgər]

v. 비틀거리다, 휘청거리다; n. 비틀거림
If you stagger, you walk very unsteadily, for example because you are ill or drunk.

clutch**
[klʌtʃ]

v. 꽉 잡다, 붙들다, 부여잡다; n. 붙잡음, 움켜쥠
If you clutch at something or clutch something, you hold it tightly, usually because you are afraid or anxious.

stumble^{복습}
[stʌ́mbəl]

v. 비틀거리며 걷다, 발부리가 걸리다; n. 비틀거림
If you stumble, you put your foot down awkwardly while you are walking or running and nearly fall over.

groan^{복습}
[groun]

v. 신음하다, 끙끙거리다; n. 신음소리
If you groan, you make a long, low sound because you are in pain, or because you are upset or unhappy about something.

grin^{복습}
[grin]

v. (이를 드러내고) 싱긋 웃다, 활짝 웃다; n. 싱긋 웃음
When you grin, you smile broadly.

imaginary^{복습}
[imǽdʒənèri]

a. 상상의, 가공의
An imaginary person, place, or thing exists only in your mind or in a story, and not in real life.

dart *
[dɑ:rt]

v. 돌진하다, 던지다, 쏘다; n. 던지는 화살, 다트
If a person or animal darts somewhere, they move there suddenly and quickly.

ambush *
[ǽmbuʃ]

n. 매복, 잠복; v. 매복하다; 매복하여 습격하다
An ambush is an attack on someone by people who have been hiding and waiting for them.

pastime *
[pǽstàim]

n. 기분 전환, 오락
A pastime is something that you do in your spare time because you enjoy it or are interested in it.

pose **
[pouz]

v. 자세를 취하(게 하)다; n. 자세, 포즈
If you pose for a photograph or painting, you stay in a particular position so that someone can photograph you or paint you.

freakish
[frí:kiʃ]

a. 별난, 기이한, 괴상한
Something that is freakish is remarkable because it is not normal or natural.

posture^{복습}
[pástʃər]

n. 자세; 태도, 마음가짐; v. 자세[태도]를 취하다
Your posture is the position in which you stand or sit.

equipment^{복습}
[ikwípmənt]

n. 장비, 설비
Equipment consists of the things which are used for a particular purpose, for example a hobby or job.

dash^{복습}
[dæʃ]

v. 돌진하다, 서둘러 가다; 내던지다; n. 돌진, 질주
If you dash somewhere, you run or go there quickly and suddenly.

horde *
[hɔ:rd]

n. 큰 떼거리; 무리
If you describe a crowd of people as a horde, you mean that the crowd is very large and excited and, often, rather frightening or unpleasant.

emerge^{복습}
[imə́:rdʒ]

vi. 나오다, 나타나다
To emerge means to come out from an enclosed or dark space.

crouch *
[krautʃ]

v. 몸을 쭈그리다, 쭈그리고 앉다; 웅크리다; n. 웅크림
If you are crouching, your legs are bent under you so that you are close to the ground and leaning forward slightly.

chest[*]
[tʃest]

① n. 가슴, 흉부 ② n. 상자, 궤
Your chest is the top part of the front of your body where your ribs, lungs, and heart are.

exaggerate^{**}
[igzǽdʒərèit]

vt. 과장하다 (exaggerated a. 과장된, 허풍떠는)
If you exaggerate, you indicate that something is, for example, worse or more important than it really is.

suppress^{**}
[səprés]

vt. 억압하다, 진압하다, 참다
If you suppress your feelings or reactions, you do not express them, even though you might want to.

surge[*]
[səːrdʒ]

v. 쇄도하다, 밀어닥치다; n. 쇄도, 돌진
If something surges, it increases suddenly and greatly, after being steady or developing only slowly.

yell^{**}
[yell]

v. 소리치다, 고함치다; n. 고함소리, 부르짖음
If you yell, you shout loudly, usually because you are excited, angry, or in pain.

lie[*]
[lai]

vi. (lay-lain) 놓여 있다, 위치하다; 눕다, 누워 있다
LAY(v. 놓다, 눕히다)와 헷갈리기 쉬우므로 유의하자.

choke^{**}
[tʃouk]

v. 숨이 막히다, 질식시키다; n. 질식 (choking a. 숨이 막히는 듯한)
When you choke or when something chokes you, you cannot breathe properly or get enough air into your lungs.

rifle^{**}
[ráifəl]

① n. 라이플총 ② vt. 샅샅이 뒤지다; 강탈하다
A rifle is a gun with a long barrel.

awkward[*]
[ɔ́ːkwərd]

a. 어색한, 불편한, 곤란한 (awkwardly ad. 어색하게, 거북하게)
Someone who feels awkward behaves in a shy or embarrassed way.

shudder[*]
[ʃʌ́dər]

vi. 떨다, 몸서리치다; n. 떨림, 전율
If you shudder, you shake with fear, horror or cold.

struggle[*]
[strʌ́gəl]

v. 고심하다, 분투하다; 발버둥 치다, 몸부림치다; n. 투쟁, 분투
If you struggle to do something, you try hard to do it, even though other people or things may be making it difficult for you to succeed.

gradual[*]
[grǽdʒuəl]

a. 점진적인, 단계적인 (gradually ad. 점진적으로)
A gradual change or process occurs in small stages over a long period of time, rather than suddenly.

ruin^{***}
[rúːin]

v. 망치다, 못쓰게 만들다; 몰락하다; n. 폐허; 파멸
To ruin something means to severely harm, damage, or spoil it.

irritate^{**}
[írətèit]

vt. 짜증나게 하다, 화나게 하다 (irritated a. 짜증난)
If something irritates you, it keeps annoying you.

plead^{**}
[pliːd]

v. 간청하다, 탄원하다; 변론하다, 변호하다
If you plead with someone to do something, you ask them in an intense, emotional way to do it.

expert[*]
[ékspəːrt]

a. 숙련된, 노련한; n. 전문가, 숙련가
Someone who is expert at doing something is very skilled at it.

expertise
[èkspərtíːz]

n. 전문적 기술, 전문적 지식
Expertise is special skill or knowledge that is acquired by training, study, or practice.

wary
[wέəri]

a. 조심성 있는, 신중한 (warily ad. 조심히, 신중하게)
If you are wary of something or someone, you are cautious because you do not know much about them and you believe they may be dangerous or cause problems.

apologize복습
[əpálədʒàiz]

v. 사과하다, 사죄하다
When you apologize to someone, you say that you are sorry that you have hurt them or caused trouble for them.

deserve복습
[dizə́ːrv]

vt. …을 할[받을] 만하다, …할 가치가 있다
If you say that a person or thing deserves something, you mean that they should have it or receive it because of their actions or qualities.

mumble복습
[mʌ́mbəl]

v. 중얼거리다, 웅얼거리다; n. 중얼거림
If you mumble, you speak very quietly and not at all clearly with the result that the words are difficult to understand.

apology복습
[əpálədʒi]

n. 사죄, 사과
An apology is something that you say or write in order to tell someone that you are sorry that you have hurt them or caused trouble for them.

weary복습
[wíəri]

a. 피로한, 지친 (wearily ad. 지쳐서, 지친 상태로)
If you are weary, you are very tired.

fleeting복습
[flíːtiŋ]

a. 순식간의, 잠깐 동안의; 어느덧 지나가는
Fleeting is used to describe something which lasts only for a very short time.

trudge*
[trʌdʒ]

v. 터벅터벅 걷다; n. 터덕터덕 걸음
If you trudge somewhere, you walk there slowly and with heavy steps, especially because you are tired or unhappy.

overwhelm복습
[òuvərhwélm]

vt. 압도하다, 제압하다; 질리게 하다
If you are overwhelmed by a feeling or event, it affects you very strongly, and you do not know how to deal with it.

carefree*
[kέərfrìː]

a. 근심 걱정 없는, 속 편한
A carefree person or period of time doesn't have or involve any problems, worries, or responsibilities.

slip복습
[slip]

v. 미끄러지다; 미끄러져 사라지다; 미끄러지듯 움직이다
If you slip somewhere, you go somewhere quickly and quietly, especially without being noticed.

chatter복습
[tʃǽtər]

v. 수다를 떨다, 재잘거리다; 지저귀다; n. 재잘거림, 수다
If you chatter, you talk quickly and continuously, usually about things which are not important.

merry***
[méri]

a. 명랑한, 유쾌한 (merrily a. 즐겁게, 흥겹게)
If you describe someone's character or behavior as merry, you mean that they are happy and cheerful.

confess^{準準}
[kənfés]

v. 자백하다, 고백하다, 인정하다
If someone confesses to doing something wrong, they admit that they did it.

sneak^準
[sni:k]

v. 몰래 움직이다, 몰래하다; 고자질하다; n. 밀고자
If you sneak somewhere, you go there very quietly on foot, trying to avoid being seen or heard.

matter-of-fact
[mǽtərɔvfækt]

a. 사무적인, 무미건조한; 사실의, 실제적인 (matter-of-factly ad. 사무적으로)
If you describe a person as matter-of-fact, you mean that they show no emotions such as enthusiasm, anger, or surprise.

occasion^{準準}
[əkéiʒən]

n. 행사, 의식; 특수한 경우, 때
An occasion is an important event, ceremony, or celebration.

celebration^{準準}
[sèləbréiʃən]

n. 축하, 축전, 기념행사
The celebration of something is praise and appreciation which is given to it.

discipline^{準準}
[dísəplin]

n. 훈련, 규율; vt. 훈련하다
Discipline is the practice of making people obey rules or standards of behavior, and punishing them when they do not.

wand^{準準}
[wɑnd]

n. (마술사의) 지팡이, 막대기
A wand is a long thin rod.

slender^準
[sléndər]

a. 호리호리한, 가느다란, 날씬한
A slender person is attractively thin and graceful.

misbehave
[mìsbihéiv]

v. 못된 짓을 하다, 품행이 좋지 못하다
If someone, especially a child, misbehaves, they behave in a way that is not acceptable to other people.

easygoing*
[í:zigóuiŋ]

a. 태평스러운, 안이한
If you describe someone as easygoing, you mean that they are not easily annoyed, worried, or upset, and you think this is a good quality.

toddler^準
[tɑ́dlər]

n. 아장아장 걷는 아이, 유아
A toddler is a young child who has only just learned to walk or who still walks unsteadily with small, quick steps.

unsteady^{準準}
[ʌnstédi]

a. 불안정한, 비틀비틀하는 (unsteadily ad. 불안정하게)
If you are unsteady, you have difficulty doing something, for example walking, because you cannot completely control your legs or your body.

chirp**
[tʃə:rp]

v. (즐거운 듯이) 말하다; 짹짹 울다; n. 짹짹 (새 등의 울음소리)
You say that a person chirps when they say something in a cheerful, high-pitched voice.

brighten^{복습}
[bráitn]

v. (사람의 얼굴이) 밝아지나, 빛내다, 밝게 하다
If someone brightens or their face brightens, they suddenly look happier.

depress[*]
[diprés]

vt. 우울하게 하다, 낙담시키다 (depressing a. 우울한)
If someone or something depresses you, they make you feel sad and disappointed.

glum
[glʌm]

a. 시무룩한, 풀죽은, 침울한
Someone who is glum is sad and quiet because they are disappointed or unhappy about something.

ceremony^{복습}
[sérəmòuni]

n. 의식, 의례
A ceremony is a formal event such as a wedding.

glee^{복습}
[gli:]

n. 기쁨, 즐거움
Glee is a feeling of happiness and excitement.

identical^{복습}
[aidéntikəl]

a. 동일한, 꼭 같은
Things that are identical are exactly the same.

chant^{복습}
[tʃænt]

v. 노래를 부르다; 일제히 외치다: n. (규칙적으로 반복되는) 구호, 문구; 노래
If you chant or if you chant something, you sing a religious song or prayer.

comfy
[kʌmfi]

a. (구어) 기분 좋은, 편안한, 안락한
A comfy item of clothing, piece of furniture, room, or position is a comfortable one.

assign^{복습}
[əsáin]

v. 맡기다, 배정하다, 임명하다, 지정하다 (assignment n. 임무, 과제, 할당된 일)
If you assign a piece of work to someone, you give them the work to do.

committee^{복습}
[kəmíti]

n. 위원회
A committee is a group of people who meet to make decisions or plans for a larger group or organization that they represent.

definite^{복습}
[défənit]

a. 확정된, 확실한, 명확한 (definitely ad. 확실히, 명확히)
If something such as a decision or an arrangement is definite, it is firm and clear, and unlikely to be changed.

elder^{복습}
[éldər]

n. 연장자, 웃어른: a. 나이가 더 많은
A person's elder is someone who is older than them, especially someone quite a lot older.

chapter eighteen

1. Which of the following character traits did not describe Rosemary when she first started her Assignment as Receiver?

    (A) She was very intelligent.

    (B) She was eager to learn.

    (C) She was unsure of herself.

    (D) She was confident.

2. What was the first unhappy memory that The Giver gave Rosemary?

    (A) War

    (B) A friend dying

    (C) A child taken from his parents

    (D) Parents watching their child die

3. What kind of memory could The Giver not share with Rosemary?

    (A) Physical Pain

    (B) Hunger

    (C) Poverty

    (D) Terror

4. For how long was Rosemary the Receiver in Training?

    (A) One year

    (B) Nine months

    (C) Ten weeks

    (D) Five weeks

5. What happened to the memories when Rosemary was released?

    (A) They went back to The Giver.

    (B) They went back to the people in the community.

    (C) They went with Rosemary.

    (D) They disappeared.

6. Why didn't The Giver help the people of the community when Rosemary was released?

    (A) He left the community for a few months.

    (B) He was angry at the people of the community.

    (C) He was too devastated with his own grief.

    (D) He was too busy looking for a new Receiver of Memories.

7. What helped Jonas deal with all of the memories?

    (A) The support of his family

    (B) His courage and bravery

    (C) His inability to allow himself to fail

    (D) The Giver

1분에 몇 단어를 읽는지 리딩 속도를 측정해보세요.

$$\frac{1{,}673 \text{ words}}{\text{reading time (\quad) sec}} \times 60 = (\qquad) \text{ WPM}$$

• *Build Your Vocabulary*

precise^{수능}
[prisáis]

a. 정확한, 정밀한; 명확한
You use precise to emphasize that you are referring to an exact thing, rather than something vague.

occasional^{수능}
[əkéiʒənəl]

a. 가끔의, 때때로의 (occasionally ad. 때때로, 가끔)
Occasional means happening sometimes, but not regularly or often.

permit^{수능}
[pə:rmít]

v. 허가하다, 허락하다; n. 허가(증)
If someone permits something, they allow it to happen.

dejected[*]
[didʒéktid]

a. 낙담한, 실의에 빠진
If you are dejected, you feel miserable or unhappy, especially because you have just been disappointed by something.

harsh^{수능}
[ha:rʃ]

a. 냉혹한, 가혹한; 거친, (소리 따위가) 귀에 거슬리는 (harshly ad. 냉혹하게)
Harsh actions or speech are unkind and show no understanding or sympathy.

hammer out

phrasal v. 고심해서 만들어내다, 고안하다
If you hammer out something, you discuss a plan or a deal for a long time and with great effort, until it is decided or agreed on.

reference^{수능}
[réfərəns]

n. 참조; 언급; 문의
A reference is a word, phrase, or idea which comes from something such as a book, poem, or play and which you use when making a point about something.

shrug^{수능}
[ʃrʌg]

v. (양 손바닥을 내보이면서 어깨를) 으쓱하다; n. 으쓱하기
If you shrug, you raise your shoulders to show that you are not interested in something or that you do not know or care about something.

frighten^{수능}
[fráitn]

v. 놀라게 하다, 섬뜩하게 하다; 기겁하다 (frightened a. 깜짝 놀란, 겁이 난)
If something or someone frightens you, they cause you to suddenly feel afraid, anxious, or nervous.

shiver^{수능}
[ʃívər]

v. 전율하다; (추위·공포로) 후들후들 떨다; n. 떨림, 전율
When you shiver, your body shakes slightly because you are cold or frightened.

remarkable^{수능}
[rimá:rkəbəl]

a. 비범한, 뛰어난; 주목할 만한
Someone or something that is remarkable is unusual or special in a way that makes people notice them and be surprised or impressed.

self-possessed
[sélfpəzést]

a. 냉정한, 침착한
Someone who is self-possessed is calm and confident and in control of their emotions.

serene^{복습}
[sirí:n]

a. 조용한, 평온한; 고요한, 잔잔한
Someone or something that is serene is calm and quiet.

eager^{복습}
[í:gər]

a. 열망하는, 간절히 하고 싶어 하는
If you are eager to do or have something, you want to do or have it very much.

hesitate^{복습}
[hézətèit]

v. 주저하다, 머뭇거리다, 망설이다
If you hesitate, you do not speak or act for a short time, usually because you are uncertain, embarrassed, or worried about what you are going to say or do.

excruciating^{복습}
[ikskrú:ʃièitiŋ]

a. 극심한 고통을 주는; 맹렬한, 극심한
If you describe something as excruciating, you are emphasizing that it is extremely painful, either physically or emotionally.

chuckle^{복습}
[tʃʌkl]

vi. 낄낄 웃다; n. 낄낄 웃음
When you chuckle, you laugh quietly.

rueful^{복습}
[rú:fəl]

a. 애처로운, 가엾은 (ruefully ad. 가엾게, 비참하게)
If someone is rueful, they feel or express regret or sorrow in a quiet and gentle way.

luminous**
[lú:mənəs]

a. 빛을 내는, 빛나는, 반짝이는
Something that is luminous shines or glows in the dark.

shred^{복습}
[ʃred]

n. 조각, 파편; v. 조각조각으로 찢다, 갈가리 찢다
If there is not a shred of something, there is not even a small amount of it.

enthusiastic^{복습}
[enθú:ziæstik]

a. 열렬한, 열광적인
If you are enthusiastic about something, you show how much you like or enjoy it by the way that you behave and talk.

falter^{복습}
[fɔ́:ltər]

vi. 불안정해지다, 흔들리다; 더듬거리다, 머뭇거리다
If something falters, it loses power or strength in an uneven way, or no longer makes much progress.

trail off

phrasal v. (목소리가) 서서히 사라지다 (trail v. 끌다; 뒤쫓다)
If a speakers voice or a speaker trails off, their voice becomes quieter and they hesitate until they stop speaking completely.

transfer**
[trænsfə́:r]

v. 옮기다, 이동하다; 갈아타다; n. 이동; 환승
If you transfer something or someone from one place to another, they go from the first place to the second.

kitten**
[kítn]

n. 새끼 고양이; (작은 동물의) 새끼
A kitten is a very young cat.

treasure^{복습}
[tréʒər]

vt. 소중히 하다, 잘 간수하다; n. 보물, 보배
If you treasure something that you have, you keep it or care for it carefully because it gives you great pleasure and you think it is very special.

stun^{복습}
[stʌn]

vt. 어리벙벙하게 하다; 기절시키다; n. 놀라게 함
If you are stunned by something, you are extremely shocked or surprised by it and are therefore unable to speak or do anything.

swallow^{복습}
[swálou]

v. 삼키다, 목구멍으로 넘기다; (초조해서) 마른침을 삼키다
If you swallow, you make a movement in your throat as if you are swallowing something, often because you are nervous or frightened.

spare***
[spɛər]

v. 피하게 해주다, 모면하게 하다; 아끼다, 절약하다; a. 예비의, 여분의
If you spare time or another resource for a particular purpose, you make it available for that purpose.

inflict**
[inflíkt]

vt. (벌 · 괴로움 등을) 가하다, 주다
To inflict harm or damage on someone or something means to make them suffer it.

Poverty**
[pávərti]

n. 빈곤, 가난
Poverty is the state of being extremely poor.

implore^{복습}
[impló:r]

vt. 애원하다, 탄원하다 (imploringly ad. 탄원하는 듯이, 애원하는 듯이)
If you implore someone to do something, you ask them to do it in a forceful, emotional way.

stroke^{복습}
[strouk]

① vt. 쓰다듬다, 어루만지다; n. 쓰다듬기, 달램 ② n. 타격, 일격, 치기
If you stroke someone or something, you move your hand slowly and gently over them.

session^{복습}
[séʃən]

n. (어느 활동을 위한) 기간; 모임, 회의
A session of a particular activity is a period of that activity.

recall^{복습}
[rikó:l]

vt. 생각해내다, 상기하다, 소환하다; n. 회상, 상기
When you recall something, you remember it and tell others about it.

notify^{복습}
[nóutəfài]

vt. 알리다, 통보하다
If you notify someone of something, you officially inform them about it.

successor^{복습}
[səksésər]

n. 후임자, 후계자
Someone's successor is the person who takes their job after they have left.

amuse^{복습}
[əmjú:z]

vt. 즐겁게 하다, 재미나게 하다 (amused a. 즐거워하는)
If something amuses you, it makes you want to laugh or smile.

grave**
[greiv]

① a. 중대한, 근엄한 (gravely ad. 근엄하게, 진지하게) ② n. 무덤, 묘
A grave person is quiet and serious in their appearance or behavior.

disaster**
[dizǽstər]

n. 재해, 재앙, 참사
If you refer to something as a disaster, you are emphasizing that you think it is extremely bad or unacceptable.

overwhelm^{복습}
[òuvərhwélm]

vt. 압도하다, 제압하다; 질리게 하다
If you are overwhelmed by a feeling or event, it affects you very strongly, and you do not know how to deal with it.

devastate*
[dévəstèit]

vt. 완전히 파괴하다; 엄청난 충격을 주다, 비탄에 빠뜨리다
If you are devastated by something, you are very shocked and upset by it.

grief^{수능}
[gri:f]

n. 슬픔, 비탄
Grief is a feeling of extreme sadness.

make a face^{수능}

idiom 얼굴을 찌푸리다, 침울한 표정을 짓다
If you make a face, you twist your face to indicate a certain mental or emotional state.

float***
[flout]

v. 뜨다, 띄우다; n. 뜨는 물건, 부유물
If something or someone is floating in a liquid, they are in the liquid, on or just below the surface, and are being supported by it.

lighthearted
[láithá:rtid]

a. 근심 걱정 없는, 마음 편한; 쾌활한, 명랑한
Someone who is lighthearted is cheerful and happy.

chapter nineteen

1. Why did Jonas ask The Giver about release?

    (A) His father released one of the twins earlier that day.

    (B) He wanted to know how they released Rosemary.

    (C) He wanted to prepare himself for his own release.

    (D) His father was going to release Gabe later that day.

2. How was Jonas able to watch the release?

    (A) Jonas asked to watch the release as it happened.

    (B) Jonas's father performed the release so Jonas was able to watch it.

    (C) The Receiver of Memory was allowed to ask anything of the people community.

    (D) The release was recorded and could be watched at the Hall of Open Records.

3. After the smaller twin was weighed, Jonas thought his father would _____.

    (A) clean up the twin and make him comfortable

    (B) immediately give the twin to a person from Elsewhere

    (C) inject the twin with a needle

    (D) perform a ceremony

4. How did The Giver do when Jonas spoke during the release?

    (A) He turned off the video screen.

    (B) He commanded Jonas to be quiet.

    (C) He told Jonas to either watch the video screen or go outside.

    (D) He ignored Jonas.

5. What happened to the baby after Jonas's father injected his forehead with a clear liquid?

    (A) He fell asleep.

    (B) He squirmed around for a few minutes.

    (C) He died.

    (D) He was given to someone to take to elsewhere.

6. What did Jonas's father do with the baby's body after the injection?

    (A) He put it in a box and gave the carton to his assistant.

    (B) He cleaned it and put it in a nice basket.

    (C) He gave it to his assistant to take outside

    (D) He put it in a carton and put the carton down a chute.

7. What was different about Rosemary's release?

    (A) Rosemary was scared of being released.

    (B) A person injected her leg instead of her forehead.

    (C) Rosemary injected herself with the syringe.

    (D) The chief elder ordered Rosemary to be released.

1분에 몇 단어를 읽는지 리딩 속도를 측정해보세요.

$$\frac{1{,}451 \text{ words}}{\text{reading time (\quad) sec}} \times 60 = (\qquad) \text{ WPM}$$

• *Build Your Vocabulary*

glance^{복습}
[glæns]

v. 흘긋 보다, 잠깐 보다; n. 흘긋 봄
If you glance at something or someone, you look at them very quickly and then look away again immediately.

seldom^{복습}
[séldəm]

ad. 드물게, 거의 ⋯않는
If something seldom happens, it happens only occasionally.

release^{복습}
[rilí:s]

n. 석방; vt. 놓아주다, 해방시키다, 풀어놓다
If a person or animal is released from somewhere where they have been looked after, they are set free or allowed to go.

solemn^{복습}
[sáləm]

a. 엄숙한, 근엄한
Someone or something that is solemn is very serious rather than cheerful or humorous.

identical^{복습}
[aidéntikəl]

a. 동일한, 꼭 같은
Things that are identical are exactly the same.

chuckle^{복습}
[tʃʌkl]

vi. 낄낄 웃다; n. 낄낄 웃음
When you chuckle, you laugh quietly.

comfy^{복습}
[kʌmfi]

a. (구어) 기분 좋은, 편안한, 안락한
A comfy item of clothing, piece of furniture, room, or position is a comfortable one.

click^{복습}
[klik]

v. 딸깍 소리를 내다; n. 딸깍[찰깍]하는 소리
If something clicks or if you click it, it makes a short, sharp sound.

blank^{복습}
[blæŋk]

a. 멍한, 얼빠진; 공허한, 공백의; n. 공백
If you look blank, your face shows no feeling, understanding, or interest.

flicker^{복습}
[flíkər]

v. (등불·희망·빛 등이) 깜박이다; n. 깜박임
If a light or flame flickers, it shines unsteadily.

astonish^{복습}
[əstániʃ]

vt. 깜짝 놀라게 하다 (astonished a. 깜짝 놀란)
If something or someone astonishes you, they surprise you very much.

equipment^{복습}
[ikwípmənt]

n. 장비, 설비
Equipment consists of the things which are used for a particular purpose, for example a hobby or job.

scale**
[skeil]

① n. 저울, 저울 접시 ② n. 규모; 비례, 비율; v. 기어오르다 ③ n. 비늘
Scales are a piece of equipment used for weighing things, for example for weighing amounts of food that you need in order to make a particular meal.

volunteer 복습
[vὰləntíər]

n. 지원자, 자원 봉사자; v. 자발적으로 나서다; a. 자발적인
A volunteer is someone who offers to do a particular task or job without being forced to do it.

cupboard 복습
[kʌ́bərd]

n. 식기장, 찬장
A cupboard is a piece of furniture that has one or two doors, usually contains shelves, and is used to store things.

carpeting 복습
[káːrpitiŋ]

n. 카펫류, 양탄자 재료
You use carpeting to refer to a carpet, or to the type of material that is used to make carpets.

ordinary 복습
[ɔ́ːrdənèri]

a. 보통의, 평범한
Ordinary people or things are normal and not special or different in any way.

auditorium 복습
[ɔ̀ːditɔ́ːriəm]

n. 강당, 회관; 청중석, 관객석
An auditorium is a large room, hall, or building which is used for events such as meetings and concerts.

cradle**
[kréidl]

v. 부드럽게 안다, 떠받치다; n. 요람, 유아용 침대
If you cradle someone or something in your arms or hands, you hold them carefully and gently.

blanket 복습
[blǽŋkit]

n. 담요, 모포
A blanket is a large square or rectangular piece of thick cloth, especially one which you put on a bed to keep you warm.

naked 복습
[néikid]

a. 나체의, 벌거벗은; 적나라한
Someone who is naked is not wearing any clothes.

fascinate 복습
[fǽsənèit]

v. 매혹하다, 반하게 하다 (fascinated a. 매혹된, 마음을 빼앗긴)
If something fascinates you, it interests and delights you so much that your thoughts tend to concentrate on it.

pound***
[paund]

① n. 파운드(무게의 단위) ② v. 쿵쿵 울리다, 마구 치다, 세게 두드리다; n. 타격 ③ n. 울타리, 우리
One pound is equal to 0.454 kilograms.

even 복습
[íːvən]

a. 딱[꼭] 맞는; 규칙적인, 한결같은; ad. 한층, 더욱
An even measurement or rate stays at about the same level.

squirm 복습
[skwəːrm]

vi. 꿈틀거리다, 몸부림치다
If you squirm, you move your body from side to side, usually because you are nervous or uncomfortable.

remark 복습
[rimáːrk]

v. 말하다, 언급하다; n. 의견, 발언
If you remark that something is the case, you say that it is the case.

obedient 복습
[oubíːdiənt]

a. 순종하는, 고분고분한 (obediently ad. 고분고분하게)
A person or animal who is obedient does what they are told to do.

concentrate[발음]
[kánsəntrèit]
v. 집중하다, 전념하다
If you concentrate on something, you give all your attention to it.

syringe
[səríndʒ]
n. 주사기; vt. 주사를 놓다; 씻다, 세척하다
Syringes are used for putting liquids into things and for taking liquids out, for example for injecting drugs or for taking blood from someone's body.

insert**
[insə́:rt]
vt. 끼워 넣다, 삽입하다, 넣다
If you insert an object into something, you put the object inside it.

wince[발음]
[wins]
vi. (아픔·무서움 때문에) 주춤하다, 움츠리다; n. 위축
If you wince, the muscles of your face tighten suddenly because you have felt a pain or because you have just seen, heard, or remembered something unpleasant.

sympathetic[발음]
[sìmpəθétik]
a. 공감하는, 동조하는; 동정적인, 동정어린
(sympathetically ad. 동정하여, 교감하여)
If you are sympathetic to someone who is in a bad situation, you are kind to them and show that you understand their feelings.

forehead[발음]
[fɔ́:rhèd]
n. 이마
Your forehead is the area at the front of your head between your eyebrows and your hair.

puncture*
[páŋktʃər]
v. (바늘 따위로) 찌르다; 펑크를 내다; n. 찌름, 구멍 뚫기
If a sharp object punctures something, it makes a hole in it.

fragile[발음]
[frǽdʒəl]
a. 부서지기 [깨지기] 쉬운
Something that is fragile is easily broken or damaged.

pulse**
[pʌls]
v. 고동치다, 맥이 뛰다; n. 맥박, 고동; 파동
If something pulses, it moves, appears, or makes a sound with a strong regular rhythm.

wail[발음]
[weil]
v. 울부짖다, 통곡하다; (큰 소리로) 투덜거리다; n. 울부짖음, 통곡
If someone wails, they make long, loud, high-pitched cries which express sorrow or pain.

vein**
[vein]
n. 혈관, 정맥; 광맥; 기질, 특질, 방식
Your veins are the thin tubes in your body through which your blood flows towards your heart.

inject*
[indʒékt]
vt. 주사하다, 주입하다
To inject someone with a substance such as a medicine means to put it into their body using a device with a needle called a syringe.

scalp*
[skælp]
n. 두피, 머리가죽
Your scalp is the skin under the hair on your head.

receptacle*
[riséptəkəl]
n. 그릇, 용기
A receptacle is an object which you use to put or keep things in.

jerk**
[dʒə:rk]
v. 갑자기 움직이다; n. 홱 움직임; 얼간이
If you jerk something or someone in a particular direction, or they jerk in a particular direction, they move a short distance very suddenly and quickly.

limp^{복습}
[limp]

① a. 약한, 기운이 없는 ② vi. 절뚝거리다; n. 절뚝거리기
If someone is limp, their body has no strength and is not moving, for example because they are asleep or unconscious.

posture^{복습}
[pástʃər]

n. 자세; 태도, 마음가짐; v. 자세[태도]를 취하다
Your posture is the position in which you stand or sit.

choke^{복습}
[tʃouk]

v. 숨이 막히다, 질식시키다; n. 질식 (choking a. 숨이 막히는 듯한)
When you choke or when something chokes you, you cannot breathe properly or get enough air into your lungs.

stun^{복습}
[stʌn]

vt. 어리벙벙하게 하다; 기절시키다; n. 놀라게 함
If you are stunned by something, you are extremely shocked or surprised by it and are therefore unable to speak or do anything.

numb*
[nʌm]

a. 망연자실한, 멍한; 감각이 없는, 마비된; vt. 감각이 없게 만들다
(numbly ad. 망연자실하게)
If you are numb with shock, fear, or grief, you are so shocked, frightened, or upset that you cannot think clearly or feel any emotion.

tidy^{복습}
[táidi]

v. 치우다, 정돈하다; a. 단정한, 말쑥한, 깔끔한
When you tidy a place such as a room or cupboard, you make it neat by putting things in their proper places.

carton^{복습}
[ká:rtən]

n. 큰 상자; 한 통
A carton is a large, strong cardboard box in which goods are stored and transported.

lid**
[lid]

n. 뚜껑
A lid is the top of a box or other container which can be removed or raised when you want to open the container.

chute
[ʃu:t]

n. 활송 장치(사람이나 물건을 미끄러뜨리듯 이동시키는 장치)
A chute is a steep, narrow slope down which people or things can slide.

deposit**
[dipázit]

vt. 두다, 놓다; 맡기다, 예금하다
To deposit something somewhere means to put them or leave them there.

load***
[loud]

v. 짐을 싣다; 장전하다; n. 적재 화물, 짐; 장전
If you load a vehicle or a container, you put a large quantity of things into it.

shove*
[ʃʌv]

n. 밀치기; v. 밀(치)다, 밀어내다
A shove is a quick, violent pushing.

glimpse^{복습}
[glimps]

v. 흘끗 보다, 잠깐보다; n. 흘끗 봄, 잠깐 봄
If you glimpse someone or something, you see them very briefly and not very well.

sleeve^{복습}
[sli:v]

n. (옷의) 소매
The sleeves of a coat, shirt, or other item of clothing are the parts that cover your arms.

bravery**
[bréivəri]

n. 용기, 용맹
Bravery is brave behavior or the quality of being brave.

wretched[**]
[rétʃid]

a. 비참한, 불쌍한, 형편없는
You use wretched to describe someone or something that you dislike or feel angry with.

bitter[수능]
[bítər]

a. 쓴, 쓰라린; 지독한, 혹독한
You can use bitter to emphasize feelings of disappointment.

rip[수능]
[rip]

v. 째다, 찢다, 집아찢다; 벗겨내다
When something rips or when you rip it, you tear it forcefully with your hands or with a tool such as a knife.

claw[**]
[klɔ:]

v. (길을) 헤치며 나아가다; (손·발톱 따위로) 할퀴다, 긁다; n. 발톱, 집게발
If you claw your way somewhere, you move there with great difficulty, trying desperately to find things to hold on to.

emerge[수능]
[imə́:rdʒ]

vi. 나오다, 나타나다
To emerge means to come out from an enclosed or dark space.

chapter twenty

1. What was different about Jonas and the rest of the community?

   (A) Jonas knew what happened during a release.

   (B) Jonas had real feelings.

   (C) Jonas was allowed to lie.

   (D) Feelings were a part of the life the people in the community learned.

2. Why did Jonas NOT care about being killed if he failed at carrying out the plan?

   (A) He didn't care about anybody in the world anymore.

   (B) He thought the community would respect him if he died.

   (C) He felt that his life in the community was no longer worth living.

   (D) He wanted the people in the community to suffer.

3. What would The Giver do when the memories came back to the people of the community?

   (A) He would leave the community.

   (B) He would be released.

   (C) He would hide in his dwelling.

   (D) He would help the people deal with the memories.

4. Which memory did The Giver NOT yet share with Jonas?

(A) Music

(B) Courage

(C) Love

(D) Family

5. What did Jonas think would be the most dangerous part of the plan?

(A) Secretly leaving his dwelling at night

(B) Entering the Annex

(C) Hiding in the storage area of the vehicle

(D) Saving food from meals during the two weeks leading up to the ceremony

6. What would The Giver tell the community about Jonas?

(A) Jonas went to another community.

(B) Jonas ran away.

(C) Jonas went searching for Elsewhere.

(D) Jonas was lost in the river.

7. Where did The Giver want to be after helping the community?

(A) Elsewhere

(B) An outlying community

(C) Be with Rosemary

(D) The House of the Old

1분에 몇 단어를 읽는지 리딩 속도를 측정해보세요.

$$\frac{2,756 \text{ words}}{\text{reading time ( ) sec}} \times 60 = (\qquad) \text{ WPM}$$

• *Build Your Vocabulary*

sob
[sɑb]
v. 흐느껴 울다; n. 흐느낌, 오열
When someone sobs, they cry in a noisy way, breathing in short breaths.

pound
[paund]
① v. 쿵쿵 울리다, 마구 치다, 세게 두드리다; n. 타격 ② n. 파운드(무게의 단위) ③ n. 울타리, 우리
If you pound something or pound on it, you hit it with great force, usually loudly and repeatedly.

fist
[fist]
n. (쥔) 주먹
Your hand is referred to as your fist when you have bent your fingers in towards the palm in order to hit someone, to make an angry gesture, or to hold something.

obey
[oubéi]
v. 복종하다, 따르다
If you obey a person, a command, or an instruction, you do what you are told to do.

weep**
[wi:p]
v. 눈물을 흘리다, 울다
If someone weeps, they cry.

shudder
[ʃʌdər]
vi. 떨다, 몸서리치다; n. 떨림, 전율
If you shudder, you shake with fear, horror or cold.

notify
[nóutəfài]
vt. 알리다, 통보하다
If you notify someone of something, you officially inform them about it.

collapse**
[kəlǽps]
v. 쓰러지다, 맥없이 주저앉다; 무너지다, 붕괴하다; n. 무너짐, 붕괴
If you collapse onto something, you sit or lie down suddenly.

huddle*
[hʌdl]
v. 몸을 움츠리다; 뒤죽박죽 쌓아 올리다; n. 집단, 군중
If you huddle somewhere, you sit, stand, or lie there holding your arms and legs close to your body, usually because you are cold or frightened.

click
[klik]
v. 딸깍 소리를 내다; n. 딸깍[찰깍]하는 소리
If something clicks or if you click it, it makes a short, sharp sound.

mimic*
[mímik]
vt. 흉내 내다, 모방하다; a. 흉내를 내는
If you mimic the actions or voice of a person or animal, you imitate them, usually in a way that is meant to be amusing or entertaining.

cruel복습
[krúːəl]

a. 잔혹한, 잔인한, 무자비한
Someone who is cruel deliberately causes pain or distress to people or animals.

sarcastic**
[saːrkǽstik]

a. 빈정대는, 비꼬는, 풍자적인
Someone who is sarcastic says or does the opposite of what they really mean in order to mock or insult someone.

grasp복습
[græsp]

v. 붙잡다, 움켜쥐다; n. 움켜잡기
If you grasp something, you take it in your hand and hold it very firmly.

successor복습
[səksésər]

n. 후임자, 후계자
Someone's successor is the person who takes their job after they have left.

spit복습
[spit]

v. (spat-spat) 뱉다, 내뿜다
If someone spits, they force an amount of liquid out of their mouth, often to show hatred or contempt.

empower복습
[empáuər]

vt. 권한을 주다, 자율권을 주다
If someone is empowered to do something, they have the authority or power to do it.

release복습
[rilíːs]

n. 석방; vt. 놓아주다, 해방시키다, 풀어놓다
If a person or animal is released from somewhere where they have been looked after, they are set free or allowed to go.

efficient**
[ifíʃənt]

a. 유능한, 실력 있는; 능률적인, 효과가 있는
If something or someone is efficient, they are able to do tasks successfully, without wasting time or energy.

rock복습
[rɑk]

① v. (앞뒤·좌우로 살짝) 흔들다, 움직이다; n. 록 음악; 흔들림, 진동
② n. 바위, 암석
When something rocks or when you rock it, it moves slowly and regularly backwards and forwards or from side to side.

nasty**
[nǽsti]

a. 심술궂은, 비열한; 더러운, 불쾌한
If you describe a person or their behavior as nasty, you mean that they behave in an unkind and unpleasant way.

rueful복습
[rúːfəll]

a. 애처로운, 가엾은
If someone is rueful, they feel or express regret or sorrow in a quiet and gentle way.

anguish복습
[ǽŋgwiʃ]

v. 괴로워하다, 괴롭히다; n. 괴로움, 고뇌, 번민 (anguished a. 번민의, 고뇌에 찬)
Anguished means showing or feeling great mental suffering or physical pain.

hunch복습
[hʌntʃ]

v. 둥글게 구부리다; n. 예감, 직감
If you hunch forward, you raise your shoulders, put your head down, and lean forwards, often because you are cold, ill, or unhappy.

puzzle복습
[pʌzl]

v. 어리둥절하게 만들다, 곤혹스럽게 하다, 난처하게 하다
(puzzled a. 당혹스러운, 어리둥절한)
If something puzzles you, you do not understand it and feel confused.

trail ^{복습}
[treil]

v. 끌다, 끌리다; 뒤쫓다, 추적하다; n. 자취, 흔적
If someone trails somewhere, they move there slowly, without any energy or enthusiasm, often following someone else.

phrase ^{복습}
[freiz]

n. 구절, 관용구
A phrase is a short group of words that people often use as a way of saying something.

barely ^{복습}
[bɛ́ərli]

ad. 간신히, 가까스로; 거의 …않다
You use barely to say that something is only just true or only just the case.

robe ^{복습}
[roub]

n. 예복, 관복; 길고 헐거운 겉옷
A robe is a loose piece of clothing which covers all of your body and reaches the ground.

belong ^{복습}
[bilɔ́(:)ŋ]

vi. 속하다, 소유물이다
If something belongs to you, you own it.

elder ^{복습}
[éldər]

n. 연장자, 웃어른; a. 나이가 더 많은
A person's elder is someone who is older than them, especially someone quite a lot older.

depend ***
[dipénd]

vi. 의존하다, 의지하다; …에 좌우되다, …에 달려 있다
If you can depend on a person, organization, or law, you know that they will support you or help you when you need them.

resident **
[rézidənt]

a. 거주하는, 살고 있는; n. 거주자
Someone who is resident in a country or a town lives there.

solemn ^{복습}
[sáləm]

a. 엄숙한, 근엄한 (solemnly ad. 엄숙하게; 진지하게)
Someone or something that is solemn is very serious rather than cheerful or humorous.

terrify ^{복습}
[térəfài]

vt. 무섭게[겁나게] 하다, 놀래다 (terrifying a. 겁나게 하는, 무서운)
If something terrifies you, it makes you feel extremely frightened.

burden ^{복습}
[bə́:rdn]

n. 짐, 부담; vt. 짐을 지우다, 부담시키다
If you describe a problem or a responsibility as a burden, you mean that it causes someone a lot of difficulty, worry, or hard work.

acquire ^{복습}
[əkwáiər]

vt. 습득하다, 배우다; 얻다, 획득하다
If you acquire something such as a skill or a habit, you learn it, or develop it through your daily life or experience.

desperate ^{복습}
[déspərit]

a. 자포자기의, 절망적인; 필사적인 (desperately ad. 절망적으로)
If you are desperate for something or desperate to do something, you want or need it very much indeed.

plead ^{복습}
[pli:d]

v. 간청하다, 탄원하다; 변론하다, 변호하다
If you plead with someone to do something, you ask them in an intense, emotional way to do it.

questioning ^{복습}
[kwéstʃəniŋ]

a. 따지는, 캐묻는; n. 의문, 질문
If someone has a questioning expression on their face, they look as if they want to know the answer to a question.

brighten^{복습}
[bráitn]

v. (사람의 얼굴이) 밝아지다; 빛내다, 밝게 하다
If someone brightens or their face brightens, they suddenly look happier.

frown^{복습}
[fraun]

vi. 얼굴을 찡그리다, 눈살을 찌푸리다; n. 찌푸린 얼굴
When someone frowns, their eyebrows become drawn together, because they are annoyed or puzzled.

remarkable^{복습}
[rimá:rkəbəl]

a. 비범한, 뛰어난; 주목할 만한
Someone or something that is remarkable is unusual or special in a way that makes people notice them and be surprised or impressed.

emphatic[*]
[imfǽtik]

a. 강한; 강조하는; 단호한 (emphatically ad. 강조하여; 단호하게)
An emphatic response or statement is one made in a forceful way, because the speaker feels very strongly about what they are saying.

startle^{복습}
[stá:rtl]

v. 깜짝 놀라게 하다; 움찔하다; n. 깜짝 놀람 (startlingly ad. 놀랄 정도로)
If something sudden and unexpected startles you, it surprises and frightens you slightly.

ceremony^{복습}
[sérəmòuni]

n. 의식, 의례
A ceremony is a formal event such as a wedding.

transfer^{복습}
[trænsfə́:r]

v. 옮기다, 이동하다; 갈아타다; n. 이동; 환승
If you transfer something or someone from one place to another, they go from the first place to the second.

dwelling^{복습}
[dwéliŋ]

n. 거처, 주소, 사는 집
A dwelling is a place where someone lives.

violation^{복습}
[vàiəléiʃən]

n. 위반, 위배; 방해, 침해
Violation is the infringement or breach, as of a law, rule or right.

emergency^{**}
[imə́:rdʒənsi]

a. 긴급한, n. 비상사태, 위급함
An emergency action is one that is done or arranged quickly and not in the normal way, because an emergency has occurred.

flee^{**}
[fli:]

vi. 달아나다, 도망치다; 사라지다
If you flee from something or someone, or flee a person or thing, you escape from them.

individual^{복습}
[ìndəvídʒuəl]

a. 개개의, 개인의; n. 개인
If you describe someone or something as individual, you mean that you admire them because they are very unusual and do not try to imitate other people or things.

forceful[*]
[fɔ́:rsfəl]

a. 단호한, 강력한; 강압적인 (forcefully ad. 강압적으로; 강력하게)
If you describe someone as forceful, you approve of them because they express their opinions and wishes in a strong, emphatic, and confident way.

errand^{**}
[érənd]

n. 심부름; 볼일, 용건
An errand is a short trip that you make in order to do a job for someone, for example when you go to a shop to buy something for them.

tease^{복습}
[ti:z]

v. 놀리다, 골리다, 괴롭히다; n. 골리기, 놀림
To tease someone means to laugh at them or make jokes about them in order to embarrass, annoy, or upset them.

slip^{복습}
[slip]

v. 미끄러지다; 미끄러져 사라지다; 미끄러지듯 움직이다
If you slip somewhere, you go somewhere quickly and quietly, especially without being noticed.

riverbank^{복습}
[rívərbæ̀ŋk]

n. 강둑, 강기슭
A riverbank is the land along the edge of a river.

annex^{복습}
[ənéks]

n. 별관, 별채; 부속물; vt. 부가하다; 합병하다
An annex is a building that is an addition to another building.

attendant^{복습}
[əténdənt]

n. 안내원, 수행원; 참석자
An attendant is someone whose job is to serve or help people in a place such as a petrol station, a car park, or a cloakroom.

irritate^{복습}
[írətèit]

vt. 짜증나게 하다, 화나게 하다 (irritated a. 짜증난)
If something irritates you, it keeps annoying you.

alarm***
[əlá:rm]

v. 놀라게 하다; 경보하다, 위급을 알리다; n. 놀람; 경보
(alarmed a. 겁먹은, 불안해하는)
If something alarms you, it makes you afraid or anxious that something unpleasant or dangerous might happen.

inconsiderate
[ìnkənsídərit]

a. 경솔한; 지각없는, 배려할 줄 모르는
If you accuse someone of being inconsiderate, you mean that they do not take enough care over how their words or actions will affect other people.

chastise^{복습}
[tʃæstáiz]

vt. 벌하다, 꾸짖다, 혼내주다
If you chastise someone, you speak to them angrily or punish them for something wrong that they have done.

mount^{복습}
[maunt]

v. 상승하다; 오르다, 타다
If something mounts, it increases in quantity.

reflect^{복습}
[riflékt]

v. 반영하다, 나타내다; 비추다, 반사하다
If something reflects an attitude or situation, it shows that the attitude or situation exists or it shows what it is like.

involve^{복습}
[inválv]

vt. 수반하다, 포함하다, 관련시키다 (involved a. 열심인, 몰두하는; 관련된)
If a situation or activity involves someone, they are taking part in it.

assume***
[əsjú:m]

vt. 추정하다, 가정하다; (역할·임무 등을) 맡다
If you assume that something is true, you imagine that it is true, sometimes wrongly.

shrug^{복습}
[ʃrʌg]

v. (양 손바닥을 내보이면서 어깨를) 으쓱하다; n. 으쓱하기
If you shrug, you raise your shoulders to show that you are not interested in something or that you do not know or care about something.

vehicle^{복습}
[ví:ikəl]

n. 탈것, 차량
A vehicle is a machine such as a car, bus, or truck which has an engine and is used to carry people from place to place.

extend^{복습}
[iksténd]

v. (손·발 등을) 뻗다, 늘이다; 연장하다
If an object extends from a surface or place, it sticks out from it.

undertaking**
[ʌndərtéikiŋ]

n. (중요한·힘든) 업무, 일
An undertaking is a task or job, especially a large or difficult one.

occasion^{복습}
[əkéiʒən]

n. 특수한 경우, 때; 행사, 의식
An occasion is a time when something happens, or a case of it happening.

bundle**
[bʌ́ndl]

n. 묶음, 꾸러미
A bundle of things is a number of them that are tied together or wrapped in a cloth or bag so that they can be carried or stored.

apparent^{복습}
[əpǽrənt]

a. 또렷한; 명백한; 외관상의
If something is apparent to you, it is clear and obvious to you.

disrupt*
[disrʌ́pt]

vt. 붕괴시키다, 분열시키다
If someone or something disrupts an event, system, or process, they cause difficulties that prevent it from continuing or operating in a normal way.

unthinkable^{복습}
[ʌnθíŋkəbəl]

a. 상상할 수 없는, 감히 생각도 할 수 없는
un (부정, 반대의 접두사) + think (v. 생각하다) + able (a. …할 수 있는)

confront**
[kənfrʌ́nt]

vt. 직면하다, 맞서다
If you are confronted with a problem, task, or difficulty, you have to deal with it.

solace*
[sáləs]

n. 위안, 위로; v. 위안[위로]하다
Solace is a feeling of comfort that makes you feel less sad.

auditorium^{복습}
[ɔ̀:ditɔ́:riəm]

n. 강당, 회관; 청중석, 관객석
An auditorium is a large room, hall, or building which is used for events such as meetings and concerts.

stride**
[straid]

v. 성큼성큼 걷다; n. 큰 걸음, 활보
If you stride somewhere, you walk there with quick, long steps.

chant^{복습}
[tʃænt]

n. (규칙적으로 반복되는) 구호, 문구; 노래; v. 일제히 외치다; 노래를 부르다
A chant is a word or group of words that is repeated over and over again.

in unison^{복습}

idiom 일제히, 한목소리로
If two or more people do something in unison, they do it together at the same time.

murmur^{복습}
[mə́:rmər]

n. 중얼거림; v. 중얼거리다; 투덜거리다
A murmur is something that is said which can hardly be heard.

overwhelm^{복습}
[òuvərhwélm]

vt. 압도하다, 제압하다; 질리게 하다 (overwhelming a. 압도적인, 저항할 수 없는)
If something is overwhelming, it affects you very strongly, and you do not know how to deal with it.

lengthy^{복습}
[léŋkθi]

a. 긴, 오랜; 장황한, 지루한
You use lengthy to describe an event or process which lasts for a long time.

plea^{복습}
[pli:]

n. 탄원, 청원; 간청, 기도
A plea is an appeal or request for something, made in an intense or emotional way.

grateful**
[gréitfəl]

a. 고맙게 여기는, 감사하는
If you are grateful for something that someone has given you or done for you, you have warm, friendly feelings towards them and wish to thank them.

figure out

phrasal v. …을 생각해내다, 이해하다, 알아내다
If you figure out a solution to a problem or the reason for something, you succeed in solving it or understanding it.

glum^{복습}
[glʌm]

a. 시무룩한, 풀죽은, 침울한 (glumly ad. 침울하게)
Someone who is glum is sad and quiet because they are disappointed or unhappy about something.

spouse^{복습}
[spaus]

n. 배우자, 남편, 아내
Someone's spouse is the person they are married to.

chapter twenty one

1. Why did Jonas's plans change?

   (A) Jonas realized it was too dangerous to go to the Annex at night.
   (B) Jonas was too close to being caught by the night crew and needed to change his route.
   (C) Jonas found out that Gabriel would be released.
   (D) Jonas's parents were suspicious.

2. Jonas didn't _____.

   (A) rob the community of food
   (B) steal his mother's bicycle
   (C) leave his dwelling at night
   (D) take Gabriel with him

3. After days had pasted, how did Jonas have enough food?

   (A) He stole a month's worth of food from the community.
   (B) He had a lot of leftovers from The Giver's dinners.
   (C) He stole food from dwellings in outlying communities.
   (D) He mixed food he found in the fields with the food scraps he stole.

4. Why would the search planes have difficulty finding Jonas?

    (A) They used heat seeking devices which could identify body warmth.

    (B) They did not fly very close to the ground.

    (C) The pilots could not see color.

    (D) Jonas learned how to hide well from his warfare memories.

5. What was the scariest thing Jonas had experienced since leaving the community?

    (A) Not finding enough clean water from the streams.

    (B) Hearing the search planes fly overhead.

    (C) Feeling like he might freeze to death in the nighttime.

    (D) Worrying about Gabriel becoming sick from the food scraps.

1분에 몇 단어를 읽는지 리딩 속도를 측정해보세요.

$$\frac{1,815 \text{ words}}{\text{reading time ( ) sec}} \times 60 = (\quad) \text{ WPM}$$

• *Build Your Vocabulary*

meticulous^{복습}
[mətíkjələs]

a. 꼼꼼한, 세심한; 정확한 (meticulously ad. 꼼꼼하게)
If you describe someone as meticulous, you mean that they do things very carefully and with great attention to detail.

flee^{복습}
[fli:]

vi. 달아나다, 도망치다; 사라지다
If you flee from something or someone, or flee a person or thing, you escape from them.

stealthy*
[stélθi]

a. 남의 눈을 피하는, 살금살금 하는, 비밀의 (stealthily ad. 몰래, 은밀히)
Stealthy actions or movements are performed quietly and carefully, so that no one will notice what you are doing.

pedal^{복습}
[pédl]

v. 페달을 밟다; n. 페달, 발판
When you pedal a bicycle, you push the pedals around with your feet to make it move.

steady^{복습}
[stédi]

a. 한결같은, 고른; 확고한; vt. 흔들리지 않게 하다, 안정시키다
(steadily ad. 끊임없이; 착실하게)
A steady situation continues or develops gradually without any interruptions and is not likely to change quickly.

churn^{복습}
[tʃəːrn]

v. (물·파도 등이) 마구 휘돌다, 휘젓다; 거품이 나게 하다; (속이) 뒤틀리다
If something churns water, mud, or dust, it moves it about violently.

capacity^{복습}
[kəpǽsəti]

n. 능력, 역량; 수용력, 용량
Your capacity for something is your ability to do it, or the amount of it that you are able to do.

chatter^{복습}
[tʃǽtər]

v. 수다를 떨다, 재잘거리다; 지저귀다; n. 재잘거림, 수다
If you chatter, you talk quickly and continuously, usually about things which are not important.

customary**
[kʌ́stəmèri]

a. 관례적인, 관습상의; 습관적인
Customary is used to describe something that a particular person usually does or has.

babble
[bǽbəl]

v. (어린아이 등이) 불명료한 소리를 내다; 쓸데없는 말을 하다; n. 재잘거림
If someone babbles, they talk in a confused or excited way.

glee^{복습}
[gli:]

n. 기쁨, 즐거움
Glee is a feeling of happiness and excitement.

(every) now and then^{복습}

idiom 가끔, 때때로, 이따금
If you do something every now and then, you do it sometimes, but not very often.

glance^{복습}
[glæns]

v. 흘긋 보다, 잠깐 보다; n. 흘긋 봄
If you glance at something or someone, you look at them very quickly and then look away again immediately.

toddler^{복습}
[tάdlər]

n. 아장아장 걷는 아이, 유아
A toddler is a young child who has only just learned to walk or who still walks unsteadily with small, quick steps.

nurture^{복습}
[nə́:rtʃər]

vt. 양육하다, 기르다; n. 양육, 양성, 교육 (nurturing n. 양육)
If you nurture something such as a young child or a young plant, you care for it while it is growing and developing.

sleep soundly^{복습}

idiom 깊이 잠들다
If someone sleep soundly, they are sleeping very deeply.

sympathetic^{복습}
[sìmpəθétik]

a. 공감하는, 동조하는; 동정적인, 동정어린
(sympathetically ad. 동정하여, 교감하여)
If you are sympathetic to someone who is in a bad situation, you are kind to them and show that you understand their feelings.

disaster^{복습}
[dizǽstər]

n. 재해, 재앙, 참사; 큰 실패(작)
If you refer to something as a disaster, you are emphasizing that you think it is extremely bad or unacceptable.

frazzled
[frǽzəld]

a. 기진맥진한
If you are frazzled, you are exhausted physically or emotionally.

naughty**
[nɔ́:ti]

a. 장난꾸러기인, 버릇없는; 부적합한, 도리에 어긋난
If you say that a child is naughty, you mean that they behave badly or do not do what they are told.

scold^{복습}
[skould]

v. 꾸짖다, 잔소리하다
If you scold someone, you speak angrily to them because they have done something wrong.

cluck*
[klʌk]

n. 혀 차는 소리; 꼬꼬댁 우는 소리; v. (닭이) 꼬꼬 울다; (혀를) 쯧쯧 차다
A cluck is a clicking sound with the tongue.

grin^{복습}
[grin]

v. (이를 드러내고) 싱긋 웃다, 활짝 웃다; n. 싱긋 웃음
When you grin, you smile broadly.

vote***
[vout]

v. 투표하다; n. 투표, 투표권
When you vote, you indicate your choice officially at a meeting or in an election.

emphatic^{복습}
[imfǽtik]

a. 강한; 강조하는; 단호한 (emphatically ad. 강조하여; 단호하게)
An emphatic response or statement is one made in a forceful way, because the speaker feels very strongly about what they are saying.

ceremony^{복습}
[sérəmòuni]

n. 의식, 의례
A ceremony is a formal event such as a wedding.

dawn^{※合}
[dɔːn]

n. 새벽, 동틀 녘; vi. 날이 새다, 밝아지다; 나타나기 시작하다
Dawn is the time of day when light first appears in the sky, just before the sun rises.

discipline^{※合}
[dísəplin]

vt. 훈련하다; n. 훈련, 규율 (disciplined a. 훈련받은)
If you discipline yourself to do something, you train yourself to behave and work in a strictly controlled and regular way.

inconvenient**
[ìnkənvíːnjənt]

a. 불편한, 곤란한
Something that is inconvenient causes problems or difficulties for someone.

condemn**
[kəndém]

vt. 규탄하다, 비난하다; 선고를 내리다
(condemned a. 유죄 선고를 받은, 구제할 길 없는)
If you condemn something, you say that it is very bad and unacceptable.

transgression^{※合}
[trænsgréʃən]

n. 위반, 범죄
Transgression is the action of going beyond or overstepping some boundary or limit.

leftover^{※合}
[léftòuvər]

n. (pl.) 나머지, 찌꺼기; a. 나머지의, 남은;
You use leftover to describe an amount of something that remains after the rest of it has been used or eaten.

hesitate^{※合}
[hézətèit]

v. 주저하다, 머뭇거리다, 망설이다
If you hesitate, you do not speak or act for a short time, usually because you are uncertain, embarrassed, or worried about what you are going to say or do.

port^{※合}
[pɔːrt]

n. 항구 (여기서는 '자전거를 세우는 곳'이라는 의미로 사용)
A port is a harbor area where ships load and unload goods or passengers.

accustom^{※合}
[əkʌ́stəm]

v. 익히다, 익숙해지다 (accustomed a. 익숙해진)
If you accustom yourself or another person to something, you make yourself or them become used to it.

attach^{※合}
[ətǽtʃ]

vt. 붙이다, 달다; 소속시키다 (attached a. 붙여진)
If you attach something to an object, you join it or fasten it to the object.

nudge^{※合}
[nʌdʒ]

vt. (주의를 끌기 위해 팔꿈치로) 슬쩍 찌르다; 주의를 환기시키다
If you nudge someone, you push them gently, usually with your elbow, in order to draw their attention to something.

strap^{※合}
[stræp]

vt. 끈으로 묶다, 잡아매다; n. 가죽 끈, 혁대 (unstrap vt. 끈을 벗기다, 풀다)
If you strap something somewhere, you fasten it there with a narrow piece of leather or cloth.

transmit^{※合}
[trænsmít]

v. 보내다, 전달하다
If you transmit an idea or feeling to someone else, you make them understand and share the idea or feeling.

soothing^{※合}
[súːðiŋ]

a. 달래는, 위로하는, 진정시키는
Something that is soothing has a calming, assuaging, or relieving effect.

languid*
[lǽŋgwid]

a. 나른한, 노곤한, 축 늘어진, 기운이 없는
If you describe someone as languid, you mean that they show little energy or interest and are very slow and casual in their movements.

lap 복습
[læp]

① v. (파도가) 찰싹거리다, (찰짝찰짝) 핥다 ② n. 무릎; (트랙의) 한 바퀴
When water laps against something such as the shore or the side of a boat, it touches it gently and makes a soft sound.

hypnotic
[hipnátik]

a. 최면을 일으키는, 최면성의 (hypnotically ad. 최면을 거는 것처럼)
Something that is hypnotic holds your attention or makes you feel sleepy, often because it involves repeated sounds, pictures, or movements.

seep
[si:p]

vi. 스며 나오다, 새다
If something such as liquid or gas seeps somewhere, it flows slowly and in small amounts into a place where it should not go.

stir 복습
[stə:r]

n. 움직임; 휘젓기; v. 휘젓다, 움직이다
A stir is a slight moving, for example because of uncomfortable or beginning to wake up.

crib 복습
[krib]

n. 유아용 침대; 여물통; 곳간, 헛간
A crib is a bed for a small baby.

mold*
[mould]

vt. 틀에 넣어 만들다, 본뜨다; n. 틀, 주형
If you mold a soft substance such as plastic or clay, you make it into a particular shape or into an object.

outlying 복습
[áutlàiiŋ]

a. 외딴, 외진, 바깥에 있는
Outlying places are far away from the main cities of a country.

gradual 복습
[grǽdʒuəl]

a. 점진적인, 단계적인 (gradually ad. 점진적으로)
A gradual change or process occurs in small stages over a long period of time, rather than suddenly.

numb 복습
[nʌm]

a. 감각이 없는, 마비된; 망연자실한, 멍한; vt. 감각이 없게 만들다
If a part of your body is numb, you cannot feel anything there.

isolate 복습
[áisəlèit]

vt. 고립시키다, 격리시키다 (isolated a. 고립된, 격리된)
To isolate a person or organization means to cause them to lose their friends or supporters.

thicket*
[θíkit]

n. 덤불, 잡목 숲
A thicket is a small group of trees or bushes which are growing closely together.

rut
[rʌt]

vt. 바퀴 자국을 내다, 홈을 내다; n. 바퀴자국, 홈 (rutted a. 바퀴자국이 깊이 난)
A rutted road or track is very uneven because it has long, deep, narrow marks in it made by the wheels of vehicles.

bumpy
[bʌ́mpi]

a. (길이) 울퉁불퉁한, 평탄치 않은
A bumpy road or path has a lot of bumps on it.

meadow 복습
[médou]

n. 목초지, 초원
A meadow is a field which has grass and flowers growing in it.

giggle
[gígəl]

v. 낄낄 웃다; n. 낄낄 웃음
If someone giggles, they laugh in a childlike way, because they are amused, nervous, or embarrassed.

jolt*
[dʒoult]

v. 거칠게 움직이다, 덜컹거리게 하다; 충격을 주다; n. 심한 요동
If something jolts or if something jolts it, it moves suddenly and quite violently.

investigate*
[invéstəgèit]

v. 조사하다, 연구하다, 심사하다
If someone, especially an official, investigates an event, situation, or claim, they try to find out what happened or what is the truth.

twig*
[twig]

n. 잔가지, 가는 가지
A twig is a very small thin branch that grows out from a main branch of a tree or bush.

exhaust*
[igzɔ́:st]

vt. 지치게 하다; 다 써버리다, 소진시키다 (exhausted a. 지칠 대로 지친)
If something exhausts you, it makes you so tired, either physically or mentally, that you have no energy left.

muscle*
[mʌ́səl]

n. 근육
A muscle is a piece of tissue inside your body which connects two bones and which you use when you make a movement.

struggle*
[strʌ́gəl]

v. 발버둥치다, 몸부림치다; 고심하다, 분투하다; n. 투쟁, 분투
If you struggle when you are being held, you twist, kick, and move violently in order to get free.

tickle*
[tíkəl]

n. 간질이기; vt. 간지럼을 태우다; 기쁘게 하다
If a part of the body tickles, or if something tickles it, it feels slightly uncomfortable and you want to rub it.

cuddle*
[kʌ́dl]

v. 꼭 껴안다
If you cuddle someone, you put your arms round them and hold them close as a way of showing your affection.

murmur*
[mə́:rmər]

v. 중얼거리다; 투덜거리다; n. 중얼거림
If you murmur something, you say it very quietly, so that not many people can hear what you are saying.

contented*
[kənténtid]

a. 만족한
If you are contented, you are satisfied with your life or the situation you are in.

exhaustion*
[igzɔ́:stʃən]

n. 기진맥진; 소모, 고갈
Exhaustion is the state of being so tired that you have no energy left.

chest*
[tʃest]

① n. 가슴, 흉부 ② n. 상자, 궤
Your chest is the top part of the front of your body where your ribs, lungs, and heart are.

fugitive*
[fjú:dʒətiv]

n. 도망자, 탈주자; a. 도망치는
A fugitive is someone who is running away or hiding, usually in order to avoid being caught by the police.

scrap*
[skræp]

n. 한 조각, 파편; 단편, 토막
A scrap of something is a very small piece or amount of it.

augment*
[ɔ:gmént]

v. 증가시키다, 늘리다
To augment something means to make it larger, stronger, or more effective by adding something to it.

taut
[tɔ:t]

a. 팽팽한, 긴장된
Something that is taut is stretched very tight.

remount
[ri:máunt]

v. 다시 타다, 다시 오르다
When you remount a bicycle or horse, you get back on it after you have got off it or fallen off it.

fearful복습
[fíərfəl]

a. 두려워하는, 겁내는; 무서운 (fearfully ad. 무서워하며, 걱정스럽게)
If you are fearful of something, you are afraid of it.

flesh복습
[fleʃ]

n. 살, 살집, 고기; 피부
Flesh is the soft part of a person's or animal's body between the bones and the skin.

smear*
[smiər]

n. 얼룩, 자국; 중상모략; v. 바르다, 문지르다; 더럽히다
A smear is a dirty or oily mark.

foliage*
[fóuliidʒ]

n. 나뭇잎
The leaves of a plant are referred to as its foliage.

heat-seeking
[hi:tsí:kiŋ]

a. 열을 추적하는, 적외선을 탐지하는
heat (n. 열, 뜨거움) + seeking (…을 찾는)

device**
[diváis]

n. 장치, 설비
A device is an object that has been invented for a particular purpose, for example for recording or measuring something.

home in on

idiom …으로 곧장 나아가다, 접근하다
If you home in on something, you move or aim straight toward them.

huddle복습
[hʌdl]

v. 몸을 움츠리다; 뒤죽박죽 쌓아 올리다; n. 집단, 군중
If you huddle somewhere, you sit, stand, or lie there holding your arms and legs close to your body, usually because you are cold or frightened.

shrubbery복습
[ʃrʌbəri]

n. 관목을 심은 길, 관목 숲
You can refer to a lot of shrubs or to shrubs in general as shrubbery.

aircraft복습
[ɛ́ərkræft]

n. 항공기 (비행기 · 비행선 · 기구 · 헬리콥터 등의 총칭)
An aircraft is a vehicle which can fly, for example an airplane or a helicopter.

shiver복습
[ʃívər]

v. (추위 · 공포로) 후들후들 떨다; 전율하다; n. 떨림, 전율
When you shiver, your body shakes slightly because you are cold or frightened.

urge***
[ə:rdʒ]

v. 몰아대다, 재촉하다; n. (강한) 충동
If you urge someone to do something, you try hard to persuade them to do it.

shallow^{복습}
[ʃǽlou]

a. 얕은, 얄팍한
If you describe a person, piece of work, or idea as shallow, you disapprove of them because they do not show or involve any serious or careful thought.

shed^{복습}
[ʃed]

① v. 없애다, 버리다 ② n. 오두막, 헛간
To shed something means to get rid of it.

cling**
[kliŋ]

vi. 매달리다, 달라붙다
If you cling to someone or something, you hold onto them tightly.

alert**
[ələ́:rt]

a. 방심하지 않는; n. 경보, 경계; v. 경고하다
If you are alert, you are paying full attention to things around you and are able to deal with anything that might happen.

intent^{복습}
[intént]

① a. 집중된, 열심인, 여념이 없는 (intently ad. 골똘하게) ② n. 의지, 의향
If someone does something in an intent way, they pay great attention to what they are doing.

occasional^{복습}
[əkéiʒənəl]

a. 가끔의, 때때로의 (occasionally ad. 때때로, 가끔)
Occasional means happening sometimes, but not regularly or often.

frighten^{복습}
[fráitn]

v. 놀라게 하다, 섬뜩하게 하다; 기겁하다 (frighteningly ad. 깜짝 놀랄 정도로)
If something or someone frightens you, they cause you to suddenly feel afraid, anxious, or nervous.

close call
[klouzkɔ:l]

n. (구어) 위기일발, 구사일생
A close call is a situation where a disaster or an accident almost happens.

habitation*
[hæbətéiʃən]

n. 거주
Habitation is the activity of living somewhere.

vigilant*
[vídʒələnt]

a. 바짝 경계하는, 방심하지 않는
Someone who is vigilant gives careful attention to a particular problem or situation and concentrates on noticing any danger or trouble that there might be.

frequency*
[frí:kwənsi]

n. 빈도; 자주 일어남, 빈번함; 주파수
The frequency of an event is the number of times it happens during a particular period.

diminish^{복습}
[dəmíniʃ]

v. 줄(이)다, 감소시키다
When something diminishes, or when something diminishes it, it becomes reduced in size, importance, or intensity.

haphazard
[hæphǽzərd]

a. 무계획적인, 되는 대로의; n. 우연(한 일)
If you describe something as haphazard, you are critical of it because it is not at all organized or is not arranged according to a plan.

chapter twenty two

1. What did NOT change as Jonas got farther away from the community?

    (A) There were more trees and the forests were dark and thick.

    (B) The road became narrower and bumpy.

    (C) The search planes only came a few times a day.

    (D) There were birds flying in the sky.

2. What did Jonas fear as he got farther away from the community?

    (A) The airplanes would find him.

    (B) Unknown landscape and perils in the new place

    (C) People from another community would find him and take Gabriel away.

    (D) Wildlife in the dense forest

3. What made Jonas feel moments of exquisite happiness?

    (A) The freedom of living in the forest and not being trapped in his community

    (B) A life of Sameness and predictability

    (C) Unknown perils and unfamiliar landscape

    (D) Pleasant surprises that lay beyond each curve of the road

4. What did Jonas get food in the forest?

   (A) He stole food from cultivated fields along the road.

   (B) He caught small animals in the forest.

   (C) He caught some fish with a net.

   (D) He caught birds with a net.

5. What would have happened if Jonas stayed in the community?

   (A) He would have had love.

   (B) He would have had real feelings.

   (C) He would have asked for release.

   (D) Gabriel would have been killed.

6. What experience did Jonas enjoy in his memories but not enjoy in reality?

   (A) Interaction with wildlife

   (B) Searching for food

   (C) Watching the way the wind shifted the trees

   (D) Being caught in the rain

7. Which of the following was a reason why Jonas cried?

   (A) He wanted to go back to his dwelling.

   (B) He was afraid he couldn't save Gabriel.

   (C) He was unhappy with his choice of leaving the community.

   (D) He missed The Giver.

1분에 몇 단어를 읽는지 리딩 속도를 측정해보세요.

$$\frac{1,946 \text{ words}}{\text{reading time (} \quad \text{) sec}} \times 60 = (\quad) \text{ WPM}$$

• *Build Your Vocabulary*

subtle**
[sʌ́tl]

a. 미묘한, 미세한; 교묘한, 솜씨 좋은
Something that is subtle is not immediately obvious or noticeable.

bumpy복습
[bʌ́mpi]

a. (길이) 울퉁불퉁한, 평탄치 않은
A bumpy road or path has a lot of bumps on it.

apparent복습
[əpǽrənt]

a. 또렷한; 명백한; 외관상의 (apparently ad. 보아하니, 명백히)
If something is apparent to you, it is clear and obvious to you.

tend복습
[tend]

① v. 돌보다, 간호하다 ② vi. 향하다, 경향이 있다
If you tend someone or something, you do what is necessary to keep them in a good condition or to improve their condition.

wobble
[wάbəl]

v. 흔들흔들하다, 비틀대다; 동요하다; n. 흔들림
If something or someone wobbles, they make small movements from side to side, for example because they are unsteady.

rut복습
[rʌt]

n. 바퀴자국, 홈; vt. 바퀴 자국을 내다, 홈을 내다
A rut is a deep, narrow mark made in the ground by the wheels of a vehicle.

jolt복습
[dʒoult]

v. 거칠게 움직이다, 덜컹거리게 하다; 충격을 주다; n. 심한 요동
If something jolts or if something jolts it, it moves suddenly and quite violently.

instinctive*
[instíŋktiv]

a. 본능적인, 직관적인 (instinctively ad. 본능적으로)
Instinctive behavior or reactions are not thought about, planned or developed by training.

strap복습
[stræp]

vt. 끈으로 묶다, 잡아매다; n. 가죽 끈, 혁대
If you strap something somewhere, you fasten it there with a narrow piece of leather or cloth.

injure복습
[índʒər]

vt. 상처를 입히다, 해치다 (uninjured a. 다치지 않은)
If you injure a person or animal, you damage some part of their body.

frighten복습
[fráitn]

v. 놀라게 하다, 섬뜩하게 하다; 기겁하다 (frightened a. 깜짝 놀란, 겁이 난)
If something or someone frightens you, they cause you to suddenly feel afraid, anxious, or nervous.

ankle**
[ǽŋkl]

n. 발목
Your ankle is the joint where your foot joins your leg.

scrape복습
[skreip]

v. 스쳐서 상처를 내다; 긁다, 긁어내다, 문지르다
If you scrape a part of your body, you accidentally rub it against something hard and rough, and damage it slightly.

raw**
[rɔ:]

a. 피부가 벗겨져 쓰라린; 생것의, 날것의
If a part of your body is raw, it is red and painful, perhaps because the skin has come off or has been burnt.

seep복습
[si:p]

vi. 스며 나오다, 새다
If something such as liquid or gas seeps somewhere, it flows slowly and in small amounts into a place where it should not go.

trousers복습
[tráuzərz]

n. (남자용) 바지
Trousers are a piece of clothing that you wear over your body from the waist downwards, and that cover each leg separately.

reassure복습
[rì:əʃúər]

vt. 안심시키다
If you reassure someone, you say or do things to make them stop worrying about something.

tentative복습
[téntətiv]

a. 머뭇거리는, 주저하는; 잠정적인, 임시의 (tentatively ad. 조심스럽게, 주저하며)
If someone is tentative, they are cautious and not very confident because they are uncertain or afraid.

peril**
[pérəl]

n. 위험, 모험; vt. 위태롭게 하다, 위험에 빠뜨리다
Perils are great dangers.

wince복습
[wins]

vi. (아픔·무서움 때문에) 주춤하다, 움츠리다; n. 위축
If you wince, the muscles of your face tighten suddenly because you have felt a pain or because you have just seen, heard, or remembered something unpleasant.

flesh복습
[fleʃ]

n. 살, 살집, 고기; 피부
Flesh is the soft part of a person's or animal's body between the bones and the skin.

swell복습
[swel]

v. (swelled-swollen) 부풀다, 팽창하다; 증가하다; n. 팽창, 증대
(swollen a. 부어오른)
If a part of your body is swollen, it is larger and rounder than normal usually as a result of injury or illness.

soak**
[souk]

v. 젖다, 스며들다; 적시다; 빨아들이다; n. 적심
If a liquid soaks something or if you soak something with a liquid, the liquid makes the thing very wet.

occasional복습
[əkéiʒənəl]

a. 가끔의, 때때로의 (occasionally ad. 때때로, 가끔)
Occasional means happening sometimes, but not regularly or often.

gully
[gʌ́li]

n. 협곡, 골짜기; 도랑, 배수구
A gully is a long narrow valley with steep sides.

depend복습
[dipénd]

vi. …에 좌우되다, …에 달려 있다; 의존하다, 의지하다
If you say that one thing depends on another, you mean that the first thing will be affected or determined by the second.

swift**
[swift]

a. 빠른, 신속한 (swiftly ad. 빨리, 즉시)
A swift event or process happens very quickly or without delay.

aircraft ^{복습}
[ɛ́ərkræ̀ft]

n. 항공기 (비행기 · 비행선 · 기구 · 헬리콥터 등의 총칭)
An aircraft is a vehicle which can fly, for example an airplane or a helicopter.

shrubbery ^{복습}
[ʃrʌ́bəri]

n. 관목을 심은 길, 관목 숲
You can refer to a lot of shrubs or to shrubs in general as shrubbery.

chubby
[tʃʌ́bi]

a. 토실토실 살찐, 오동통한
A chubby person is rather fat.

terrify ^{복습}
[térəfài]

vt. 무섭게[겁나게] 하다, 놀래다 (terrified a. 무서워하는, 겁먹은)
If something terrifies you, it makes you feel extremely frightened.

soar**
[sɔːr]

vi. 높이 치솟다, 날아오르다; n. 높이 날기, 비상
If something such as a bird soars into the air, it goes quickly up into the air.

deer**
[diər]

n. 사슴
A deer is a large wild animal that eats grass and leaves. A male deer usually has large, branching horns.

predictable ^{복습}
[pridíktəbl]

a. 예상[예측, 예언]할 수 있는 (predictability n. 예측 가능성)
If you say that an event is predictable, you mean that it is obvious in advance that it will happen.

awe ^{복습}
[ɔː]

vt. 경외심을 갖게 하다; n. 경외, 외경심
If you are awed by someone or something, they make you feel respectful and amazed, though often rather frightened.

throaty
[θróuti]

a. 목이 쉰 듯한
A throaty voice or laugh is low and rather rough.

warble*
[wɔ́ːrbəl]

n. 지저귐; 떨리는 목소리; v. 목소리를 떨며 노래하다; (새가) 지저귀다
Warble is a succession of constant soft song by birds.

shift ^{복습}
[ʃift]

v. 옮기다, 방향을 바꾸다; n. 변화, 이동; 교대
If you shift something or if it shifts, it moves slightly.

exquisite**
[ikskwízit]

a. 정교한, 절묘한; 우아한, 섬세한
Something that is exquisite is extremely beautiful or pleasant, especially in a delicate way.

relentless*
[riléntlis]

a. 집요한, 끊임없는; 냉혹한, 가차 없는
Something bad that is relentless never stops or never becomes less intense.

starve ^{복습}
[staːrv]

v. 굶주리다, 굶어죽다
If people starve, they suffer greatly from lack of food which sometimes leads to their death.

cultivate**
[kʌ́ltəvèit]

vt. 경작하다, 재배하다; 양성하다 (cultivated a. 경작된)
If you cultivate land or crops, you prepare land and grow crops on it.

meager*
[míːgər]

a. 빈약한, 결핍한; 메마른
If you describe an amount or quantity of something as meager, you are critical of it because it is very small or not enough.

agricultural [ægrikʌltʃərəl]
a. 농업의, 농사의
Agricultural means involving or relating to farming and the methods that are used to raise and look after crops and animals.

kneel [ni:l]
vi. (knelt–knelt) 무릎 꿇다
When you kneel, you bend your legs so that your knees are touching the ground.

frustrate [frʌstreit]
v. 좌절시키다, 불만스럽게 만들다; 방해하다 (frustrated a. 실망한, 좌절한)
If something frustrates you, it upsets or angers you because you are unable to do anything about the problems it creates.

desperation [dèspəréiʃən]
n. 절망, 자포자기; 필사적임
Desperation is the feeling that you have when you are in such a bad situation that you will try anything to change it.

fashion [fǽʃən]
vt. 만들어내다, 형성하다; n. 유행
If you fashion an object or a work of art, you make it.

makeshift [méikʃìft]
a. 임시변통의, 일시적인; n. 임시 수단, 미봉책
Makeshift things are temporary and usually of poor quality, but they are used because there is nothing better available.

loop [lu:p]
v. 고리로 만들다; 고리로 두르다; n. 고리, 올가미
If you loop something such as a piece of rope around an object, you tie a length of it in a loop around the object, for example in order to fasten it to the object.

strand [strænd]
n. (실 · 전선 · 머리카락 등의) 가닥, 꼰 줄
A strand of something such as hair, wire, or thread is a single thin piece of it.

countless [káuntlis]
a. 셀 수 없는, 무수한
Countless means very many.

yield [ji:ld]
v. 산출하다, 생산하다; 넘겨주다, 양도하다; n. 산출
If an area of land yields a particular amount of a crop, this is the amount that is produced.

flop [flɑp]
v. 퍼덕거리다, 털썩 쓰러지다
If something flops onto something else, it falls there heavily or untidily.

silvery [sílvəri]
a. 은빛의; 은과 같은
Silvery things look like silver or are the color of silver.

methodical [məθádikəl]
a. 체계적인, 꼼꼼한 (methodically ad. 체계적으로, 찬찬히)
If you describe someone as methodical, you mean that they do things carefully, thoroughly, and in order.

hack [hæk]
v. 마구 자르다; (흙을) 파 뒤집다; 경작하다
If you hack something or hack at it, you cut it with strong, rough strokes using a sharp tool such as an axe or knife.

shred [ʃred]
n. 조각, 파편; v. 조각조각으로 찢다, 갈가리 찢다
If there is not a shred of something, there is not even a small amount of it.

torture^{出る}
[tɔ́ːrtʃər]

vt. 고문하다, 고통을 주다; n. 고문, 고뇌
To torture someone means to cause them to suffer mental pain or anxiety.

dwelling^{出る}
[dwéliŋ]

n. 거처, 주소, 사는 집
A dwelling is a place where someone lives.

flag***
[flæg]

① v. (활력 · 활동 · 흥미 · 기력 등이) 떨어지다, 풀리다; 시들해지다 ② n. 기, 깃발
If you flag or if your spirits flag, you begin to lose enthusiasm or energy.

recreate^{出る}
[rékrièit]

vt. (과거에 존재하던 것을) 되살리다, 재현하다
If you recreate something, you succeed in making it exist or seem to exist in a different time or place to its original time or place.

tantalize
[tǽntəlàiz]

vt. 애타게 하다, 감질나게 하다 (tantalizing a. 애타게 하는, 감질나게 하는)
If someone or something tantalizes you, they make you feel hopeful and excited about getting what you want.

fragment^{出る}
[frǽgmənt]

n. 조각, 파편, 단편
A fragment of something is a small piece or part of it.

banquet**
[bǽŋkwit]

n. 연회
A banquet is a grand formal dinner.

frost**
[frɔːst]

v. (케이크에) 설탕을 입히다; 서리로 덮다, 서리가 앉다; n. 서리
If you frost something such as a cake, you give a frostlike surface by putting sugar on it.

lush
[lʌʃ]

a. 무성한, 우거진
Lush fields or gardens have a lot of very healthy grass or plants.

drip^{出る}
[drip]

v. 물방울이 떨어지다, 뚝뚝 흐르다
When something drips, drops of liquid fall from it.

glimpse^{出る}
[glimps]

v. 흘끗 보다, 잠깐보다; n. 흘끗 봄, 잠깐 봄
If you get a glimpse of someone or something, you see them very briefly and not very well.

subside^{出る}
[səbsáid]

vi. 가라앉다, 진정되다
If a feeling or noise subsides, it becomes less strong or loud.

gnaw*
[nɔː]

v. 갉아먹다, 물어뜯다, 괴롭히다 (gnawing a. 갉는, 쏘는; 괴롭히는)
If a feeling or thought gnaws at you, it causes you to keep worrying.

grim^{出る}
[grim]

a. 암울한, 음산한; 엄한, 엄격한 (grimly ad. 암울하게, 음울하게)
If you say that something is grim, you think that it is very bad, ugly, or depressing.

chastise^{出る}
[tʃæstáiz]

vt. 벌하다, 꾸짖다, 혼내주다
If you chastise someone, you speak to them angrily or punish them for something wrong that they have done.

yearn**
[jəːrn]

vi. 동경하다, 갈망하다
If someone yearns for something that they are unlikely to get, they want it very much.

struggle ^{복습}
[strʌ́gəl]

n. 투쟁, 분투; v. 고심하다, 분투하다; 발버둥치다, 몸부림치다
A struggle is a long and difficult attempt to achieve something such as freedom or political rights.

encounter **
[enkáuntər]

v. 만나다, 마주치다; n. 마주침
If you encounter problems or difficulties, you experience them.

sprain
[sprein]

vt. (발목·손목 등을) 삐다; n. 삠, 접질림
If you sprain a joint such as your ankle or wrist, you accidentally damage it by twisting it or bending it violently.

throb ^{복습}
[θrɑb]

vi. (심장이) 고동치다, 맥이 뛰다; n. 고동, 맥박
If part of your body throbs, you feel a series of strong and usually painful beats there.

chapter twenty three

1. How did Jonas know that his destination was ahead of him?

    (A) He saw it in the distance ahead.

    (B) He heard sounds ahead.

    (C) He could see light on the horizon.

    (D) He could feel that it was not far away.

2. What final challenge did Jonas meet in this chapter?

    (A) Riding up a narrow hill with his bicycle

    (B) Trying to remember a memory of courage

    (C) Climbing up a steep hill covered in snow without his bicycle

    (D) Hiking through a snow filled forest in the dark

3. Why didn't Jonas keep the memory of sunshine for himself?

    (A) He was not cold.

    (B) He couldn't remember what sunshine felt like.

    (C) He wanted to give it to Gabe.

    (D) He had many more memories of sunshine he could keep for himself.

4. What helped Jonas reach the top of the hill?

    (A) He used his last memory of warmth and gave it to Gabriel.

    (B) He recalled his own memories of his family, friends, and The Giver.

    (C) He thought about his goal to reach Elsewhere.

    (D) He used his final memories of courage and strength.

5. What did Jonas find at the top of the hill?

    (A) A sled

    (B) Elsewhere

    (C) Warmth and light

    (D) A rope

6. What did Jonas believe was waiting for him at the bottom of the hill?

    (A) His family and friends

    (B) A place where families celebrated love

    (C) A large community

    (D) A person who could save Gabriel

7. Jonas thought he heard _____ as he approached the bottom of the hill.

    (A) laughing

    (B) talking

    (C) music

    (D) a Christmas party

1분에 몇 단어를 읽는지 리딩 속도를 측정해보세요.

$$\frac{1{,}368 \text{ words}}{\text{reading time ( ) sec}} \times 60 = (\qquad) \text{ WPM}$$

• *Build Your Vocabulary*

destination^{복습}
[dèstənéiʃən]

n. 목적지, 행선지
The destination of someone or something is the place to which they are going or being sent.

diminish^{복습}
[dəmíniʃ]

v. 줄(이)다, 감소시키다
When something diminishes, or when something diminishes it, it becomes reduced in size, importance, or intensity.

blur^{복습}
[blə:r]

v. (광경·의식·눈 등을) 흐리게 하다; n. 흐림, 침침함; 더러움, 얼룩
When a thing blurs or when something blurs it, you cannot see it clearly because its edges are no longer distinct.

swirl^{복습}
[swə:rl]

vi. 소용돌이치다, 빙빙 돌다
If liquid or flowing swirls, it moves round and round quickly.

inadequate^{복습}
[inǽdikwit]

a. 부적당한, 부적절한; 불충분한
If something is inadequate, there is not enough of it or it is not good enough.

blanket^{복습}
[blǽŋkit]

n. 담요, 모포
A blanket is a large square or rectangular piece of thick cloth, especially one which you put on a bed to keep you warm.

hunch^{복습}
[hʌntʃ]

v. 둥글게 구부리다; n. 예감, 직감
If you hunch your shoulders, you raise them and lean forwards slightly.

shiver^{복습}
[ʃívər]

v. (추위·공포로) 후들후들 떨다; 전율하다; n. 떨림, 전율
When you shiver, your body shakes slightly because you are cold or frightened.

weary^{복습}
[wíəri]

a. 피로한, 지친 (wearily ad. 지쳐서, 지친 상태로)
If you are weary, you are very tired.

freeze^{복습}
[fri:z]

v. 얼다, 얼어붙다 (freezing a. 어는, 얼어붙은)
If you say that something is freezing or freezing cold, you are emphasizing that it is very cold.

mound^{복습}
[maund]

n. 더미, 무더기, 언덕
A mound of something is a large rounded pile of it.

numb^{복습}
[nʌm]

a. 감각이 없는, 마비된; 망연자실한, 멍한; vt. 감각이 없게 만들다
If a part of your body is numb, you cannot feel anything there.

tunic^{복습}
[tjú:nik]

n. 튜닉 (고대 그리스나 로마인들이 입던, 무릎까지 내려오는 헐렁한 가운 같은 옷옷)
A tunic is a loose piece of clothing covering the body down to the knees, usually without sleeves.

bare^{복습}
[bɛər]

a. 발가벗은; 있는 그대로의
If a part of your body is bare, it is not covered by any clothing.

chest^{복습}
[tʃest]

① n. 가슴, 흉부 ② n. 상자, 궤
Your chest is the top part of the front of your body where your ribs, lungs, and heart are.

feeble**
[fí:bəl]

a. 연약한, 허약한 (feebly ad. 약하게)
If you describe someone or something as feeble, you mean that they are weak.

whimper^{복습}
[hwímpər]

v. 훌쩍이다, 울먹이다; 낑낑거리다
If someone whimpers, they make quiet unhappy or frightened sounds, as if they are about to start crying.

dim^{복습}
[dim]

a. 어둑한, 흐릿한, 희미한; v. 어둑하게 하다, 흐려지다 (dimly ad. 어렴풋이)
If you have a dim memory or understanding of something, it is difficult to remember or is unclear in your mind.

recall^{복습}
[rikɔ́:l]

vt. 생각해내다, 상기하다, 소환하다; n. 회상, 상기
When you recall something, you remember it and tell others about it.

snowflake^{복습}
[snóuflèik]

n. 눈송이
A snowflake is one of the soft, white bits of frozen water that fall as snow.

dusk*
[dʌsk]

n. 땅거미, 황혼, 어스름
Dusk is the time just before night when the daylight has almost gone but when it is not completely dark.

matted^{복습}
[mǽtid]

a. 텁수룩한, 헝클어진; 매트를 깐
If you describe someone's hair as matted, you mean that it has become a thick untidy mass, often because it is wet or dirty.

filthy*
[fílθi]

a. 불결한, 더러운
Something that is filthy is very dirty indeed.

drift^{복습}
[drift]

v. 표류하다, 떠돌다; 모르는 사이에 빠져들다; n. 표류; 흐름
When something drifts somewhere, it is carried there by the movement of wind or water.

sparkle^{복습}
[spá:rkəl]

n. 반짝거림, 광채; v. 반짝이다; 생기 넘치다
Sparkles are small points of light caused by light reflecting off a clear bright surface.

flutter^{복습}
[flʌ́tər]

v. (깃발 등이) 펄럭이다, (새 등이) 날갯짓하다; n. 펄럭임
If something thin or light flutters, or if you flutter it, it moves up and down or from side to side with a lot of quick, light movements.

eyelash
[áilæ̀ʃ]

n. 속눈썹
Your eyelashes are the hairs which grow on the edges of your eyelids.

remount^{복습}
[ri:máunt]

v. 다시 타다, 다시 오르다
When you remount a bicycle or horse, you get back on it after you have got off it or fallen off it.

steep^{복습}
[sti:p]

① a. 가파른, 험한; 급격한 ② v. 적시다, 담그다; 열중하다
A steep slope rises at a very sharp angle and is difficult to go up.

loom*
[lu:m]

vi. 어렴풋이 나타나다, 흐릿하게 보이다
If something looms over you, it appears as a large or unclear shape, often in a frightening way.

obscure**
[əbskjúər]

vt. 가리다, 덮다; a. (소리 · 모양 등이) 분명치 않은, 흐릿한
If one thing obscures another, it prevents it from being seen or heard properly.

imperceptible
[ìmpərséptəbəl]

a. 감지할 수 없는, 아주 미세한 (imperceptibly ad. 아주 미세하게)
Something that is imperceptible is so small that it is not noticed or cannot be seen.

pedal^{복습}
[pédl]

n. 페달, 발판; v. 페달을 밟다
The pedals on a bicycle are the two parts that you push with your feet in order to make the bicycle move.

exhaust^{복습}
[igzɔ́:st]

vt. 지치게 하다; 다 써버리다, 소진시키다 (exhausted a. 지칠 대로 지친)
If something exhausts you, it makes you so tired, either physically or mentally, that you have no energy left.

flicker^{복습}
[flíkər]

v. (등불 · 희망 · 빛 등이) 깜박이다; n. 깜박임
If a light or flame flickers, it shines unsteadily.

creep**
[kri:p]

vi. 살금살금 움직이다, 기다; n. 포복
If something creeps somewhere, it moves very slowly.

glow^{복습}
[glou]

v. 상기되다, 발개지다, 달아오르다; 빛을 내다, 빛나다; n. 빛, 밝음
If your body or face glows, it looks pink or you feel warm, especially after exercise or because of excitement or embarrassment.

tense^{복습}
[tens]

a. 긴장한, 긴박한; 팽팽한; v. 팽팽하게 하다
A tense situation or period of time is one that makes people anxious, because they do not know what is going to happen next.

fleeting^{복습}
[flí:tiŋ]

a. 순식간의, 잠깐 동안의; 어느덧 지나가는
Fleeting is used to describe something which lasts only for a very short time.

bathe^{복습}
[beið]

v. (열 · 빛 등이) 뒤덮다, 감싸다; 목욕시키다, 씻다
If a place is bathed in light, it is covered with light, especially a gentle, pleasant light.

burden^{복습}
[bɔ́:rdn]

vt. 짐을 지우다, 부담시키다; n. 짐, 부담 (unburden v. 짐을 덜다, 덜어 주다)
If someone burdens you with something that is likely to worry you, for example a problem or a difficult decision, they tell you about it.

urge^{복습}
[ə:rdʒ]

n. (강한) 충동; v. 촉구하다, 충고하다, 몰아대다, 재촉하다
If you have an urge to do or have something, you have a strong wish to do or have it.

passionate 복습
[pǽʃənit]

a. 열정적인, 열렬한, 격정적인
A passionate person has very strong feelings about something or a strong belief in something.

yearn 복습
[jə:rn]

vi. 동경하다, 갈망하다 (yearning n. 동경, 열망)
If someone yearns for something that they are unlikely to get, they want it very much.

stir 복습
[stə:r]

v. 휘젓다, 움직이다; n. 움직임; 휘젓기
If you stir, you move slightly, for example because you are uncomfortable or beginning to wake up.

blind 복습
[blaind]

vt. 눈멀게 하다; a. 눈먼, 장님인 (blinding a. 눈을 멀게 하는)
If something blinds you, it makes you unable to see, either for a short time or permanently.

agonizing
[ǽgənàiziŋ]

a. 고뇌하게 하는, 괴로워하는 (agonizingly ad. 고뇌할 정도로)
Something that is agonizing causes you to feel great physical or mental pain.

trudge 복습
[trʌdʒ]

v. 터벅터벅 걷다; n. 터덕터덕 걸음
If you trudge somewhere, you walk there slowly and with heavy steps, especially because you are tired or unhappy.

lethargy
[léθərdʒi]

n. 무기력, 무감각
Lethargy is the condition or state of being not having much energy or enthusiasm.

resignation *
[rèzignéiʃən]

n. 체념, 포기; 사직, 사임
Resignation is the acceptance of an unpleasant situation or fact because you realize that you cannot change it.

restore 복습
[ristɔ́:r]

vt. 되돌리다, 복구하다, 회복시키다
To restore someone or something to a previous condition means to cause them to be in that condition once again.

treacherous *
[trétʃərəs]

a. 믿을 수 없는, 신뢰할 수 없는; (보기와는 달리) 위험한
(treacherously ad. 위험할 정도로)
If you say that something is treacherous, you mean that it is very dangerous and unpredictable.

impede *
[impí:d]

vt. 방해하다, 지연시키다
If you impede someone or something, you make their movement, development, or progress difficult.

stumble 복습
[stʌ́mbəl]

v. 비틀거리며 걷다, 발부리가 걸리다; n. 비틀거림
If you stumble, you put your foot down awkwardly while you are walking or running and nearly fall over.

grasp 복습
[græsp]

v. 붙잡다, 움켜쥐다; n. 움켜잡기
If you grasp something, you take it in your hand and hold it very firmly.

wisp 복습
[wisp]

n. 단편, 조각; 한 줌, 작은 묶음
A wisp of something such as smoke or cloud is an amount of it in a long thin shape.

desperate^{복습}
[déspərit]

a. 필사적인; 자포자기의, 절망적인 (desperately ad. 필사적으로)
If you are desperate for something or desperate to do something, you want or need it very much indeed.

enlarge^{복습}
[enlá:rdʒ]

v. 크게 하다, 확대하다
When you enlarge something or when it enlarges, it becomes bigger.

concentration^복
[kànsəntréiʃən]

ᵃn. 집중, 전념
Concentration on something involves giving all your attention to it.

scrap^{복습}
[skræp]

n. 한 조각, 파편; 단편, 토막
A scrap of something is a very small piece or amount of it.

summit**
[sʌ́mit]

n. 정상, 꼭대기
The summit of a mountain is the top of it.

leaden
[lédn]

a. 나른한, 뻐근한; 납의, 납빛의
If your movements are leaden, you move slowly and heavily, usually because you are tired.

barely^{복습}
[béərli]

ad. 간신히, 가까스로; 거의 …않다
You use barely to say that something is only just true or only just the case.

flood^{복습}
[flʌd]

v. (갑자기 강하게) 밀려들다; 범람하다, 넘치다; n. 홍수
If an emotion, feeling, or thought floods you, you suddenly feel it very intensely.

crest**
[krest]

vt. 꼭대기에 이르다, 최고조에 달하다; n. 산등성이, 산마루; (새의) 볏
To crest means to reach the top of a hill or mountain.

recollection^{복습}
[rèkəlékʃən]

n. 회상, 회고
If you have a recollection of something, you remember it.

brisk^{복습}
[brisk]

a. 활발한, 활기찬, 기운찬 (briskly ad. 활발하게)
A brisk activity or action is done quickly and in an energetic way.

bitter^{복습}
[bítər]

a. 지독한, 혹독한; 쓴, 쓰라린 (bitterly ad. 지독하게; 씁쓸하게)
Bitter weather, or a bitter wind, is extremely cold.

sled^{복습}
[sled]

n. 썰매
A sled is an object used for travelling over snow.

fumble*
[fʌ́mbəl]

vi. 손으로 더듬어 찾다; (말을) 더듬거리다
If you fumble for something or fumble with something, you try and reach for it or hold it in a clumsy way.

powdery
[páudəri]

a. 가루 같은, 가루의
Something that is powdery looks or feels like powder.

surge^{복습}
[səːrdʒ]

v. 쇄도하다, 밀어닥치다; n. 쇄도, 돌진
If something surges, it increases suddenly and greatly, after being steady or developing only slowly.

will[쪽음]
[wil]

v. 의지를 발동하다; 뜻하다; n. 의지; 유언장
If you will something to happen, you try to make it happen by using mental effort rather than physical effort.

upright[쪽음]
[ʌ́pràit]

a. 똑바른, 꼿꼿한, 수직으로 선
If you are sitting or standing upright, you are sitting or standing with your back straight, rather than bending or lying down.

clutch[쪽음]
[klʌtʃ]

v. 꽉 잡다, 붙들다, 부여잡다; n. 붙잡음, 움켜쥠
If you clutch at something or clutch something, you hold it tightly, usually because you are afraid or anxious.

whip**
[hwip]

v. 채찍질하다; 급히 움직이다, 홱 잡아채다; n. 채찍(질)
If something, for example the wind, whips something, it strikes it sharply.

incision
[insíʒən]

n. 절개, 베기, 째기
An incision is a sharp cut made in something, for example by a surgeon who is operating on a patient.

twinkle*
[twíŋkəl]

v. 반짝거리다, 빛나다; (눈이 행복감·흥분으로) 반짝거리다; n. 반짝거림
If a star or a light twinkles, it shines with an unsteady light which rapidly and constantly changes from bright to faint.

celebrate[쪽음]
[séləbrèit]

v. 기념하다, 축하하다
If you celebrate, you do something enjoyable because of a special occasion.

수고하셨습니다!

드디어 끝까지 다 읽으셨군요! 축하드립니다! 여러분은 이 책을 통해 총 43,617개의 단어를 읽으셨고, 1,120개 이상의 어휘와 표현들을 익히셨습니다. 이 책에 나온 어휘는 다른 원서를 읽을 때에도 빈번히 만날 수 있는 필수 어휘들입니다. 이 책을 읽었던 경험은 비슷한 수준의 다른 원서들을 읽을 때 큰 도움이 될 것입니다.
이제 자신의 상황에 맞게 원서를 반복해서 읽거나, 오디오북을 들어 볼 수 있습니다. 혹은 비슷한 수준의 다른 원서를 찾아 읽는 것도 좋습니다. 일단 원서를 완독한 뒤에 어떻게 계속 영어 공부를 이어갈 수 있을지, 아래에 제시되는 도움말을 꼼꼼히 살펴보고 각자 상황에 맞게 적용해 보세요!

리딩(Reading)을 확실하게 다지고 싶다면? 반복해서 읽어 보세요!

리딩 실력을 탄탄하게 다지고 싶다면, 같은 원서를 2~3번 반복해서 읽을 것을 권합니다. 같은 책을 여러 번 읽으면 지루할 것 같지만, 꼭 그렇지도 않습니다. 반복해서 읽을 때 처음과 주안점을 다르게 두면, 전혀 다른 느낌으로 재미있게 읽을 수 있습니다.
처음 원서를 읽을 때는 생소한 단어들과 스토리로 인해 읽으면서 곧바로 이해하기가 매우 힘들 수 있습니다. 전체 맥락을 잡고 읽어도 약간 버거운 느낌이지요. 하지만 반복해서 읽기 시작하면 달라집니다. 일단 내용을 파악한 상황이기 때문에 문장 구조나 어휘의 활용에 더 집중하게 되고, 조금 더 깊이 있게 읽을 수 있습니다. 좋은 표현과 문장을 수집하고 메모할 만한 여유도 생기게 되지요. 어휘도 많이 익숙해졌기 때문에 리딩 속도에도 탄력이 붙습니다. 처음 읽을 때는 '내용'에서 재미를 느꼈다면, 반복해서 읽을 때에는 '영어'에서 재미를 느끼게 되는 것입니다. 따라서 리딩 실력을 더욱 확고하게 다지고자 한다면, 같은 책을 2~3회 정도 반복해서 읽을 것을 권해 드립니다.

리스닝(Listening) 실력을 늘리고 싶다면?
귀를 통해서 읽어 보세요!

많은 영어 학습자들이 '리스닝이 안 돼서 문제'라고 한탄합니다. 그리고 리스닝 실력을 늘리는 방법으로 무슨 뜻인지 몰라도 반복해서 듣는 '무작정 듣기'를 선택합니다. 하지만 뜻도 모르면서 무작정 듣는 일에는 엄청난 인내력이 필요합니다. 그래서 대부분 며칠 시도하다가 포기해 버리고 말지요.

따라서 모르는 내용을 무작정 듣는 것보다는 어느 정도 알고 있는 내용을 반복해서 듣는 것이 더 효과적인 듣기 방법입니다. 그리고 이런 방식의 듣기에 활용할 수 있는 가장 좋은 교재가 오디오북입니다.

리스닝 실력을 향상하고 싶다면, 이 책에서 제공하는 오디오북을 이용해서 듣는 연습을 해 보세요. 활용법은 간단합니다. 일단 책을 한 번 완독했다면, 오디오북을 통해 다시 들어 보는 것입니다. 휴대 기기에 넣어 시간이 날 때 틈틈이 듣는 것도 좋고, 책상에 앉아 눈으로는 텍스트를 보며 귀로 읽는 것도 좋습니다. 이미 읽었던 내용이라 이해하기가 훨씬 수월하고, 애매했던 발음들도 자연스럽게 교정할 수 있습니다. 또 성우의 목소리 연기를 듣다 보면 내용이 더욱 생동감 있게 다가와 이해도가 높아지는 효과도 거둘 수 있습니다.

반대로 듣기에 자신 있는 사람이라면, 책을 읽기 전에 처음부터 오디오북을 먼저 듣는 것도 좋은 방법입니다. 귀를 통해 책을 쭉 읽어 보고, 이후에 다시 눈으로 책을 읽으면서 잘 들리지 않았던 부분을 보충하는 것이지요.

중요한 것은 내용을 따라가면서, 내용에 푹 빠져서 반복해 들어야 한다는 것입니다. 이렇게 연습을 반복해서 눈으로 읽지 않은 책이라도 '귀를 통해' 읽을 수 있을 정도가 되면, 리스닝으로 고생하는 일은 거의 없을 것입니다.

왼쪽의 QR코드를 스마트폰으로 인식하여 정식 오디오북을 들어 보세요!
더불어 롱테일북스 홈페이지(www.longtailbooks.co.kr)에서도
오디오북 MP3 파일을 다운로드 받을 수 있습니다.

스피킹(Speaking)이 고민이라면? 소리 내어 읽어 보세요!

스피킹 역시 많은 학습자들이 고민하는 부분입니다. 스피킹이 고민이라면, 원서를 큰 소리로 읽는 낭독 훈련(Voice Reading)을 해 보세요!

'소리 내어 읽는 것이 말하기에 정말로 도움이 될까?'라고 의아한 생각이 들 수도 있습니다. 하지만 인간의 두뇌 입장에서 봤을 때, 성대 구조를 활용해서 '발화'한다는 점에서는 소리 내어 읽기와 말하기에 큰 차이가 없다고 합니다. 소리 내어 읽는 것은 '타인의 생각'을 전달하고, 직접 말하는 것은 '자신의 생각'을 전달한다는 차이가 있을 뿐, 머릿속에서 문장을 처리하고 조음기관(혀와 성대 등)을 움직여 의미를 만든다는 점에서 같은 과정인 것이지요. 따라서 소리 내어 읽는 연습을 꾸준히 하는 것은 스피킹 연습에 큰 도움이 됩니다.

소리 내어 읽기를 하는 방법은 간단합니다. 일단 오디오북을 들으면서 성우의 목소리를 최대한 따라 하며 같이 읽어 보세요. 발음뿐 아니라 억양, 어조, 느낌까지 완벽히 따라 한다고 생각하면서 소리 내어 읽습니다. 따라 읽는 것이 조금 익숙해지면, 옆의 누군가에게 이 책을 읽어 준다는 생각으로 소리 내어 계속 읽어 나갑니다. 한 번 눈과 귀로 읽었던 책이기 때문에 보다 수월하게 진행할 수 있고, 자연스럽게 어휘와 표현을 복습하는 효과도 거두게 됩니다. 또 이렇게 소리 내어 읽은 것을 녹음해서 들어 보면 스스로에게도 좋은 피드백이 됩니다.

최근 말하기가 강조되면서 소리 내어 읽기가 크게 각광을 받고 있긴 하지만, 그렇다고 소리 내어 읽기가 무조건 좋은 것만은 아닙니다. 책을 소리 내어 읽다 보면, 무의식적으로 속으로 발음을 하는 습관을 가지게 되어 리딩 속도 자체는 오히려 크게 떨어지는 현상이 발생할 수 있습니다. 따라서 빠른 리딩 속도가 중요한 수험생이나 고학력 학습자들에게는 소리 내어 읽기가 적절하지 않은 방법입니다. 효과가 좋다는 말만 믿고 무턱대고 따라 하기보다는 자신의 필요에 맞게 우선순위를 정하고 원서를 활용하는 것이 좋습니다.

※이 책 The Giver는 소리 내어 읽기에 적절하지 않은 책입니다. 소리 내어 읽기를 한다면, 더 짧고 간단한 책을 골라 보세요!

라이팅(Writing)까지 욕심이 난다면? 요약하는 연습을 해 보세요!

원서를 라이팅 연습에 직접적으로 활용하는 데에는 한계가 있지만, 적절히 활용하면 원서도 유용한 라이팅 자료가 될 수 있습니다.

특히 책을 읽고 그 내용을 요약하는 연습은 큰 도움이 됩니다. 요약 훈련의 방식도 간단합니다. 원서를 읽고 그날 읽은 분량만큼 혹은 책을 다 읽고 전체 내용을 기반으로, 책 내용을 한번 요약하고 나의 느낌을 영어로 적어 보는 것입니다.

이때 그 책에 나왔던 단어와 표현을 최대한 활용하여 요약하는 것이 중요합니다. 영어 표현력은 결국 얼마나 다양한 어휘로 많은 표현을 해 보았느냐가 좌우하게 됩니다. 이런 면에서 내가 읽은 책을, 그 책에 나온 문장과 어휘로 다시 표현해 보는 것은 매우 효율적인 방법입니다. 책에 나온 어휘와 표현을 단순히 읽고 무슨 말인지 아는 정도가 아니라, 실제로 직접 활용해서 쓸 수 있을 만큼 확실하게 익히게 되는 것이지요. 여기에 첨삭까지 받을 수 있는 방법이 있다면 금상첨화입니다.

이러한 '표현하기' 연습은 스피킹 훈련에도 그대로 적용될 수 있습니다. 책을 읽고 그 내용을 3분 안에 다른 사람에게 영어로 말하는 연습을 해 보세요. 순발력과 표현력을 기르는 좋은 훈련이 될 것입니다.

꾸준히 원서를 읽고 싶다면? 뉴베리 수상작을 계속 읽어 보세요!

뉴베리 상이 세계 최고 권위의 아동 문학상인 만큼, 그 수상작들은 확실히 완성도를 검증받은 작품이라고 할 수 있습니다. 특히 '쉬운 어휘로 쓰인 깊이 있는 문장'으로 이루어졌다는 점이 영어 학습자들에게 큰 호응을 얻고 있습니다. 이렇게 '검증된 원서'를 꾸준히 읽는 것은 영어 실력 향상에 큰 도움이 됩니다.

아래에 수준별로 제시된 뉴베리 수상작 목록을 보며 적절한 책들을 찾아 계속 읽어 보세요. 꼭 뉴베리 수상작이 아니더라도 마음에 드는 작가의 다른 책을 읽어 보는 것 또한 아주 좋은 방법입니다.

• 영어 초보자도 쉽게 읽을 만한 아주 쉬운 수준. 소리 내어 읽기에도 아주 적합.
Sarah, Plain and Tall*(Medal, 8,331단어), The Hundred Penny Box (Honor, 5,878단어),
The Hundred Dresses*(Honor, 7,329단어), My Father's Dragon (Honor, 7,682단어), 26
Fairmount Avenue (Honor, 6,737단어)

영어원서 읽기 TIPS

- 중 · 고등학생 정도 영어 학습자라면 쉽게 읽을 수 있는 수준. 소리 내어 읽기에도 비교적 적합한 편.

Because of Winn-Dixie★ (Honor, 22,123단어), What Jamie Saw (Honor, 17,203단어), Charlotte's Web (Honor, 31,938단어), Dear Mr. Henshaw (Medal, 18,145단어), Missing May (Medal, 17,509단어)

- 대학생 정도 영어 학습자라면 무난한 수준. 소리 내어 읽기에는 적합하지 않음.

Number The Stars★ (Medal, 27,197단어), A Single Shard (Medal, 33,726단어), The Tale of Despereaux★ (Medal, 32,375단어), Hatchet★ (Medal, 42,328단어), Bridge to Terabithia (Medal, 32,888단어), A Fine White Dust (Honor, 19,022단어), Jennifer, Hecate, Macbeth, William McKinley and Me, Elizabeth (Honor, 23,266단어)

- 원서 완독 경험을 가진 학습자에게 적절한 수준. 소리 내어 읽기에는 적합하지 않음.

The Giver★ (Medal, 43,617단어), From the Mixed-Up Files of Mrs. Basil E. Frankweiler (Medal, 30,906단어), The View from Saturday (Medal, 42,685단어), Holes★ (Medal, 47,079단어), Criss Cross (Medal, 48,221단어), Walk Two Moons (Medal, 59,400단어), The Graveyard Book (Medal, 67,380단어)

뉴베리 수상작과 뉴베리 수상 작가의 좋은 작품을 엄선한 「뉴베리 컬렉션」에도 위 목록에 있는 도서 중 상당수가 포함될 예정입니다.

★ 「뉴베리 컬렉션」으로 이미 출간된 도서

어떤 책들이 출간되었는지 확인하려면, 지금 인터넷 서점에서
뉴베리 컬렉션을 검색해 보세요.

뉴베리 수상작을 동영상 강의로 만나 보세요!

영어원서 전문 동영상 강의 사이트 영서당(yseodang.com)에서는 뉴베리 컬렉션 『Holes』, 『Because of Winn-Dixie』, 『The Miraculous Journey of Edward Tulane』, 『Wayside School 시리즈』 등의 동영상 강의를 제공하고 있습니다. 뉴베리 수상작이라는 최고의 영어 교재와 EBS 출신 인기 강사가 만난 명강의! 지금 사이트를 방문해서 무료 샘플 강의를 들어 보세요!

'스피드 리딩 카페'를 통해 원서 읽기 습관을 길러 보세요!

일상에서 영어를 한마디도 쓰지 않는 비영어권 국가에서 살고 있는 우리가 영어 환경에 가장 쉽고, 편하고, 부담 없이 노출되는 방법은 바로 '영어원서 읽기'입니다. 언제 어디서든 원서를 붙잡고 읽기만 하면 곧바로 영어를 접하는 환경이 만들어지기 때문이지요. 하루에 20분씩만 꾸준히 읽는다면, 1년에 무려 120시간 동안 영어에 노출될 수 있습니다. 이러한 이유 때문에 영어 교육 전문가들이 영어 원서 읽기를 추천하는 것이지요.

하지만 원서 읽기가 좋다는 것을 알아도 막상 꾸준히 읽는 것은 쉽지 않습니다. 그럴 때에는 13만 명 이상의 회원을 보유한 국내 최대 원서 읽기 동호회 〈스피드 리딩 카페〉(cafe.naver.com/readingtc)를 방문해보세요.

원서별로 정리된 무료 PDF 단어장과 수준별 추천 원서 목록 등 유용한 자료는 물론, 뉴베리 수상작을 포함한 다양한 원서의 리뷰를 무료로 확인할 수 있습니다. 특히 함께 모여서 원서를 읽는 '북클럽'은 중간에 포기하지 않고 원서를 끝까지 읽는 습관을 기르는 데 큰 도움이 될 것입니다.

Answer Key

chapter one

1. C   Occasionally, when supplies were delivered by cargo planes to the landing field across the river, the children rode their bicycles to the riverbank and watched, intrigued, the unloading and then the takeoff directed to the west, always away from the community.

        But the aircraft a year ago had been different. It was not a squat, fat-bellied cargo plane but a needle-nosed single-pilot jet.

2. D   Then all of the citizens had been ordered to go into the nearest building and stay there. IMMEDIATELY, the rasping voice through the speakers had said. LEAVE YOUR BICYCLES WHERE THEY ARE.

3. B   "I apologize for inconveniencing my learning community." Asher ran through the standard apology phrase rapidly, still catching his breath. The Instructor and class waited patiently for his explanation. The students had all been grinning, because they had listened to Asher's explanations so many times before.

4. B   It was almost December, and Jonas was beginning to be frightened. No. Wrong word, Jonas thought.

        …

        Thinking, still, as he wheeled his bike into its narrow port beside the door, he realized that frightened was the wrong word to describe his feelings, now that December was almost here. It was too strong an adjective.

        …

        Jonas sighed. This evening he almost would have preferred to keep his feelings hidden. But it was, of course, against the rules.

        "I'm feeling apprehensive," he confessed, glad that the appropriate descriptive word had finally come to him.

5. A   "Who wants to be the first tonight, for feelings?" Jonas's father asked, at the conclusion of their evening meal. It was one of the rituals, the evening telling of feel-

ings.

6. B   "Male," Father said. "He's a sweet little male with a lovely disposition. But he isn't growing as fast as he should, and he doesn't sleep soundly. We have him in the extra care section for supplementary nurturing, but the committee's beginning to talk about releasing him."

7. D   There were only two occasions of release which were not punishment. Release of the elderly, which was a time of celebration for a life well and fully lived; and release of a newchild, which always brought a sense of what-could-we-have-done.

    ...

    Next, Mother, who held a prominent position at the Department of Justice, talked about her feelings. Today a repeat offender had been brought before her, someone who had broken the rules before.

    ...

    "I feel frightened, too, for him," she confessed. "You know that there's no third chance. The rules say that if there's a third transgression, he simply has to be released."

chapter two

1. C   He remembered when his family received Lily, the day she was named, the day that she had become a One.

    The Ceremony for the Ones was always noisy and fun. Each December, all the newchildren born in the previous year turned One.

    ...

    Though Jonas had only become a Five the year that they acquired Lily and learned her name, he remembered the excitement, the conversations at home, wondering about her: how she would look, who she would be, how she would fit into their established family unit. He remembered climbing the steps to the stage with his parents, his father by his side that year instead of with the Nurturers, since it was the year that he would be given a newchild of his own.

    He remembered his mother taking the newchild, his sister, into her arms, while the document was read to the assembled family units. "Newchild Twenty-three," the Namer had read. "Lily."

2. D   "As a matter of fact," he went on, "I feel a little guilty about this. But I did go in this afternoon and looked to see if this year's Naming list had been made yet. It

was right there in the office, and I looked up number Thirty-six—that's the little guy I've been concerned about—because it occurred to me that it might enhance his nurturing if I could call him by a name. Just privately, of course, when no one else is around."

"Did you find it?" Jonas asked. He was fascinated. It didn't seem a terribly important rule, but the fact that his father had broken a rule at all awed him.

3. D   She became a Nine that year, and got her bicycle. I'd been teaching her to ride mine, even though technically I wasn't supposed to."

Jonas laughed. It was one of the few rules that was not taken very seriously and was almost always broken.

4. A   Rules were very hard to change. Sometimes, if it was a very important rule—unlike the one governing the age for bicycles—it would have to go, eventually, to The Receiver for a decision.

5. D   "But to be honest, Jonas," his father said, "for me there was not the element of suspense that there is with your Ceremony. Because I was already fairly certain of what my Assignment was to be."

...

There was no way, really, to know in advance. It was a secret selection, made by the leaders of the community, the Committee of Elders, who took the responsibility so seriously that there were never even any jokes made about Assignments.

...

"Well, it was clear to me—and my parents later confessed that it had been obvious to them, too—what my aptitude was. I had always loved the newchildren more than anything.

...

But again and again, during free time, I found myself drawn to the newchildren. I spent almost all of my volunteer hours helping in the Nurturing Center.

6. A   Jonas nodded. During the past year he had been aware of the increasing level of observation. In school, at recreation time, and during volunteer hours, he had noticed the Elders watching him and the other Elevens. He had seen them taking notes. He knew, too, that the Elders were

meeting for long hours with all of the instructors that he and the other Elevens had had during their years of school.

7. B   "But, Jonas, let me warn you about something that may not have occurred to you. I know I didn't think about it until after my Ceremony of Twelve."

...

"But it means," his mother went on, "that you'll move into a new group. And each of your friends will. You'll no longer be spending your time with your group of Elevens. After the Ceremony of Twelve, you'll be with your Assignment group, with those in training. No more volunteer hours. No more recreation hours. So your friends will no longer be as close."

chapter three

1. D "Oh, look!" Lily squealed in delight. "Isn't he cute? Look how tiny he is! And he has funny eyes like yours, Jonas!" Jonas glared at her. He didn't like it that she had mentioned his eyes. He waited for his father to chastise Lily. But Father was busy unstrapping the carrying basket from the back of his bicycle.

...

Almost every citizen in the community had dark eyes. His parents did, and Lily did, and so did all of his group members and friends. But there were a few exceptions: Jonas himself, and a female Five who he had noticed had the different, lighter eyes. No one mentioned such things; it was not a rule, but was considered rude to call attention to things that were unsettling or different about individuals.

2. B "I think newchildren are so cute," Lily sighed. "I hope I get assigned to be a Birthmother."

"Lily!" Mother spoke very sharply. "Don't say that. There's very little honor in that Assignment."

3. C Father turned the newchild onto his tummy in the basket. He sat beside it and rubbed its small back with a rhythmic motion. "Anyway, Lily-billy," he said affectionately, "the Birthmothers never even get to see newchildren. If you enjoy the little ones so much, you should hope for an Assignment as Nurturer."

"When you're an Eight and start your volunteer hours, you can try some at the Nurturing Center," Mother suggested.

...

Jonas turned to the school assignments on his desk. Some chance of that, he thought. Lily was never quiet. Probably she should hope for an Assignment as Speaker, so that she could sit in the office with the microphone all day, making announcements.

4. B No one had mentioned it, not even his parents, because the public announcement had been sufficient to produce the appropriate remorse. He had, of course, disposed of the apple and made his apology to the Recreation Director the next morning, before school.

5. C   Jonas thought again about that incident. He was still bewildered by it. Not by the announcement or the necessary apology; those were standard procedures, and he had deserved them—but by the incident itself.

…

But suddenly Jonas had noticed, following the path of the apple through the air with his eyes, that the piece of fruit had—well, this was the part that he couldn't adequately understand—the apple had changed. Just for an instant. It had changed in mid—air, he remembered.

chapter four

1. D   Jonas was impressed by the things Benjamin had achieved. He knew him, of course, since they had always been groupmates, but they had never talked about the boy's accomplishments because such a conversation would have been awkward for Benjamin. There was never any comfortable way to mention or discuss one's successes without breaking the rule against bragging, even if one didn't mean to.

2. B   "Hello, Jonas," the attendant at the front desk said. She handed him the sign-up sheet and stamped her own official seal beside his signature. All of his volunteer hours would be carefully tabulated at the Hall of Open Records.

3. B   Then he checked those outside Food Distribution; it was always fun to help with the deliveries, and he hoped he would find his friend there so that they could go together on the daily rounds, carrying the cartons of supplies into the dwellings of the community.

4. C   He liked the feeling of safety here in this warm and quiet room; he liked the expression of trust on the woman's face as she lay in the water unprotected, exposed, and free.

5. A   Larissa opened her eyes happily. "They told his whole life before they released him," she said. "They always do. But to be honest," she whispered with a mischievous look, "some of the tellings are a little boring.

6. B, D, F, G, C, A, E

B: "Well, there was the telling of his life. That is always first.

D: Then the toast.

F: We all raised our glasses and cheered.

G: We chanted the anthem.

C: He made a lovely good-bye speech.

A: And several of us made little speeches wishing him well. ···

E: He just bowed to all of us and then walked, like they all do, through the special door in the Releasing Room. But you should have seen his look. Pure happiness, I'd call it."

chapter five

1. B   Usually, at the morning ritual when the family members told their dreams, Jonas didn't contribute much. He rarely dreamed.

2. A   Jonas nodded. "But it wasn't really the same. There was a tub, in the dream. But only one. And the real bathing room has rows and rows of them. But the room in the dream was warm and damp. And I had taken off my tunic, but hadn't put on the smock, so my chest was bare. I was perspiring, because it was so warm. And Fiona was there, the way she was yesterday."

3. D   "No. It was only me and Fiona, alone in the room, standing beside the tub. She was laughing. But I wasn't. I was almost a little angry at her, in the dream, because she wasn't taking me seriously."

...

"I wanted her to take off her clothes and get into the tub," he explained quickly. "I wanted to bathe her. I had the sponge in my hand. But she wouldn't. She kept laughing and saying no."

4. B   Jonas thought about it. The details were murky and vague. But the feelings were clear, and flooded him again now as he thought. "The wanting," he said. "I knew that she wouldn't. And I think I knew that she shouldn't. But I wanted it so terribly. I could feel the wanting all through me."

5. B   "Jonas," she said with a smile, "the feeling you described as the wanting? It was your first Stirrings. Father and I have been expecting it to happen to you. It happens to everyone. It happened to Father when he was your age. And it happened to me. It will happen someday to Lily.

6. C   But his mother laughed again in a reassuring, affectionate way. "No, no," she said. "It's just the pills. You're ready for the pills, that's all. That's the treatment for Stirrings."

...

"How long will I have to take them?"

"Until you enter the House of the Old," she explained.

7. D   Pedaling rapidly down the path, Jonas felt oddly proud to have joined those who took the pills. For a moment, though, he remembered the dream again. The dream had felt pleasurable. Though the feelings were confused, he thought that he had liked the feelings that his mother had called Stirrings. He remembered that upon waking, he had wanted to feel the Stirrings again.

chapter six

1. B   Fours, Fives, and Sixes all wore jackets that fastened down the back so that they would have to help each other dress and would learn interdependence.

2. D   The bicycle, at Nine, would be the powerful emblem of moving gradually out into the community, away from the protective family unit.

3. B   Gabe was back at the Nurturing Center today, being cared for by the night crew. He had been given an unusual and special reprieve from the committee, and granted an additional year of nurturing before his Naming and Placement. Father had gone before the committee with a plea on behalf of Gabriel, who had not yet gained the weight appropriate to his days of life nor begun to sleep soundly enough at night to be placed with his family unit.

4. C   This new Caleb was a replacement child. The couple had lost their first Caleb, a cheerful little Four. Loss of a child was very, very rare. The community was extraordinarily safe, each citizen watchful and protective of all children. But somehow the first little Caleb had wandered away unnoticed, and had fallen into the river. The entire community had performed the Ceremony of Loss together, murmuring the name Caleb throughout an entire day, less and less frequently, softer in volume, as the long and somber day went on, so that the little Four seemed to fade away gradually from everyone's consciousness.

Now, at this special Naming, the community performed the brief Murmur-of-Replacement Ceremony, repeating the name for the first time since the loss: softly and slowly at first, then faster and with greater volume, as the couple stood on the stage with the newchild sleeping in the mother's arms. It was as if the first Caleb were returning.

5. C   Jonas watched and cheered as Lily marched proudly to the stage, became an Eight and received the identifying jacket that she would wear this year, this one with smaller buttons and, for the first time, pockets, indicating that she was mature enough now to keep track of her own small belongings.

6. C   Jonas could see them applauding dutifully as the Nines, one by one, wheeled their new bicycles, each with its gleaming nametag attached to the back, from the stage.

…

Then the Tens. Jonas never found the Ceremony of Ten particularly interesting—only time-consuming, as each child's hair was snipped neatly into its distinguishing cut: females lost their braids at Ten, and males, too, relinquished their long childish hair and took on the more manly short style which exposed their ears.

…

Lily grinned and wriggled away from her mother. "And this year you get your Assignment," she said to Jonas in an exited voice.

7. A   Even the Matching of Spouses was given such weighty consideration that some-times an adult who applied to receive a spouse waited months or even years before a Match was approved and announced.

…

Like the Matching of Spouses and the Naming and Placement of newchildren, the Assignments were scrupulously thought through by the Committee of Elders.

chapter seven

1. C   Jonas was Nineteen. He had been the nineteenth newchild born his year. It had meant that at his Naming, he had been already standing and bright-eyed, soon to walk and talk. It had given him a slight advantage the first year or two, a little more maturity than many of his groupmates who had been born in the later months of that year.

2. D   But the duplication was only for these few hours. Very soon he would not be an Eleven but a Twelve, and age would no longer matter. He would be an adult, like his parents, though a new one and untrained still.

…

"This is the time," she began, looking directly at them, when we acknowledge differences. You Elevens have spent all your years till now learning to fit in, to standardize your behavior, to curb any impulse that might set you apart from the group.

"But today we honor your differences. They have determined your futures."

Finally the Chief Elder paid tribute to the hard work of her committee, which had performed the observations so meticulously all year. The Committee of Elders stood and was acknowledged by applause. Jonas noticed Asher yawn slightly, covering his mouth politely with his hand.

Then, at last, the Chief Elder called number One to the stage, and the Assignments began.

3. B But the mistake had been made. And precision of language was one of the most important tasks of small children. Asher had asked for a smack.

4. A They were fingering them as they sat, and Jonas knew that each one was thinking about the training that lay ahead.

5. B A mistake. She made a mistake. But Jonas knew, even as he had the thought, that she hadn't.

chapter eight

1. C Jonas moved his hands together, clapping, but it was an automatic, meaningless gesture that he wasn't even aware of. His mind had shut out all of the earlier emotions: the anticipation, excitement, pride, and even the happy kinship with his friends. Now he felt only humiliation and terror.

2. A "We failed in our last selection," the Chief Elder said solemnly. "It was ten years ago, when Jonas was just a toddler. I will not dwell on the experience because it causes us all terrible discomfort."

3. B "But the Receiver-in-training cannot be observed, cannot be modified. That is stated quite clearly in the rules. He is to be alone, apart, while he is prepared by the current Receiver for the job which is the most honored in our community."

4. C "Intelligence," she said. "We are all aware that Jonas has been a top student throughout his school days.

"Integrity," she said next. "Jonas has, like all of us, committed minor transgressions." She smiled at him. "We expect that. We hoped, also, that he would present himself promptly for chastisement, and he has always done so.

"Courage," she went on. "Only one of us here today has ever undergone the rigorous training required of a Receiver.

...

"The fourth essential attribute," the Chief Elder said, "is wisdom. Jonas has not yet acquired that. The acquisition of wisdom will come through his training.

5. B   "Finally, The Receiver must have one more quality, and it is one which I can only name, but not describe. I do not understand it. You members of the community will not understand it, either. Perhaps Jonas will, because the current Receiver has told us that Jonas already has this quality. He calls it the Capacity to See Beyond."

6. D   With the chant, Jonas knew, the community was accepting him and his new role, giving him life, the way they had given it to the newchild Caleb. His heart swelled with gratitude and pride.

But at the same time he was filled with fear. He did not know what his selection meant. He did not know what he was to become.

7. A   Then she turned and left the stage, left him there alone, standing and facing the crowd, which began spontaneously the collective murmur of his name.

"Jonas." It was a whisper at first: hushed, barely audible. "Jonas. Jonas."

Then louder, faster. "JONAS. JONAS. JONAS."

With the chant, Jonas knew, the community was accepting him and his new role, giving him life, the way they had given it to the newchild Caleb.

chapter nine

1. B   Now, for the first time in his twelve years of life, Jonas felt separate, different. He remembered what the Chief Elder had said: that his training would be alone and apart.

2. A   "Right! See you!" Asher called back. Once again, there was just a moment when things weren't quite the same, weren't quite as they had always been through the long friendship. Perhaps he had imagined it. Things couldn' change, with Asher.

3. B   Jonas was shocked. A name designated Not-to-Be- Spoken indicated the highest degree of disgrace.

4. A   But he was a little dismayed that his schedule left no time, apparently, for recreation.

5. C   He felt no reaction to rule number 7 at all. It had never occurred to him that under any circumstances, ever, he might apply for release.

6. B   Now Jonas had a thought that he had never had before. This new thought was frightening. What if others—adults—had, upon becoming Twelves, received in their instructions the same terrifying sentence?

What if they had all been instructed: You may lie?

His mind reeled. Now, empowered to ask questions of utmost rudeness—and promised answers—he could, conceivably (though it was almost unimaginable), ask someone, some adult, his father perhaps: "Do you lie?"

But he would have no way of knowing if the answer he received were true.

chapter ten

1. A   The lobby was very small and contained only a desk at which a female Attendant sat working on some papers. She looked up when he entered; then, to his surprise, she stood. It was a small thing, the standing; but no one had ever stood automatically to acknowledge Jonas's presence before.

2. C   She smiled, pushed a button, and he heard a click that unlocked the door to her left. "You may go right on in," she told him.

Then she seemed to notice his discomfort and to realize its origin. No doors in the community were locked, ever. None that Jonas knew of, anyway.

3. B   But the most conspicuous difference was the books.

4. A   "I have been The Receiver for a long time. A very, very long time. You can see that, can't you?"

Jonas nodded. The man was wrinkled, and his eyes, though piercing in their unusual lightness, seemed tired.

5. B   He sat forward suddenly, opened his eyes, and said, "You may ask questions. I have so little experience in describing this process. It is forbidden to talk of it."

6. B   He leaned back, resting his head against the back of the upholstered chair. "It's the memories of the whole world," he said with a sigh. "Before you, before me, before the previous Receiver, and generations before him."

7. D   "It's as if ..." The man paused, seeming to search his mind for the right words of description. "It's like going downhill through deep snow on a sled," he said, finally. "At first it's exhilarating: the speed; the sharp, clear air; but then the snow accumulates, builds up on the runners, and you slow, you have to push hard to keep going, and—"

He shook his head suddenly, and peered at Jonas. "That meant nothing to you, did it?" he asked.

Jonas was confused. "I didn't understand it, sir."

"Of course you didn't. You don't know what snow is, do you?"

Jonas shook his head.

chapter eleven

1. C   Now he became aware of an entirely new sensation: pinpricks? No, because they were soft and without pain. Tiny, cold, featherlike feelings peppered his body and face. He put out his tongue again, and caught one of the dots of cold upon it. It disappeared from his awareness instantly; but he caught another, and another. The sensation made him smile.

    …

    Beyond, through the swirl of what he now, somehow, perceived was the thing the old man had spoken of—snow—he could look out and down a great distance. He was up high someplace. The ground was thick with the furry snow, but he sat slightly above it on a hard, flat object.

2. B   Even as he thought the word "mound," his new consciousness told him hill.
    Then the sled, with Jonas himself upon it, began to move through the snowfall, and he understood instantly that now he was going downhill. No voice made an explanation. The experience explained itself to him.

3. A   Then the sled, with Jonas himself upon it, began to move through the snowfall, and he understood instantly that now he was going downhill.

4. B   "Do you mean that now you don't have the memory of it—of that ride on the sled—anymore?"
    "That's right. A little weight off this old body."
    "But it was such fun! And now you don't have it anymore! I took it from you!"

5. C   "But what happened to those things? Snow, and the rest of it?"
    "Climate Control. Snow made growing food difficult, limited the agricultural periods. And unpredictable weather made transportation almost impossible at times. It wasn't a practical thing, so it became obsolete when we went to Sameness.

6. A   The old man nodded to him. He looked drained, and a little sad.

7. B   Jonas felt nothing unusual at first. He felt only the light touch of the old man's hands on his back.

chapter twelve

1. C   Jonas listened. He was very aware of his own admonition not to discuss his training. But it would have been impossible, anyway. There was no way to describe to

his friends what he had experienced there in the Annex room.

…

Even trained for years as they all had been in precision of language, what words could you use which would give another the experience of sunshine?

2. C Jonas closed his eyes again. He took a deep breath and sought the sled and the hill and the snow in his consciousness.

3. C Dumbfounded, he stared at it. This time it was not a fleeting impression. This time the sled had—and continued to have, as he blinked, and stared at it again—that same mysterious quality that the apple had had so briefly. And Fiona's hair. The sled did not change. It simply was—whatever the thing was.

4. C The Giver chuckled, suddenly. "We've never completely mastered Sameness. I suppose the genetic scientists are still hard at work trying to work the kinks out. Hair like Fiona's must drive them crazy."

5. D "I'll tell you another day. Now we must work. And I've thought of a way to help you with the concept of color.

"Close your eyes and be still, now. I'm going to give you a memory of a rainbow."

6. A "Our people made that choice, the choice to go to Sameness. Before my time, before the previous time, back and back and back. We relinquished color when we relinquished sunshine and did away with differences." He thought for a moment. "We gained control of many things. But we had to let go of others."

chapter thirteen

1. B "But I want them!" Jonas said angrily. "It isn't fair that nothing has color!"

"Not fair?" The Giver looked at Jonas curiously. "Explain what you mean."

"Well …" Jonas had to stop and think it through. "If everything's the same, then there aren't any choices! I want to wake up in the morning and decide things! A blue tunic, or a red one?"

…

"It's the choosing that's important, isn't it?" The Giver asked him.

…

"We really have to protect people from wrong choices."

2. B "Or what if," he went on, almost laughing at the absurdity, "they chose their own jobs?"

"Frightening, isn't it?" The Giver said.

Jonas chuckled. "Very frightening. I can't even imagine it. We really have to protect people from wrong choices."

3. A   But when the conversation turned to other things, Jonas was left, still, with a feeling of frustration that he didn't understand.

4. B   Jonas went and sat beside them while his father untied Lily's hair ribbons and combed her hair. He placed one hand on each of their shoulders. With all of his being he tried to give each of them a piece of the memory: not of the tortured cry of the elephant, but of the being of the elephant, of the towering, immense creature and the meticulous touch with which it had tended its friend at the end.

But his father had continued to comb Lily's long hair, and Lily, impatient, had finally wiggled under her brother's touch. "Jonas," she said, "you're hurting me with your hand."

5. A   "You'll be able to apply for a spouse, Jonas, if you want to. I'll warn you, though, that it will be difficult. Your living arrangements will have to be different from those of most family units, because the books are forbidden to citizens. You and I are the only ones with access to the books."

...

"When you become the official Receiver, when we're finished here, you'll be given a whole new set of rules. Those are the rules that I obey. And it won't surprise you that I am forbidden to talk about my work to anyone except the new Receiver."

...

Jonas nodded again, but he was puzzled. Didn't life consist of the things you did each day? There wasn't anything else, really. "I've seen you taking walks," he said.

6. D   The Giver smiled grimly. "When the new Receiver failed, the memories that she had received were released. They didn't come back to me. They went . . ."

He paused, and seemed to be struggling with the concept. "I don't know, exactly. They went to the place where memories once existed before Receivers were created. Someplace out there—" He gestured vaguely with his arm. "And then the people had access to them. Apparently that's the way it was, once. Everyone had access to memories.

"It was chaos," he said. "They really suffered for a while. Finally it subsided as the memories were assimilated. But it certainly made them aware of how they need a Receiver to contain all that pain. And knowledge."

7. C   He wondered what lay in the far distance where he had never gone. The land didn't end beyond those nearby communities. Were there hills Elsewhere? Were there vast wind-torn areas like the place he had seen in memory, the place where the elephant died?

chapter fourteen

1. A   It was much the same, this memory, though the hill seemed to be a different one, steeper, and the snow was not falling as thickly as it had before.

    It was colder, also, Jonas perceived. He could see, as he sat waiting at the top of the hill, that the snow beneath the sled was not thick and soft as it had been before, but hard, and coated with bluish ice.

2. B   He fell with his leg twisted under him, and could hear the crack of bone.

    …

    Then, the first wave of pain. He gasped. It was as if a hatchet lay lodged in his leg, slicing through each nerve with a hot blade. In his agony he perceived the word "fire" and felt flames licking at the torn bone and flesh.

3. C   They have never known pain, he thought. The realization made him feel desperately lonely, and he rubbed his throbbing leg.

4. C   "It gives us wisdom," The Giver replied. "Without wisdom I could not fulfill my function of advising the Committee of Elders when they call upon me."

5. B   The Giver sighed. "You're right" he said. "But then everyone would be burdened and pained. They don't want that. And that's the real reason The Receiver is so vital to them, and so honored. They selected me—and you—to lift that burden from themselves."

chapter fifteen

1. C   "I'll come back tomorrow, sir," he said quickly. Then he hesitated. "Unless maybe there's something I can do to help."

    The Giver looked up at him, his face contorted with suffering. "Please," he gasped, "take some of the pain."

    Jonas helped him to his chair at the side of the bed. Then he quickly removed his tunic and lay face down. "Put your hands on me," he directed, aware that in such anguish The Giver might need reminding.

2. A   Around him, everywhere, far across the expanse of what seemed to be a field, lay groaning men.

3. D   Jonas heard a voice next to him. "Water," the voice said in a parched, croaking whisper.

4. B   One of Jonas's arms was immobilized with pain, and he could see through his

own torn sleeve something that looked like ragged flesh and splintery bone.

5. A   The boy sighed. His head fell back, his lower jaw dropping as if he had been surprised by something. A dull blankness slid slowly across his eyes. He was silent.

6. D   From the distance, Jonas could hear the thud of cannons. Overwhelmed by pain,
he lay there in the fearsome stench for hours, listened to the men and animals die,
and learned what warfare meant.

7. B   Finally, when he knew that he could bear it no longer and would welcome death
himself, he opened his eyes and was once again on the bed.

chapter sixteen

1. C   Jonas did not want to go back. He didn't want the memories, didn't want the
honor, didn't want the wisdom, didn't want the pain. He wanted his childhood
again, his scraped knees and ball games.

        …

        But the choice was not his. He returned each day to the Annex room.

2. D   He had seen a birthday party, with one child singled out and celebrated on his
day, so that now he understood the joy of being an individual, special and unique
and proud.

3. A   Now he understood about animals; and in the moment that the horse turned
from the stream and nudged Jonas's shoulder affectionately with its head, he per-
ceived the bonds between animal and human.

        He had walked through woods, and sat at night beside a campfire. Although he
had through the memories learned about the pain of loss and loneliness, now he
gained, too, an understanding of solitude and its joy.

        …

        "It works," The Giver agreed.

        Jonas hesitated. "I certainly liked the memory, though. I can see why it's your
favorite. I couldn't quite get the word for the whole feeling of it, the feeling that
was so strong in the room."

        "Love," The Giver told him.

        Jonas repeated it. "Love." It was a word and concept new to him.

4. D   He was in a room filled with people, and it was warm, with firelight glowing on
a hearth. He could see through a window that outside it was night, and snowing.
There were colored lights: red and green and yellow, twinkling from a tree which
was, oddly, inside the room. On a table, lighted candles stood in a polished gold-

en holder and cast a soft, flickering glow. He could smell things cooking, and he heard soft laughter. A golden-haired dog lay sleeping on the floor.

On the floor there were packages wrapped in brightly colored paper and tied with gleaming ribbons. As Jonas watched, a small child began to pick up the packages and pass them around the room: to other children, to adults who were obviously parents, and to an older, quiet couple, man and woman, who sat smiling together on a couch.

While Jonas watched, the people began one by one to untie the ribbons on the packages, to unwrap the bright papers, open the boxes and reveal toys and clothing and books. There were cries of delight. They hugged one another.

5. B Jonas thought. "Oh," he said slowly. "When I finish my training and become a full adult, I'll be given my own dwelling. And then when Lily does, a few years later, she'll get her own dwelling, and maybe a spouse, and children if she applies for them, and then Mother and Father—"

"That's right."

"As long as they're still working and contributing to the community, they'll go and live with the other Childless adults. And they won' be part of my life anymore."

6. A "And they'll be well cared for, and respected, and when they're released, there will be a celebration."

"Which you won't attend," The Giver pointed out.

"No, of course not, because I won't even know about it. By then I'll be so busy with my own life."

7. D "Do you love me?"

There was an awkward silence for a moment. Then Father gave a little chuckle. Jonas. You, of all people. Precision of language, please!"

...

"Your father means that you used a very generalized word, so meaningless that it's become almost obsolete," his mother explained carefully.

Jonas stared at them. Meaningless? He had never before felt anything as meaningful as the memory.

"And of course our community can't function smoothly if people don't use precise language. You could ask, 'Do you enjoy me?' The answer is 'Yes,'" his mother said.

"Or," his father suggested, "'Do you take pride in my accomplishments?' And the answer is wholeheartedly 'Yes.'"

"Do you understand why it's inappropriate to use a word like 'love'?" Mother asked.

Jonas nodded. "Yes, thank you, I do," he replied slowly.

It was his first lie to his parents.

chapter seventeen

1. C   He had not taken the pills, now, for four weeks. The Stirrings had returned, and he felt a little guilty and embarrassed about the pleasurable dreams that came to him as he slept. But he knew he couldn't go back to the world of no feelings that he had lived in so long.

And his new, heightened feelings permeated a greater realm than simply his sleep.

2. D   Now he could see all of the colors; and he could keep them, too, so that the trees and grass and bushes stayed green in his vision.

...

Thinking, as he always did, about precision of language, Jonas realized that it was a new depth of feelings that he was experiencing.

...

But Lily had not felt anger, Jonas realized now. Shallow impatience and exasperation, that was all Lily had felt. He knew that with certainty because now he knew what anger was.

...

"I felt sad today," he had heard his mother say, and they had comforted her.

But now Jonas had experienced real sadness. He had felt grief. He knew that there was no quick comfort for emotions like those.

These were deeper and they did not need to be told. They were felt.

3. B   He had never recognized it before as a game of war.

...

Jonas stood alone in the center of the field. Several of the children raised their heads and looked at him uneasily. The attacking armies slowed, emerged from their crouched positions, and watched to see what he was doing.

In his mind, Jonas saw again the face of the boy who had lain dying on a field and had begged him for water. He had a sudden choking feeling, as if it were difficult to breathe.

4. A   Jonas trudged to the bench beside the Storehouse and sat down, overwhelmed with feelings of loss. His childhood, his friendships, his carefree sense of securi-

ty—all of these things seemed to be slipping away.

5. C   "No, I just have to make the selection. I weigh them, hand the larger over to a Nurturer who's standing by, waiting, and then I get the smaller one all cleaned up and comfy. Then I perform a small Ceremony of Release and—" He glanced down, grinning at Gabriel. "Then I wave bye-bye," he said, in the special sweet voice he used when he spoke to the newchild. He waved his hand in the familiar gesture.

Gabriel giggled and waved bye-bye back to him. "And somebody else comes to get him? Somebody from Elsewhere?"

"That's right, Jonas-bonus."

chapter eighteen

1. C   The Giver looked sad, thinking about it. "She was a remarkable young woman. Very self-possessed and serene. Intelligent, eager to learn."

2. C   The Giver shook his head and sighed. "No. And I didn't give her physical pain. But I gave her loneliness. And I gave her loss. I transferred a memory of a child taken from its parents. That was the first one. She appeared stunned at its end."

3. A   "I couldn't bring myself to inflict physical pain on her. But I gave her anguish of many kinds. Poverty, and hunger, and terror.

4. D   Jonas held his breath for a moment. "You didn't give her war, did you? Not after just five weeks?"

    ...

"Rosemary had only those five weeks worth, and most of them were good ones.

5. B   "I think I mentioned to you once," The Giver reminded him, "that when she was gone, the memories came back to the people. If you were to be lost in the river, Jonas, your memories would not be lost with you. Memories are forever.

6. C   "I was so devastated by my own grief at her loss, and my own feeling of failure, that I didn't even try to help them through it. I was angry, too."

7. D   Jonas made a face. "They'd hate that."

"They certainly would. They wouldn't know how to deal with it at all."

"The only way I deal with it is by having you there to help me," Jonas pointed out with a sigh.

The Giver nodded. "I suppose," he said slowly, "that I could—"

chapter nineteen

1. A   "I'm sorry that I wasted so much time with my questions," Jonas said. "I was only asking about release because my father is releasing a newchild today.

2. C   "Jonas," The Giver told him, "I know that you read your training instructions very carefully. Don't you remember that you are allowed to ask anyone anything?"

     …

     The Giver told him, then, something he had not known. "All private ceremonies are recorded. They're in the Hall of Closed Records. Do you want to see this morning's release?"

3. A   Jonas watched as his father bent over the squirming newchild on the bed. "And you, little guy, you're only five pounds ten ounces. A shrimp!"

     …

     "Now he cleans him up and makes him comfy," Jonas told him. "He told me."

4. B   "Be quiet, Jonas," The Giver commanded in a strange voice. "Watch."

     …

     "Why's he—"

     "Shhh," The Giver said sharply.

5. C   He pushed the plunger very slowly, injecting the liquid into the scalp vein until the syringe was empty.

     …

     As he continued to watch, the newchild, no longer crying, moved his arms and legs in a jerking motion. Then he went limp. His head fell to the side, his eyes half open. Then he was still.

     …

     He killed it! My father killed it! Jonas said to himself, stunned at what he was realizing. He continued to stare at the screen numbly.

6. D   His father tidied the room. Then he picked up a small carton that lay waiting on the floor, set it on the bed, and lifted the limp body into it. He placed the lid on tightly.

     He picked up the carton and carried it to the other side of the room. He opened a small door in the wall; Jonas could see darkness behind the door. It seemed to be the same sort of chute into which trash was deposited at school.

7. C   "You suggested, Jonas, that perhaps she wasn't brave enough? I don't know about bravery: what it is, what it means. I do know that I sat here numb with horror. Wretched with helplessness. And I listened as Rosemary told them that she

would prefer to inject herself.

"Then she did so. I didn't watch. I looked away."

chapter twenty

1. B   The Giver gave a rueful, anguished, empty laugh. "Jonas, you and I are the only ones who have feelings. We've been sharing them now for almost a year."

2. C   It was possible, what they had planned. Barely possible. If it failed, he would very likely be killed.

But what did that matter? If he stayed, his life was no longer worth living.

3. D   "No. I have to stay here," The Giver said firmly. "I want to, Jonas. If I go with you, and together we take away all their protection from the memories, Jonas, the community will be left with no one to help them. They'll be thrown into chaos. They'll destroy themselves. I can't go."

4. A   "Because I've been a little selfish. I haven't given any of it to you. I wanted to keep it for myself to the last."

"Keep what?"

…

"Music," The Giver said, smiling. "I began to hear something truly remarkable, and it is called music. I'll give you some before I go."

5. A   Jonas would secretly leave his dwelling. This was probably the most dangerous part, because it was a violation of a major rule for any citizen not on official business to leave a dwelling at night.

6. D   He(The Giver) would make the solemn announcement that Jonas had been lost in the river. He would immediately begin the Ceremony of Loss.

7. C   The Giver hugged him. "I love you, Jonas," he said. "But I have another place to go. When my work here is finished, I want to be with my daughter."

…

"Her name was Rosemary," The Giver said.

chapter twenty one

1. C   But that evening everything changed. All of it—all the things they had thought through so meticulously—fell apart.

...

Father went on, "we obviously had to make the decision. Even I voted for Gabriel's release when we had the meeting this afternoon."

2. B   First, he had left the dwelling at night. A major transgression.

Second, he had robbed the community of food: a very serious crime, even though what he had taken was leftovers, set out on the dwelling doorsteps for collection.

Third, he had stolen his father's bicycle.

...

And he had taken Gabriel, too.

3. D   The journey had become automatic: the sleep by days, hidden in underbrush and trees; the finding of water; the careful division of scraps of food, augmented by what he could find in the fields. And the endless, endless miles on the bicycle by night.

4. C   He knew that they could not see color, and that their flesh, as well as Gabriel's light golden curls, would be no more than smears of gray against the colorless foliage.

5. B   The most terrifying thing was the planes. By now, days had passed; Jonas no longer knew how many.

...

But when the planes came, he wished that he could have received the courage.

chapter twenty two

1. C   Trees became more numerous, and the forests beside the road were dark and thick with mystery.

...

Now the landscape was changing. It was a subtle change, hard to identify at first. The road was narrower, and bumpy, apparently no longer tended by road crews.

...

Tentatively he began to ride in daylight. He had forgotten the fear of the searchers, who seemed to have diminished into the past.

...

Terrified, he looked up, but it was not a plane at all. Though he had never seen one before, he identified it from his fading memories, for The Giver had given them to him often. It was a bird.

2. B   Tentatively he began to ride in daylight. He had forgotten the fear of the searchers, who seemed to have diminished into the past. But now there were new fears; the unfamiliar landscape held hidden, unknown perils.

3. D   All of it was new to him. After a life of Sameness and predictability, he was awed by the surprises that lay beyond each curve of the road. He slowed the bike again and again to look with wonder at wildflowers, to enjoy the throaty warble of a new bird nearby, or merely to watch the way wind shifted the leaves in the trees. During his twelve years in the community, he had never felt such simple moments of exquisite happiness.

4. C   After countless tries, the net yielded two flopping silvery fish. Methodically Jonas hacked them to pieces with a sharp rock and fed the raw shreds to himself and to Gabriel. They ate some berries, and tried without success to catch a bird.

5. D   Once he had yearned for choice. Then, when he had had a choice, he had made the wrong one: the choice to leave. And now he was starving.

But if he had stayed . . .

His thoughts continued. If he had stayed, he would have starved in other ways. He would have lived a life hungry for feelings, for color, for love.

And Gabriel? For Gabriel there would have been no life at all. So there had not really been a choice.

6. D   And the weather was changing. It rained for two days. Jonas had never seen rain, though he had experienced it often in the memories. He had liked those rains, enjoyed the new feeling of it, but this was different. He and Gabriel became cold and wet, and it was hard to get dry, even when sunshine occasionally followed.

7. B   Gabriel had not cried during the long frightening journey. Now he did. He cried because he was hungry and cold and terribly weak. Jonas cried, too, for the same reasons, and another reason as well. He wept because he was afraid now that he could not save Gabriel. He no longer cared about himself.

chapter twenty three

1. D   He saw nothing ahead except the endless ribbon of road unfolding in twisting narrow curves. He heard no sound ahead.

Yet he felt it: felt that Elsewhere was not far away.

2. C   A steep hill loomed ahead. In the best of conditions, the hill would have been a difficult, demanding ride. But now the rapidly deepening snow obscured the nar-

row road and made the ride impossible. His front wheel moved forward imperceptibly as he pushed on the pedals with his numb, exhausted legs. But the bicycle stopped. It would not move.

…

But he had come this far. He must try to go on.

3. C   For a fleeting second he felt that he wanted to keep it for himself, to let himself bathe in sunlight, unburdened by anything or anyone else.

But the moment passed and was followed by an urge, a need, a passionate yearning to share the warmth with the one person left for him to love.

4. B   But he began, suddenly, to feel happy. He began to recall happy times. He remembered his parents and his sister. He remembered his friends, Asher and Fiona. He remembered The Giver.

Memories of joy flooded through him suddenly.

He reached the place where the hill crested and he could feel the ground under his snow-covered feet become level. It would not be uphill anymore.

5. A   Using his final strength, and a special knowledge that was deep inside him, Jonas found the sled that was waiting for them at the top of the hill. Numbly his hands fumbled for the rope.

6. B   He forced his eyes open as they went downward, downward, sliding, and all at once he could see lights, and he recognized them now. He knew they were shining through the windows of rooms, that they were the red, blue, and yellow lights that twinkled from trees in places where families created and kept memories, where they celebrated love.

7. C   For the first time, he heard something that he knew to be music. He heard people singing.

Behind him, across vast distances of space and time, from the place he had left, he thought he heard music too. But perhaps it was only an echo.

THE GIVER

1판 1쇄   2010년 12월 20일
2판 5쇄   2024년 8월 11일

지은이   Lois Lowry
기획   이수영
책임편집   김보경 유난영 이수영
콘텐츠제작및감수   롱테일 교육 연구소
저작권   명채린
마케팅   두잉글 사업 본부

펴낸이   이수영
펴낸곳   롱테일북스
출판등록   제2015-000191호
주소   04033 서울특별시 마포구 양화로 113, 3층 (서교동, 순흥빌딩)
전자메일   help@ltinc.net

ISBN 979-11-91343-86-1 14740